Psychotherapy in Ireland

Edited by

Edward Boyne

the columba press

First edition, 1993, published by
the columba press
93 The Rise, Mount Merrion, Blackrock, Co Dublin

Second, revised edition 1995
Third, revised edition 2003

Cover by Bill Bolger
Origination by The Columba Press
Printed in Ireland by
Colour Books Ltd, Dublin

ISBN 1 85607 368 8

Contents

Foreword

Vincent Browne

Mental illness is an epidemic. The predominant health care system for dealing with the phenomenon is failing to cope. Other strategies are urgently required. Psychotherapy must play a prominent role in a revised approach.

In her introduction to *The World Health Report 2001: Mental Health – New Understanding, New Hope,* the Director General of the WHO, Gro Harlem Brundtland wrote:

> Initial estimates suggest that about 450 million people alive today suffer from mental or neurological disorders or from psychosocial problems such as those related to alcohol and drug abuse. Many of them suffer silently. Many of them suffer alone. Beyond the suffering and beyond the absence of care lie the frontiers of stigma, shame, exclusion and more often than we care to know, death. Major depression is now the leading cause of disability globally and ranks fourth in the ten leading causes of the global burden of disease. If projections are correct, within the next 20 years, depression will have the dubious distinction of becoming the second cause of the global disease burden.

In the year 2000, there were 24,100 admissions to psychiatric hospitals in Ireland.[1] About 230,000 people attend out-patient psychiatric clinics.[2]

The government's Health Strategy, published in 2001, states:

> More than one in four adults will suffer from mental illness at some point during their lives. Twenty five per cent of families are likely to have at least one member who suffers from mental illness ... In Ireland it has been estimated that 10 per cent of the general population suffers from depression and 1 per cent from schizophrenia.

> It is likely that the numbers of people presenting to the mental health services for treatment will increase in the coming years, due in part to the modernisation of the services and the reduction in the stigma associated with their use. The ageing population and the increasing incidence of social problems such as drug abuse and family breakdown, are also likely to contribute to increasing demands on the services in the future.[3]

Another indicator of mental illness is the suicide rate. There have been around 500 suicides in Ireland per year for the last decade with the main incidence of suicide being in the category of males in the age group 15-24 with mental illness being a major contributory factor.[4]

There is evidence that the current prescriptions for dealing with mental illness are not, on their own at least, sufficient to deal with the problem. The 2000 Report of the Inspector of Mental Hospitals states that of the 24,100 admissions to mental hospitals, 17,350 (72%) were readmissions. That report also notes: 'Few psychologists, social workers or occupational therapists were employed (in the psychiatric service) and those that were often felt professionally isolated in the smaller services.'[5]

Is it not likely there is a link between the high failure rate of in-patient treatment (and even if temporary relief, for instance, from depression is considered a success, the overall readmissions rate suggests a deficiency in the system) and the absence of adequate psychological back-up?

The 2000 report continues: 'Many patients have complained that they don't have the option of psychotherapy or psychological treatments which they feel would be of greater help to them (than the drug treatments).'[6]

Since I started writing and broadcasting on the psychiatric services in 1997 I have received literally hundreds of letters and heard countless people at seminars and conferences telling of how they felt the prevalent psychiatric treatments, primarily drug treatments, have failed them. How they have felt abused and neglected by the psychiatric services, how their stories of pain and anger have been unheard, how they have been excluded from decisions on their own treatments and the management of their own lives.

I do not have the knowledge or expertise to determine which of the therapies in the treatment of mental illness is likely to be the most successful. But it is evidence that the psychiatric model on its own is not working adequately and that many people who suffer mental illness want a range of treatments to be available to them. Among such treatments must be psychotherapy. And psychotherapy must be generally available within the health service.

The *Irish Psychiatric Hospitals and Units Census 2001* report[7] shows that the unskilled had the highest rate of hospitalisation among residents on census night at 314.3 per 100,000 population. A report on inequalities in the health system[8] stated: '… in 1996 you were almost four times as likely to be admitted to hospital for the first time for schizophrenia if you were in the unskilled manual category than if you were a higher professional.'

Since the incidence of mental illness seems very much more prevalent among the lower social economic groups, it is obvious that psychotherapy treatment must be part of the public health system. Whatever complications remain with regard to the registration and recognition of the psychotherapy profession should be quickly resolved between members of the profession and the Department of Health and Children.

Notes

1. Report of the Inspector of Mental Hospitals 2000, page 1.
2. According to the Health Statistics 1999 report published by The Department of health and Children, there were 233,512 attendances at out-patient psychiatric clinics in 1996 (Table F10C, page 127), of which 13,781 were new attendees and 219,731 were return attendees.
3. *Quality and Fairness: A Health System for You*, published in November 2001 by the Department of Health and Children (pages 34 and 35).
4. *Suicide in Ireland: A global Perspective and A National Strategy* by Aware.
5. Report of the Inspector of Mental Hospitals 2000.
6. Ibid pages 5 and 6.
7. *Irish Psychiatric Hospitals and Units Census 2001* by Antoinette Daly and Dermot Walsh, published by the Health Research Board.
8. *Inequalities in Health in Ireland – Hard Facts* by Barry et al, published by the Department of Community Health and General Practice, Trinity College, Dublin, September 200.

Introduction

Since the 1970s Ireland has seen a steady growth in the range and availability of psychotherapy services. It is now not uncommon to hear psychotherapy mentioned in various contexts and as a possible response to a wide range of personal issues including depression, post traumatic stress disorder, anxiety etc. However, the very diverse nature of psychotherapy and the differences between the multiple schools and approaches can cause confusion and misunderstanding. Indeed rather than referring to 'psychotherapy' as a single discipline it may be more accurate to refer to 'the psychotherapies' instead.

In this book, some of the leading practitioners of psychotherapy working in Ireland offer an overview of the approach or school of psychotherapy which is within their competence. They offer an indication of their individual perspective or style, and in some cases of the way they combine or are informed by different psychotherapy approaches within their practice. A total of ten different perspectives or styles are outlined and discussed.

Irish cultural, socio-political and historical circumstances are also reflected in these essays, including the ways in which aspects of the Irish psyche, or psychological issues frequently observed in Ireland, emerge within the process of psychotherapy.

Structure and content of the essays

Every approach to non-medical psychotherapy has its own philosophy or 'theory of the person', of what it is to be a human being. This theory of the person may be implicit rather than self-evident to the client. Certainly the assumptions made about what it is to be human within a particular school of psychotherapy dictate to a considerable extent the techniques and interventions used, the nature of the therapy process and the sort of therapeutic outcome that can be anticipated. For example, in psychoanalytic psychotherapy, emphasis is placed on the 'unconscious' in the model of the person, whereas this is not the emphasis in cognitive or in systemic therapy.

'Change' is also an important concept within psychotherapy and most approaches contain a notion of what 'change' means and how it may come about within the therapeutic process. Barriers and resistances to change and how they are dealt with are also important.

The various schools of psychotherapy also differ in the way they understand psychopathology, illness or dis-ease. For some the elimination of illness is emphasised while for other approaches, symptoms are seen as indicators of deeper issues which may have their origin, for example, in early childhood experiences.

By and large the issues which are the stuff of psychotherapy are both commonplace and unusual. They include feelings of loneliness, meaninglessness and alienation, rejection, love, intimacy, self doubt and fears of being overwhelmed, unable and constrained. As Dr Mark Aveline puts it:

> The focus of psychotherapy is the contribution that the individual ... in the context of his circumstances makes to the problem or difficulty. Psychotherapy assumes that people are responsible for their lives and have choice.

A more fundamental assumption in psychotherapy is that one person can help, support or enable another to resolve difficult and painful personal issues. Within the therapy the client or patient is the focus in her own right and not only in terms of the function or role she performs in the world. The realm of psychotherapy is the subjective experience of the individual person and the personal meanings placed on that experience. In an increasingly consumerist and materialist society where much human interaction is more often a function of economic roles, psychotherapy is an important activity.

Mental health services in Ireland

The mental health system in Ireland is still very much the preserve of psychiatry and the medical model. In practice the psychiatric profession largely controls policy in relation to the provision of most mental health services. While improvements have taken place in recent years and models of best-practice are available, there is growing concern at the general state of these services and growing doubt that the needs of the community are being fully served. The services are seriously under-resourced relative to need and there is also what has been described as a 'poverty of ideas' within the system. There is much anecdotal evidence to suggest that human rights transgressions are endemic . Amnesty International (Irish Section) has expressed concern on this issue. Amnesty International and the Irish Penal Reform Trust have also expressed concern about the very high proportion of people with mental illness and personality disorders among the prison population.

Non-medical psychotherapy occupies an ambiguous position with uneven and inconsistent recognition within the various State agencies, the mental health system and within the health insurance system.

Psychotherapy is therefore among the most privatised of all the caring services meaning that it tends to be availed of more by people in the higher socio-economic groups who have sufficient disposable income to pay private fees. By and large it is not available through the medical card system and is not easily accessible to those on lower incomes.

Ireland is not unique in this respect. Holmes and Lindley, writing with reference to the position in the UK, point out that: 'A working-class patient presenting to a doctor with emotional distress is likely to be prescribed a tranquilliser. Middle-class patients are more likely to see a doctor who offers psychotherapy rather than a prescription. Tranquillisers are often a token currency of heteronomous dependency which inhibits change; psychotherapeutic dependency, on the other hand, can be a precursor to greater understanding and autonomy. On the face of it, it does not seem fair that distressed working-class people should be tranquillised while their middle-class counterparts are more likely to receive psychotherapy.'

The question in relation to psychotherapy and its role in society has arisen in official reports in recent years. For example the Bloomfield report (1998) on the victims of the troubles in Northern Ireland highlighted the obvious dearth of psychotherapy services and the lack of a coherent strategy to address this issue. In the Irish Republic the report of the Commission on the Family (1999) called for an integrated government policy in relation to psychotherapy and noted the widespread interest in the area as evidenced by the very large number of submissions made on the subject.

Psychotherapy as a profession

One of the problems inhibiting the expansion of psychotherapy services has been the ambiguous position of psychotherapy as a profession. Some have argued that psychotherapy should be merely an ancillary activity of certain 'core' professions, i.e. medicine, psychology and social work. Others suggest that psychotherapy should be a profession in its own right with its own standards of entry and training, open to as wide a group of suitably qualified students as is possible or reasonable. As Holmes and Lindley put it:

> Psychotherapy has a separate and special contribution to make within a state-funded service and ... the training needed for this, while overlapping to some extent with that undergone by other professions, is unique.

The Irish Council for Psychotherapy (ICP) has for the past 10 years or so been the premier professional body in the field of psychotherapy in Ireland. The ICP is strongly in favour of psychotherapy as a profession in its own right. The ICP consists of 5 divisions each corresponding to a major approach to psychotherapy. Each section operates its own accreditation system. The ICP has its own national register of accredited practitioners and issues *The Guide to Psychotherapy in Ireland* (Columba Press) as a useful information source for the public. It is hoped that this register will ultimately form the basis of a statutory register along the lines of the General Medical Council with statutory powers of enforcement for the accrediting body.

Training for psychotherapy in Ireland

The training process to become a psychotherapist is by and large different from other forms of training for the caring services.

Usually trainees are expected to undergo their own personal therapy as part of the training. Assessment within the training course includes assessment of the trainee's personal growth and awareness. Trainees are also assessed on their standard of work with actual clients. All of this presents particular challenges for the course organisers and trainers involved.

A noticeable gap in ICP`s current information service to the public is in relation to training courses for those who wish to become practitioners. The ICP does not at present issue a list of accredited or recognised courses. Aspiring therapists wishing to find a reputable course currently have difficulty discerning which courses are accepted for the purposes of individual accreditation with ICP.

This lack of official information has arguably restricted the development of psychotherapy in Ireland. The criteria for what is an acceptable standard of training course are not published by ICP. There is no official mechanism by which new training courses can become recognised. New training courses and training initiatives are likely to be inhibited and discouraged.

In practice certain courses have been accepted for the purpose of accreditation for many years, but information on them is provided informally.

A list of those courses known to the editor to be recognised by ICP through precedent via the individual practitioner's accreditation system, is at Appendix A. This list is offered here by way of guideline only.

It should be noted that the Irish Association for Counselling and Psychotherapy (IACP) has a significant number of psychotherapists as members as well as many counsellors.

The IACP has a training course recognition system and a list of recognised courses in counselling. Most agencies which exclusively offer psychotherapy courses operate under the umbrella of the ICP and do not participate in the IACP course recognition system.

Group Analysis

Although not directly within the scope of this book, there has been a welcome increase in recent years in the number of qualified group analysts in Ireland and in the availability of group analytic psychotherapy. This has been largely due to the activities of the Group Analytic training course at St Vincent's Hospital, Dublin (see Appendix A).

The third revised edition

This book was first published ten years ago in 1993. Since then it has established itself as a recognised and respected text, in particular for students of psychotherapy and of the social sciences. I hope with this, the third revised edition, that it will find a wider readership and continue as the standard introductory text on psychotherapy in Ireland in the years to come.

Edward Boyne
Galway, 2003

CHAPTER 1

Psychoanalysis

Ross M. Skelton

Psychoanalysis, which will shortly be one hundred years old, was discovered by Sigmund Freud and developed by Melanie Klein and others. The reader may be surprised that the name of Carl Jung is not included. There is a reason for this. Although Freud and Jung worked in tandem for some years, and there is considerable overlap in their interests, Jung did not wish to be known as a psychoanalyst after his split with Freud, and to this day the Jungians call themselves 'Analytical Psychologists'.

Classical psychoanalysis, as practiced by the members of the International Psychoanalytic Association, requires that the client attend five fifty-minute sessions per week for a number of years. This classical psychoanalysis is not yet practiced in Ireland. What we do practice is called 'psychoanalytic psychotherapy' which requires that a client attend at least once a week but preferably twice or three times, usually for fifty-minute sessions. Psychoanalytic psychotherapy differs from psychoanalysis only in its intensity, as the same working concepts are used.

Psychoanalysis is a process which takes place in a relationship between the psychoanalyst and client, working together to explore in detail and depth the client's current distress in relation to his or her childhood and family backround. In this it does not differ greatly from other therapies but in its means it has the extra tool of a special access to unconscious processes. Thus analysts can gain access to memories and ideas that were once consciously active but became repressed because they were 'too true to be good'. The thesis of psychoanalysis is this: these memories and ideas may be repressed and forgotten, but they remain active and continue to exert a secret powerful influence on the client's life. The aim of psychoanalysis is to relieve neurosis. Freud says to an imaginary client: 'No doubt fate would find it easier than I do to relieve you of your illness. But you will be able to convince yourself that much will be gained if we succeed in transforming your hysterical (neurotic) misery into common unhappiness. With a mental life that has been restored to health, you will be better armed against that unhappiness.' The reader may be shocked by this sombre, even pessimistic outlook, but on the other side it must be said that psychoanalysis does not make false promises of happiness. On a more optimistic note, it is often said that the aim of psychoanalysis is to enable the client to love and to work.

Psychoanalysis does not investigate the past for its own sake, but in order to see what is really underpinning current anxieties. However it is not enough just to *recall* the past, a great deal of the mutual task in analysis is in allowing a *reliving* of the past in the present. The link between the present and the past thus becomes 'alive' in the *relationship* with the analyst.

In the initial interviews, the client is given freedom to speak openly and frankly, initially about their distress and eventually about their feelings for family members and the people in their life. The client is usually quite anxious about these initial sessions since it may be the first time that they have ever spoken about distressing thoughts, feelings and memories, which up until then have remained totally secret. Even talking about secret feelings for the first time can bring a great deal of relief to the client living in a very private 'hell'.

If there is mutual agreement between the analyst and client to work together, an informal agreement is drawn up about fees and frequency of attendance. This also includes the more flexible proviso, that missed sessions shall be paid for and that as far as possible the client will take holidays at the same time as the analyst.

As the analysis proceeds, there is usually surprise on the part of the client about the levels of frankness that are acceptable to the analyst. Hand in hand with this usually goes a greater spontaneity in expression, leading eventually to the ultimate fluency of 'free association' where the conscious prejudice of 'sticking to the point' can be suspended at will. It is sometimes said that the only people who can 'free associate' well are the analysts themselves and there is some truth in this. All analysts have undergone intensive psychoanalysis, usually of at least five years duration and this is, among other things, a training in free association. (Incidentally this must make psychoanalysts the only physicians who have to actually take their own medicine!) In many ways, it could be said that the ability to free associate well is more indicative of well-being than distress in a person. Thus the melting away of inhibitions makes free association easier and free associations enable the trained 'ear' of the analyst to make new connections between the present and the past.

Since the psychoanalyst says little and listens with great care to what is said, the overall impression can be a little 'eerie', and the client can experience this as being aimless and chaotic as the old order of experience begins to dissolve and before the new order begins to emerge out of the joint task. In some ways, the enterprise resembles scuba diving where the novice dives *in the company of* an experienced diver who does not intervene but watches and only intervenes when necessary. Thus the client has the satisfaction of 'doing the discovering by themselves' but with the security of knowing that the analyst, though distant, is benevolent but watchful. However, as we shall see, this simple picture is to become complicated by the emerging nature of the 'analytic relationship' which is not merely of the doctor / patient kind.

The psychoanalytic process is very rich in human experience. In fact, it takes the whole of human experience as its field of interest. One reason for this richness is that it was conceived out of the living experience of its founder, Sigmund Freud. We can understand a great deal about psychoanalysis from examining Freud's own life, for Freud was his own first real psychoanalytic patient.

It comes as a surprise to us to discover that Freud was actually Slavic, for he was was born in Czechoslovakia in 1856 and his first words were to be spoken in Czech, although he was later to disclaim any knowledge of this language. His father, Jakob, had two sons, Emmanuel and Philip, by a previous marriage. Philip had a son John who was Freud's age, with whom he often played. This meant that he constantly struggled with the question: why did his playmate John Freud call his father 'grandfather'?

Thus we can see that Freud was born into a two-tier family, where his step brothers were more like uncles and his father seemed more of an age with the old nanny who looked after them, so in his young imagination he paired them off. His step brother Philip seemed more of an age with his mother and so, in imagination, he paired them off too. This would have made him Philip's son and not his father's son. Already we see the seeds of the Oedipus complex in Freud's own life.

The Freuds moved to Leipzig in Germany but settled later in the Austrian capital,Vienna, when their young Sigmund was four years old. In Vienna he was to assimilate the Classical Greek culture of the educated classes to complement the strong Jewish culture that was his birthright. At the university he studied medicine, neurology and psychiatry, but perhaps more importantly he was to attend the classes of the great German philosopher, Franz Brentano. Brentano was at that time pioneering a revolutionary theory of how human *subjective* experience was to be understood and, in those classes, Freud was to sit in the same room with Edmund Husserl, the founder of phenomenology, which became the great rival theory of subjectivity to psychoanalysis.

At the age of 26, he went to study in Paris and this too was to have a momentous impact on him, for he was to meet Charcot, the great hypnotist who was at that time investigating hysteria from the point of view of unconscious processes. Hysteria is a psychological process where the body of an individual is modified in accordance with their unconscious wishes.The simplest example of this, known to all, is hysterical pregnancy, where a woman exhibits every sign of pregnancy imaginable but does not have any baby in the womb. There are many dramatic examples of paralysed limbs, usually in women – although it would be a mistake to think that there are no hysterical men. Charcot was able to cure many hysterics by putting them into a trance in order to recover repressed memories and relieve physical symptoms. He was also a consummate performer and Freud wrote at the time: 'I believe I am changing a great deal. Charcot who is both one of the great physicians and a man whose common sense is the order of genius simply demolishes my views and aims. Many a time after a lecture I go out as from Notre Dame with new impressions to work over, but he engrosses me. When I go away from him I have no more wish to work at my own simple things. My brain is sated as after an evening at the theatre. Whether the seed will ever bring forth fruit I do not know, but what I certainly know is that no other human being has ever affected me in such a way.'

When Freud returned to Vienna from Paris, full of enthusiasm for these new ideas, he delivered a lecture to his colleagues on Charcot's ideas on hysteria, which was very badly received. Nevertheless, at the age of 27, newly married, he commenced his therapeutic work as a hypnotist. Interestingly, this is where the use of the couch originated in psychoanalysis. The patient would lie down and be put into a trance and, in the early days of his practice, Freud would place a hand on the patient's forehead. Five years into his practice, one of his patients, Elizabeth von R, told him to keep quiet during one of his 'suggestions' in order to let her talk more freely and 'free assosiation' was born, called in those early days 'chimney sweeping'.

By the age of 37, the year of his father's death, another ingredient of psychoanalysis was to come into Freud's life in the shape of an upsurge of violent feelings towards his friend and mentor Joseph Breuer, which were later to be replicated with his friend Wilhelm Fleiss. This was a pointer towards what would later become a foundation-stone of psychoanalysis, namely the notion of ambivalence. We never have *fully* positive feelings towards anyone at all; there is always a repressed negative side. These feelings were later to be conceptualised as 'the transference', the hidden negative feelings towards apparently loved parent figures. In Freud's case, both Breuer and Fleiss were father-substitutes, and so he acted out his feelings towards them instead of his real father.

By the age of 37 then, Freud had assembled the main ingredients of his theory: from Brentano he had received a profound teaching about the subjectivity of human experience, from Charcot he had seen with his own eyes the unconscious power of repressed ideas, from Elizabeth von R he was inspired to free association, and in his relation with Breuer we find the first nudge towards what will become the theory of transference.

The great emotional crisis in Freud's life came when his father died and this was to prompt a flow of dreams whose analysis was to provide the core of his masterpiece, *The Interpretation of Dreams*, published in 1900. He wrote: 'By one of the dark ways behind the official consciousness, my father's death has affected me profoundly. I had treasured him highly and understood him exactly. With his peculiar mixture of deep wisdom, fantastic lightness, he had meant very much in my life. He had passed his time when he died, but inside me the occasion of his death has reawakened all my feelings. Now I feel quite uprooted.' However, despite these warm feelings, during his self analysis of this period he discovered an ambivalence in himself about his father. Underlying his filial affection he discovered, mainly through his dreams, that he was ashamed of his father for being uneducated and of not being a warrior-father like his hero Hannibal.

In this connection there is a fascinating 'Freudian slip' in the early editions of the Dreambook which Freud himself points out. When he writes of Hannibal's father, Hamilcar, instead of writing 'Hamilcar' he writes 'Hasdrubal', and he makes this slip no fewer than three times in the text! Now Hasdrubal was the brother of Hannibal with whom the young Freud was deeply identified, so in substituting Hasdrubal for Hamilcar he has effectively substituted brother for father, that is, his (step) brother Philip for his father Jakob. We have already noted that the young Freud paired his mother off with Philip in his fantasy as a couple, and we can recall that Freud was a playmate of Philip's son John. Now Philip had gone to England when Freud was 14 and this was generally perceived as a definite move 'up in the world' because England was seen as a country tolerant towards Jews. Freud analyses this slip himself: 'How different it would have been if I had been my brother's son.' In other words, the slip of his pen had revealed a wish to have another father. We have just seen that an apparently elementary slip can have a highly significant meaning, and anyone who doubts this need only recall a friend's failing to turn up for an important meeting or forgetting their birthday! Just as a slip can reveal an unconscious wish, so we shall see that dreams reveal unexpected fulfillment of wishes.

Freud was not the first to indicate the importance of dreams but he was instrumental in implementing a thorough-going method of deciphering them. Freud also thought symptoms like, for example, phobias had meaning and Freud's lecture, 'The Sense of Symptoms', gives an admirable account of this. More importantly, this axiom that slips, dreams and symptoms had meaning led him to investigate in detail the living history of the client.

A client's biography is of paramount importance in psychoanalysis and through that biography runs the red thread of sexuality. Now what Freud discovered about *human* sexuality, unlike the sexuality of apes, is that it is not a single strand, that is, it is not originally a single instinct or drive. More specifically, he found that it is rooted in the partial oral, anal and genital drives which do not form a confluence until puberty. We shall see that this successful confluence depends on the identification of the child with the parent of the same sex .This notion of 'identification' is a discovery of the first importance. When one person identifies with another, they feel that they *are* that person, so the notion of identification goes much further than the familiar 'mimicry'. Identification with another person is a deep and usually unconscious emotional experience. When, for example, a little girl identifies with her mother, she feels that she *is* her mother and takes on some of mother's functions in imagination. She may put her dollies to bed the way mother puts her to bed or, perhaps more vividly, she may express her identification with mummy by stepping literally into her shoes and parading around the house.

For Freud, 'the self' is formed by identification with the same sex parent and, although each of us identifies with the opposite sex parent too, the first kind of identification, namely with the same sex parent, must be securely installed. Broadly speaking, we identify with those we like and so our personalities are built up in layers as we grow up. However we shall see later that, because of rivalry in the Oedipal situation, we are forced to identify with our rivals in love. This sets up a tension in the mind of some people that is sometimes so great that it becomes the central feature of their future therapy.

It is a little acknowledged fact that there is an attraction between father and daughter and son and mother. Now, in some ways, this fact of attraction of parent for child is covertly recognised. We speak habitually of a 'Mummy's boy' or'Daddy's girl' and this is usually a condemnation. In many such cases, love has stagnated into an unhealthy attachment. If this attachment is further eroticised, the parent moves over into the realm of perversion. But the general point is this, that there is not a family where this subject has not been touched upon and, in most families, these little romances do not go unnoticed.

It is often said of Freud that for him 'everything is down to sex' and there is no doubt that he did make us aware of the omnipresence of sexuality in everyday living. What person has not used their charm to get what they want from another person by flirting? Certain jobs in society are always done by carefully chosen sexually attractive men and women who are skilled at flirting and flattery. Freud was to direct our attention towards attractions felt within the family and not just in the marketplace. He called these attractions the 'family romance'. The attraction of parent for children is becoming increasingly recognised in today's society, but what Freud discovered goes further, namely that children have precocious sexual feelings of their own which emerge between the ages of three and five years. After this early emergence, the sexual feelings go underground again until puberty, but not without having been shaped by this precocious phase which remains repressed but active. Thus we are led into the field of the Oedipus Complex.

If there is a single idea which towers in significance above all others in the practice of psychoanalysis, it is the notion of the Oedipus Complex. It has become something of a cliché in modern times and this conceals the radical nature of what Freud actually discovered. In the original Oedipus myth of the Greeks, Oedipus does actually have sexual intercourse with his mother, and goes further to murder his father, his chief rival in love. Now Oedipus does not know at the time that he has done these two things; in other words he is unconscious of this and so, too, is the child unconscious of his or her wishes. This is the basis for the so-called Oedipal Phase in development when, between the ages of three and five, a boy will actively imagine and talk about a 'romance' with Mummy. He may say such things as: 'Will I marry you when I grow up Mummy?'. Similarly with the girl who often fantasises having a romance with Daddy or even having his baby. Most parents have a story along these lines, usually told humourously, but it was Freud who revealed the truth masked by the laughter, namely that the child's percocious sexual drive has prompted a childhood 'romance'.

There are countless illustrations of this from literature. Thus Diderot: 'If the little savage were left to his own devices, and could match that passion and strength of thirty with the unreason of the cradle, he would break his father's neck and dishonour his mother.' Now we can see why Freud called the family history a 'family romance', because of father loving wife, wife loving son, and daughter loving father, and it is easy to see that such a web of loves is bound to set up rivalries and hates. Thus if mother loves son, the son will see father as rival, and similarly daughter's love for father will set her in a rivalry against mother. This is a very important and useful fact about family life.

Here then is the core of the Oedipus complex, perhaps better called the 'Oedipus Problem', which according to Freud no human being ever completely resolves. However, every human being must attempt a solution. I must stress the absolute centrality of the Oedipus problem for psychoanalysis. Centuries ago, when men wanted to test a piece of metal to see if it was gold, they scratched it on a special stone called a 'touchstone'. If it was gold then it left a certain colour scratch on the stone, so this was a rough and ready check to see if a piece of metal was valuable or not. In clinical work with neurosis, we can say that the Oedipus problem (and its attempted solutions) is the touchstone of psychoanalytic technique, to which we now turn.

A word like 'technique' is not an attractive one to the psychoanalyst, for it implies that there is one method to be applied to all patients. Similarly words like 'skills', 'clinic','cure' which stress the idea of objectivity, are usually avoided. Psychoanalysis takes its departure from the subjectivity of the client – how the client *privately feels* about themselves and others. The client's uniqueness is thus axiomatic in this very personal process. Now, how are we to contact that private world that the client has probably never told anyone about in their whole lives?

To answer this let us go back to Husserl, Freud's contemporary at the University of Vienna and inventor of phenomenology. Our view of the world, Husserl thought, was encrusted with familiarity. Visual artists are able to see the world in a fresh way, and Husserl set himself the task of bringing this idea into philosophy. Husserl thought that we could 'bracket out' our usual scientific factual attitudes to objects and clear the way for a fresh subjective vision of the same objects, rather like the way an artist achieves a fresh vision. Now it is this idea that we use in psychoanalysis, for when a client comes to us for the first time, we bracket out the usual conventional responses by saying very little except for an occasional question or a request to enlarge on some point. This generally has the effect of loosening the encrusted and cliché-ridden self-vision which the client has acquired over the years. As a way of listening, it is very difficult to acquire without going through the process of psychoanalysis yourself, but then all psychoanalysts have, by definition, been themselves analysed, usually at some length.

When sessions begin, the client is encouraged to lie on the couch, with the analyst out of sight or side by side in chairs like in a railway carriage. The reason for this is to encourage freer expression, for a face to face encounter has a 'civilising' effect on the client which will cause inhibition. Thus there is a partial taboo on seeing the listening analyst. In addition to this, the client is temporarily immobilised on the couch or chair which minimises expressions of feelings in physical action. There is no touching at all in psychoanalysis and so this means of expression is removed from the client. The only means of expression left to the client is talking, and this why psychoanalysis is often called 'the talking cure'.

In general, the taboos of not looking, not touching and not moving, tend to increase the 'bracketing out' effect, often releasing fantasies about the person of the analyst. This is because the client, being deprived of information about the thoughts and feelings of the analyst, tries (unconsciously) to fill the gap in his knowledge of the analyst with a fantasy. Thus for example, the silent listening analyst may find himself accused of harbouring hostile feelings towards the client. This can be extremely informative about the client as this persecuted feeling will probably lead back to its roots in the client's history. The client is further enjoined to say *anything and everything* that comes into their head. This 'free association' is not at all as easy as it sounds.

The hallmark of free association is spontaneity, and this can be illustrated by an example: A client came for analysis after having had therapy for some time. Soon he presented me with a dream. This dream involved the image of a boat to which I invited him to free associate, that is, to say whatever came into his head in connection with this boat. He said: 'Well a boat represents movement and this signifies a journey … perhaps life's journey …,' he tailed away. I told him to say quickly, *without thinking*, what came into his mind when he thought of the boat. He suddenly said: 'When I was six, on holiday in Killarney, my parents had a violent fight in a rowing boat where I was crouched in the stern.' He had thought the boat must surely tip over. This association allowed access to the feeling of terror he had felt when trapped between two warring parents, whereas his own 'interpretation', namely that 'a boat suggested a journey', led further into cliché within which he was already trapped. In the event, the very bad parental relationship played a major part in this man's analysis.

What this illustrates is how free association can bring a freshness to a biography which had become lost. It can also bring out the differences between people extremely well, since associations are specific to each person doing free association.

One way in which free association is crucial is in the interpretation of dreams and, in the opinion of the author, a single dream can tell the analyst more about what is going on in the mind of the client than almost anything else. Dreams and their associations often bring forgotten experience to light in a most unexpected way. For this reason, Freud called dreams 'the royal road' to what is "unconscious', and it is why many psychoanalysts regard dream interpretation as the very heart of psychoanalysis.

There are two aspects of a dream that the analyst must understand: The first is that the dream is an expression which the dreamer constructs, rather like the way of communicating in the old parlour game 'charades'. In charades the gesturing usually uses similarity to indicate things to be guessed. For example, imitating the movement of a film camera signifies 'I am referring to a film'. Events in a dream refer either to those events themselves or to similar persons and events. Here is an example of a dream with associations and interpretation: *She was arranging stalks of corn or long grasses or bull rushes. She was trying to get them to stand, which they would not.* Her associations were as follows:In India they were afraid to walk in the long grass because of dangerous snakes. As children they hid to watch the bull with a cow on her uncle's farm (the 'bull rushes'). It was big and fierce, the cow was passive. This very much corresponded to how she saw (heard) her parents' intercourse and this had a very deep influence on what she thought a woman should be and how she herself had behaved for many years. As well as visual similarities, we have in this dream also an auditory similarity, that is a pun, namely, 'bull rushes'. Manifestly this refers to a kind of water plant, but latently it refers to the father in violent intercouse. I hasten to add that there are other ways of interpreting this dream. The important point is that these were *her* associations. Another person might easily have associated, for example, Moses with the bull-rushes.

This brings up the very important point that psychoanalysis is often caricatured as interpreting dreams in accordance with fixed symbols. It is true that Freud did speak of, and use, symbolism in the interpretations of dreams – for example, symbols of the penis and vagina, womb and siblings – but he did not use them as a short-cut method. Any fixed notion of what symbols mean leads to bad psychoanalysis, in that the uniqueness of the individual becomes lost in the generality of symbols. Thus, for example, if a market gardener dreams of cucumbers it would be foolish to interpret this as a phallic dream without waiting patiently for the client's associations.

The free associations of the individual in analysis are the supreme touchstone in the direction of interpretation. However, in the absence of associations, symbols can be extremely useful. I recall seeing a young woman who had the most perplexing dreams with no associations. I noticed that they all involved water in some way or other and remembered that this was a symbol of birth. I tried a 'birth interpretration' and, to my surprise, a veritable flood of material emerged connected with the circumstances of her birth. So although the over use of fixed symbols can lead to slavish interpretation of the client's material, I would be against leaving them out completely.

Aristotle once said that good dream interpreters are good at recognising similarities, and it is worthwhile pausing at this point to explain a fundamental principle of the process of interpreting, not only of dreams but interpreting the action of the unconscious in a variety of activities.

The tendency of the unconscious is to equate objects it perceives as similar. The notion of symbolism makes this immediately clear because most symbols in Freud are based on visual resemblances. Thus things that 'stick out', like swords and pens, visually resemble the erect penis and come to symbolise it. Similarly, containers like boats, houses or caves come to symbolise women and the inside of their bodies. Now although I have played down symbolism, there is no doubt that we can learn something important from it. That is, the unconscious will substitute, say, one person for another in a dream because they have a single feature in common, and so the analysts enquiry, 'Does this person remind you of anyone?', often elicts the original figure whilst revealing the similarity. A patient who was anxious about board meetings discovered that they reminded him of mealtimes around the family table when father would 'discipline' the children. Thus the similarity between the two situations evoked anxieties about the earlier childhood scene, which lent terror to the contemporary board meetings.

This principle of similarity, sometimes called 'predicate thinking', is universally applied by analysts, therapists, psychologists and psychiatrists when they say to the client: 'What does this situation remind you of?' The operation of the principle can be startling when working with patients in psychotic states such as schizophrenia. Here is an example: A patient thought that Jesus, cigar boxes and sex were identical. Some conversation with this man revealed that the link in this improbable trio was the notion of being 'encircled'. He thought that Jesus was encircled by a halo, cigar boxes were encircled by the tax band and, most bizarre of all, a woman was encircled by the sexual glance of the man. You might think that he only had these thoughts 'because he was mad', but if that is so, how is it that we can all understand his thought process so well? The tendency to predicate thinking is deeply embedded in human nature. For example, how often do we hear the cliche, 'All men are the same', and yet there are women who believe this to be literally true at a deep level. They trust no man because 'they are all the same'. Predicate thinking can also be inherent in more everyday prejudice. For example, we can equate whole classes of individuals, who are similar in a superficial way, under a despised name such as 'culchies'. Racial prejudice works by the equation of different individuals under the predicate, 'has the same colour'. Thus unconscious connections influence our prejudice and dominate our everyday perceptions.

I hope I have made clear dream as *ex*-pression. Now I would like to show that the dream can also be the product of *re*-pression, sometimes called 'the censorship'. It can be useful for the moment to regard the dream like a film. A film, as you know, is shot with diferent cameras and the thousands of feet of film are delivered to the cutting-room for editing. The film editor selects the sequences he favours and forms a seamless whole. Now the dream is like this. A huge amount of dream 'footage' is left on the cutting-room floor and, since the dream editor (the dreamer), is anything but impartial, we must gain access in analysis to the film which has been edited out and left lying on the floor. This is done by free association to what *is* in the dream. This is one form of dream censorship. Another common form of censorship is the substitution of another dream figure to stand in for the person who is really on the mind of the deamer.

A young married woman recently mentioned a dream fragment in a session. She dreamed of a couple; the woman held a baby and the man was touched but inhibited. In reality, they were a couple whom she had recently helped adopt a child. The man was ungainly and clumsy but clearly moved at the sight of the new baby. I asked her to describe the man in detail and, as she warmed to her subject, I could not help noticing that she was speaking of him in exactly the same way as she had often spoken of her husband. I hinted at the similarity and she said that they had been at the christening of her niece where her husband had said something to the effect that perhaps having a baby would be more important than their emigration to England for the sake of his career. The disguise now fell from the dream. It now showed the wish to have her husband's baby. The censorship was probably brought about by the fact that they had posponed babies until far into the future. Thus dreams should not be taken at face value; we must bracket out the 'natural attitude' if we are to get at the underlying thoughts.

Now this whole question of the censorship reveals a very important notion in psychoanalysis. It is at this point that we finally come to where a person identifies with someone whom they don't much like. We come to the notion of the so-called *super ego.* This is a notion that has the greatest weight in psychoanalysis. It is the mental agency resulting from the internalisation of authority in the individual.

As a mental agency, the super ego combines the kinder guiding of oneself towards ideals, with the more ferocious self-critical tendencies in all of us. Freud thought that its installation took place as the resolution of the Oedipus complex and he explained it as follows: A boy only emerges from his romance with mother by an eventual, if uneasy, identification with father. In his young mind, his love of mother puts him in an imaginary (often real) rivalry with father, who normally bars the way to the furthering of his young 'romance' with mother. Similarly, the girl in her romance with father is, through her love, moved imperceptibly into a position of rivalry with mother who stands in the path of this pairing. In the spirit of 'if you cant beat them, join them', the boy or girl is cornered into identifying with the image of a loved opposite sex parent, now coloured by hostility. The girl may love her mother very much but the romantic feeling for father will inevitably set her on a collision course with mother, and similarly the boy may love his father very much until this Oedipal rivalry starts. Because of this intense emotional rivalry, the figures of the rivalled parents are internalised in exaggerated form, called 'parental imagoes'.

These internalised versions of parents, coloured by imagination, become the 'super' or 'over ego'. This identification becomes the internal benevolent and malevolent critical agency called the *super ego*. Notice that it exerts both a positive and negative effect on the *ego* or *self*, but usually it is the negative aspects that are stressed, since they so often lead to psychic pain. As someone once said, 'the super ego is soluble in alcohol!' This old joke still tells us today that, for many people, the pain of the internal criticisms can only be daily dissolved by the appliance of alcohol. Unsurprisingly a lot of analytic work is devoted to a slow dissolving of the internal criticisms that paralyse the internal world of the lives of so many people. In the Irish context, the internal criticisms are particularly clear in the analysis of members of religious orders, where a severely punitive attitude to erotic feelings in masturbation is evident. In many ways, they represent the distillation and transmission of sexual guilt in Irish society.

For the moment let us stay with the super ego, for its existence is central to a very important process in the psychoanalytic relationship. As I have already mentioned, Freud discovered in himself unexpectedly hostile feelings towards both Breuer and Fleiss, and it was only subsequently that he discovered that they had become unwitting recipients of his repressed negative feelings towards his father. In analysis, the development of the intimate relationship furthered by free association can lead to the person of the analyst being recreated in the imago of one or both parents. Now this is extremely useful, for it means that the patient can re-live parental relationships with the analyst and come to an insight about what really happened all those years ago. This re-living is called in analysis, the transference, wherein the client's feelings for the key people in his or her life are transferred onto the person of the analyst. This is the origin and inspiration for all those jokes about patients being 'in love' with their analysts. It would, however, be a great mistake to assume that a transference interpretation was merely of the order 'I remind you of your father', uttered by the analyst. The interpretation of transference is a very subtle matter and can certainly not be reduced to simple formulae. The whole subject is further complicated by the discoveries of Melanie Klein, to which we now turn.

All that I have said above applies more or less well to neurotic clients, that is, those who have had their first real life difficulties in the attempt to resolve the Oedipus complex, between the ages of three and five, and the kind of super ego acquired in the process. On Freud's account it would appear obvious that the more severe the parents, the more severe the super ego will be and thus the greater the level of mental disturbance. However, Melanie Klein showed that there were clear cases of disturbed children whose parents showed no sign of having been harsh in rearing their children. She also emphasised the love feelings of the child for the same sex parent and this complicates the more traditional Oedipal triangle explanations which I have used above. Klein discovered that children who really did have gentle parents could sometimes have extremely fierce super egos. This, of course, ran counter to Freud's theory and led to her discovery of an earlier, more primitive super ego that had its origins in the first and second years of life. A client I recall felt most strongly that in the sessions she was on a slide under the microscope, and this made her very anxious. This is a good example of a primitive super ego, which had been projected on to the analyst so that she experienced me as sadistic, cruel and merciless. In the transference I was seen as a 'witch mother'. My describing this feeling back to her eventually had an effect and her super ego became much less relentless.

Now for Klein, there is a crucial developmental bridge to be crossed in the earliest months of life and it involves relinquishing one world view in favour of another. To understand this, we must attempt to describe what the baby's view of the world is like in the first months and years. The first thing to notice is that for the baby, 'objectivity' is at an 'all time low', and it seems that the notion of an inanimate object is alien to the baby. We can see this in older children of two or three who persist in seeing, for example, furniture as 'alive'. How often do we see a child bump its head on a table, only to be reassured by mother's remark that that was a 'bold' table? This shows that the table can be viewed by the child as a malevolent agent, deserving of punishment. I recall a two year old who insisted on naming each peanut she took from the packet as a 'mummy one' or 'daddy one' or a 'baby one'.

Now what this animism means is that, for the baby, the mother's feeding breast is experienced as being alive separately from the mother, who is not seen as a whole person. According to Klein, the baby internalises good feeding experiences and this is symbolised by the 'good breast'. Thus an alive, sustaining good breast is 'inside the mind' and provides the basis for mental stability. However, the best of mothers will sometimes fail to anticipate baby's needs and, for example, the baby may be left hungry or in a screaming panic. Now this experience of an absent breast is not seen by the infant in the adult style of something being missing. According to Klein, it is experienced as the presence of a malevolent agent actually causing the pangs of hunger in the stomach. (This is reminiscent of the 'bold table' example above.) All such bad experiences are symbolised and internalised as the 'bad breast'. On a more commonsense level, it is easy to see that the baby, at the mercy of mother's changes, is splitting bad experiences off from good experiences in staying stable.

Melanie Klein's conception of the infant mind is dominated by the two processes that we can only presume actually occupy the mind of the baby: taking in food by the mouth (introjection) and evacuating waste by the bowels (projection). Thus good experiences are introjected or internalised, and bad experiences are projected. But since bad experiences are persecuting, their projection into mother makes baby's world more paranoid. It is probably best to think of this process of projection, not in isolation, but together with splitting as a kind of double action: baby splits off a bad experience, say dread, and projects or evacuates it into mother, making her seem more frightening. These remarks add up to what Klein called the 'paranoid-schizoid' position (schizoid = split), which is not a phase but a perspective which we never lose all our lives. This position is dominated by persecutory anxiety.

In the second position, the so-called 'depressive' position, there is a healing of splits. In the paranoid-schizoid position, the child believes that the good mother and the bad mother are completely separate. In this new position, however, he comes to realise that the two are in reality one and the same. There is then a feeling that the loved mother is in fact the same one that has been attacked in anger, and a kind of healing regret is felt, sometimes called 'reparation'. This position is then dominated by depressive anxiety. The Kleinian view is that creativity is rooted in this reparative process. Broadly speaking, the task of the psychoanalyst is to enable the patient to pass more securely out of the paranoid-schizoid position and further into the depressive position.

It is possible to analyse neurosis using only the ideas that Freud discovered and which I have tried to explain above. However, with the more disturbed client, in the opinion of the author, the ideas of Klein are indispensible. One consequence of her ideas is the introduction of the so-called 'countertransference', which is the analyst's reaction to the client's transference on to the analyst. Klein herself disliked this word, preferring her own term 'projective identification' to explain the evocation of strong feelings in the analyst, particularly by the more disturbed client. This notion has often been criticised, seeming somewhat 'telepathic' – it has to be experienced to be believed.

Klein taught us that a client with psychotic tendencies will need to gain access to the earlier layers of experience, and these are dominated by the mother and the breast feeding experience. Thus the mother/baby situation is recreated symbolically in the session. This can be made clearer by reference to an idea of Klein's most distinguished follower, Wilfred Bion. Bion thought that the baby evacuates into mother the feelings it cannot cope with. For example, if the baby has a sudden premonition of dying, it evacuates this into mother. Now if the mother has the capacity for what he called 'reverie', which is the ability to absorb and transmute baby's projections, she will be able to reassure the baby that 'all is well' despite what he feels. Now some mothers, often disturbed themselves, are unable to provide this reverie. Such a mother cannot manage to accept baby's projections, which are consequently never transformed and build up into a persecuting presence in the mind of the baby. The analyst, like the mother, can transmute these projections by giving an interpretation which can assist the client in taking back the projection and re-owning a split-off part of themselves.

This is not to say that the client suffering from neurosis cannot benefit from such 'deep' analysis. It is just that in the case of neurosis it is not essential to go so deep to have any success at all. The Kleinian analyst takes up the position of a mother in reverie, who transmutes the client's primitive emotion into something the client can deal with, rather than something that must be got rid of by being evacuated into the analyst.

In her later career, Klein introduced an idea into psychoanalysis that has influenced many practicioners, the notion of envy, which must be carefully distinguished from jealousy. Jealousy involves three people, for example a mother may be jealous of her daughter's relationship with her father. In such a case the mother actually wants the love of her husband and wants to be in her daughter's shoes for this very reason. On the other hand, the daughter may envy her brother's relationship with the mother, even though she actively detests her mother, that is, she has no wish for mother's love but attacks her brother in order to spoil the love he is receiving. Thus, for Klein, the impulse to spoil another's enjoyment characterises envy. She traces the roots of envy to the breast feeding experience where, she claims, a baby finds it difficult to tolerate the notion that there is a source of goodness that has an independent existence from the baby. The envious person has great difficulty expressing gratitude, since this involves recognising an external source of goodness. Klein claimed that the intensity of envy was a constitutional factor – different for each individual baby.

In the clinical situation, we see envy in the client who refuses to give the analyst the satisfaction of seeing an improvement, through analysis, in their lives. Such a client may keep improvements a secret and remain resolutely negative in sessions. At the more extreme end of the spectrum, just as there are babies whose envy interferes with breast feeding, so there are clients whose

It is not hard to see that this form of analysis is dominated by the mother/baby situation, and the father somehow gets ignored. Some would say that the father, in most cases, does not have much to do with the actual looking after of the baby, so there is no need to mention him at all. However, the father's role emerges as the child grows up. More than this, the father's relationship with the mother, before and during birth, can exercise an influence on the early relation with the baby. Supposing, for example, the husband does not love his wife at all and she feels this very keenly. She may unconsciously turn to her baby for comfort and upset the delicate 'give and take' of good mothering.

This powerful stressing of the mother at the expense of the father stimulated the French analyst, Jacques Lacan, to start a 'back to Freud' movement, for Freud did stress the father in childhood, although Lacan develops a 'theory of the father' very much his own. Broadly speaking, we have seen that Klein takes up the position of the mother in the analysis, Lacan takes up the position of the father – the 'giver of language' and representative of the 'law'.

His central idea is that man is essentially a language-using creature and the child is 'born into language' almost as if he were born on to a stage where a play is being performed. Mother and father are on stage and their scripts have been 'written' by their parents, just as they will now give the new baby its script, or part in the play. The play takes place in a theatre which inhabits a certain culture, and so the child finds its entry into the larger culture by way of the parents' perception of it. Thus if the parent's view of society is skewed in any way, the child will acquire this same vision.

The area Klein studied is, of course, pre-linguistic and Lacan sets this aside, calling it the 'imaginary order' or system, dominated as it is by the mother/baby relation – that is a relation between only two persons. This early phase, dominated as we have seen by projections on the part of the baby, is an extremely subjective period. It may not be actually psychotic but it is the stuff of madness. Lacan thought that the father's role was to provide a model of separateness or distance. Father is the first distant, that is, non-merging, figure in the child's life. It is important to note that he does not stress the physical presence of the father in the home but, rather, the presence of his symbolic fathering function that will enable the child to separate out as an individual properly. This is Lacan's version of the successful resolution of the Oedipal problem.

According to Lacan, the child will acquire its own script only by individuation into a grammar of living – the network of family relationships and human institutions in society called by him the 'symbolic order'. This access to the symbolic order signals that the individual's 'desire' is coming to fruition and that they have left what he calls 'demand' behind.

'Demand' is the wish for instant and total gratification, often seen in children when they, for example, insist on a bar of chocolate that they will certainly drop on the floor and forget when they get it. Demand, then, is the wish to have every last lack filled, but what children (and adults) must come to learn is that there is nothing that will fill every last lack in their lives. Lacan elevates this idea to a critique of modern society, in condemning the utopian impulse in all of us to 'find the answer' (life, the universe and everything!). Utopianism is the wish to obliterate lack once and for all, but Lacan's message is that the lack in each of us is a blessing in disguise, for it conceals the 'someting wanting' in us which will hopefully issue in action.

If Klein is the analyst of 'content' or emotion, Lacan is the analyst of form or structure, for Lacanian technique stresses the family structures at the expense of emotions. This assists the client in 'taking up a position' towards family members in the process of resolving the Oedipal problem. Thus the client is enabled to find an Archimidean point in the family network on which to stand and move their world. As we have seen, Kleinian analysis enables the client to relinquish the paranoid-schizoid position and gain access to the depressive position, and similarly, Lacanian analysis enables the client to relinquish the demand for total completion by another, in favour of the imperfections of putting desire into action.

Looking back over this essay, I am struck by the fact that it seems to be divided into schools: Freudian, Kleinian and Lacanian, whereas most practitioners in Dublin (and elsewhere) draw inspiration from more than one school. Thus we have here in Ireland a healthy mix of differing ideas which is the precondition of growth, and today we have a distinct and individual voice which is increasingly making itself felt in international psychoanalytic circles.

Selected Reading

Bowie, M., *Lacan* (London: Fontana Modern Masters). Advanced treatment of good quality.

Freud, S., *Introductory Lectures on Psychoanalysis* (Harmondsworth: Penguin, 1973).

Freud, S., 'The Interpretation of Dreams'(Section on 'The Dream Work') *(Collected Works,* Vol 4).

Jones, E., *The Life and Work of Sigmund Freud* (Harmondsworth: Penguin, 1964).

Klein, M., 'Infantile Anxiety-Situations' in *Love, Guilt and Reparation* (London: Hogarth, 1975). Introduction via the analysis of a work of art.

Macey, D., *Lacan in Contexts* (Verso, 1988). Introduction which contains a useful summary of Lacan's career.

Meltzer, D., *The Kleinian Development* (Clunie Press, 1978). Advanced but well written account including a section on Bion.

Mitchell, J., *The Selected Melanie Klein* (Harmondsworth: Penguin, 1978).Contains an early lecture on Envy.

Skelton, R., 'Generalisation from Freud to Matte Blanco' in *International Review of Psychoanalysis* Vol 17, 1990.

CHAPTER 2

Child Psychoanalytic Psychotherapy

Michael Fitzgerald

The two main assumptions of psychoanalysis are the principle of psychic determinism, or causality, and the importance of the unconscious in the understanding of the human mind.

The principle of psychic determinism states that nothing in the mind is arbitrary or undetermined or happens by chance. A mental event has a meaning and a cause and is determined by the those that preceded it. A person cannot therefore dismiss dreams, obsessive thoughts, or slips of the tongue, but must ask themselves 'What caused it?', 'Why did it happen?' Dreams follow the same principle of psychic determinism and psychoanalysis traditionally looks for hidden wishes beneath the remembered dream.

The second main assumption is that only a small amount of mental activity is conscious at any one time and that unconscious factors are important in understanding the human mind. Psychoanalysis is fundamentally about the study of the unconscious, about the study of how deep-seated, unconscious factors determine feelings, attitudes and patterns of behaviour. The unconscious contains early childhood memories and childhood wishes as well as many desires and fantasies that would be unacceptable to the conscious mind, for example, sexual and aggressive wishes or impulses.

While the conscious mind takes reality into account, the unconscious is governed by the pleasure principle, which means that all impulses and wishes demand immediate satisfaction. It is hardly surprising that the contents of the unconscious are therefore repressed because if they became conscious they would cause the individual anxiety. In central Europe, around the end of the nineteenth century, and in Ireland in the first half or more of the twentieth century, sexual impulses were connoted as 'bad' and so a large amount of psychological energy was expended on keeping these impulses repressed and in the unconscious. Instead of energy being available for work, for relating to people and for creative activities, it is expended in repressing unconscious impulses, for example sexual and aggressive wishes.

To take another example, the problem of repressed anger could be seen in a child who began to steal because he could not express anger at an ill father who was neglecting him. He repressed the anger at the father and began to steal as a symptom of his distress. In treatment, it was possible to make the anger conscious and to give him insight into the problems between himself and his father. He was able to express his anger directly at his father and the symptoms of stealing ceased.

Three women are most associated with the birth of child psychoanalysis and psychotherapy – Anna Freud, Hermine Hug-Hellmuth and Melanie Klein. While there is no doubt that Sigmund Freud was the 'father' of psychoanalysis and psychotherapy, child psychoanalysis and child psychotherapy had three 'mothers'.

At first, the psychoanalytic study of childhood was conducted through adult patients. Adult psychoanalysis set out to discover new information about childhood trauma through the reconstruction of childhood events within the analytic process.

After the publication of the *Three Essays on the Theory of Sexuality* by Freud in 1905, psychoanalysts began direct observation of children. These studies confirmed some psychoanalytic theories at that time and also provided alternative hypothesis. Nursery school teachers who had undergone analysis, and those working with delinquents, continued this work in the 1920s and 1930s. Indeed, psychoanalytic ideas which emphasised honesty, openness and freedom began to have increasing influence on child-rearing practices in this period.

In the 1920s, papers on child psychoanalysis, based on work conducted directly with children, began to be published using psychoanalytic theory but also using a technique modified from adult psychoanalysis with the analysis of the young child's free play as well as the spoken word. Anna Freud, a pioneer in the area, wished to eliminate suggestion as an element of treatment and achieved this by not using her authority in relation to the child.

Her aim was to help the child understand the meaning of the symptom and to resolve it in that way, rather than telling the child to give up the symptom. She kept management of the patient to a minimum except where they were seriously harmful forces at work.

An important feature of child therapy is the analysis of 'resistance', i.e. resistance by the child to the work of analytic psychotherapy and to increased self knowledge. The child can be frightened of the child psychotherapist because of previous unpleasant experiences with authority figures and is therefore frightened of showing unacceptable parts of his personality which he may define as 'bad'. He then goes into resistance and censors this part of himself and does not communicate these thoughts to the therapist. These problem parts of the child cannot then be analysed or dealt with, as they are censored. It is the therapist's task to help the child to trust him and to overcome his resistance by telling the therapist about the censored thoughts.

An example of these censored thoughts could be death wishes towards a sibling. The fears or fantasies of a child in any particular situation are often greater than would be appropriate for that situation. If the child imagines that the therapeutic situation is threatening, it is hardly surprising that they will be resistant to taking part in it. The role of the therapist is to reality test,that is to help the child to see what the real situation is. Indeed, this reality testing of the child's fantasies is a significant feature of child psychotherapeutic work. This has to be so because the child often imagines adults to be more threatening, non-accepting and punishing than they are in reality. When this has been achieved the child will speak much more freely in psychotherapy and make more rapid progress.

Indeed, children coming for psychotherapy can fear that they will be given brain surgery or hypnosis or electrical treatment. If a child is thinking about this, it is hardly surprising that they will find it difficult to speak. A child may also not speak because he feels his problems are too great to be helped by psychotherapy. He may feel that it is better to keep his feelings of upset than face what he sees as an even greater threat, that is exposing the unacceptable side of himself, e.g. his hatred of other children or of a parental figure. Children also sometimes don't want to talk in psychotherapy and want to stop because they see every interpretation by the therapist as a criticism of them. A child may feel that it is safer to censor feelings of hate, longing, pain, jealousy and anger than to admit them to the therapist whom he feels will be unaccepting.

Other forms of resistance can be seen in bodily attitudes, e.g. fixed smile, stiffness and rigidity or arrogant behaviour. The origin of these bodily attitudes in the earlier childhood need to be understood. For example, a child with a very rigid perfectionist father may identify with this father and therefore demonstrate the same patterns himself. The therapist is trying to make the child more flexible and more free to express himself by:
a) the analysis of the 'transference', i.e. feelings, attitudes and experience towards parental figures which are transferred by the child onto the therapist in the present;
b) the interpretation of unconscious material, e.g. memories, wishes and desires which the child has but is not aware of, and which are currently causing conflict.

This form of treatment is useful to children who are anxious or depressed or in psychological turmoil. It is also of value to children who are in conflict because of physical illness, or who are having difficulty coming to terms with disability. It is helpful in treating children with unresolved grief reactions because of the death of a parent. These reactions can make the child more vulnerable to depression in later life if not dealt with satisfactorily. Psychoanalysis can help children who are having difficulty resolving stress due to some overwhelming trauma, for example a serious accident or other traumatic life event.

Analysis is not for everyone, however, and it will not reverse biological brain pathology. It is a treatment of the mind rather than the brain. Psychotherapy does not attempt to alter directly chemical imbalances in the brain as psychothrophic drugs like antidepressants do. To be helpful the problem must have a psychological basis.

In general, patients with mental handicap, schizophrenia and autism, would not be treated with psychoanalysis as a first line treatment. These patients would benefit from behaviour therapy, which is based on learning theory – elements of which would include social skills training or the rewarding of positive behaviour in a systematic way. In addition, psychopharmacology approaches would be relevant to children with schizophrenia. In recent years there has been some new interest in applying child psychoanalytic psychotherapy to patients with mental handicap who tend to have more psychological problems than children with average I.Q..

If the parents and teachers are extremely negative and critical, children develop very low self-esteem which makes them vulnerable to anxiety and depression and other conditions. Unfortunately, in Ireland there has been a fear of praising children and an idea that continuous criticism is good for them. Nothing could be further from the truth. A child with low self-esteem is very prone to psychological problems. The voices of critical parents, critical teachers and others are internalised in the child and echo throughout the rest of their lives with very serious consequences for their happiness. All of this leaves children in a very anxious, unhappy, negative and pessimistic state, with a very poor quality of life. I have never known a child who grew up psychologically healthy who was continually criticised.

In Ireland, it has been shown that children from large families are more at risk from psychological problems. It is more difficult for parents to be sensitive to each member of a large family. The economic stresses also undermine parents by distracting them from the needs of their children. Anything that impacts on parents will also impact on the children. If the parents are distracted by the multiple stresses of disadvantage, mental illness or marital breakdown, they will have much less mental energy to tune in to the needs of their children, and their children are more likely to become psychologically stressed. In order to grow healthily, children need a secure environment, reasonable limits placed on their behaviour, and parents who are in tune with their needs and their developmental stage or level of maturity.

Age is a critical factor in determining what is appropriate to demand of a child. For example, to demand that a six month old child be toilet-trained is quite excessive. At the same time, a child will also be damaged if normal demands are not made at the appropriate time. Over indulgence or spoiling is as damaging as neglect or rejection. Sometimes children and adolescents from extremely wealthy families who over-indulge their children, have children who have difficulty in developing definite identities of themselves or knowing what they want or what true value is.

One of the first tasks of healthy development is the acquisition of basic trust which will grow in the child in a good enough family. Children who are physically abused, sexually abused or suffer serious neglect, grow up very mistrustful and fearful of people. Child psychotherapy takes a very long time to reverse this mistrust of people and, indeed, an element of it probably always persists.

When unconscious impulses, for example sexual or aggressive impulses, seek discharge, they put the child into conflict with his or her super ego (conscience) and the outside world. A pathological solution to this conflict is the development of a compromise formation (symptom), for example, phobia, obsessional symptom (for example, hand washing) or a conversion symptom (for example, paralysed limb). A phobia is a condition where there is an avoidance of a specific situation or object, although not dangerous, which causes anxiety to the child. Here the defence mechanism of displacement can occur where, for example, a fear of father can be displaced onto a fear of animals.

In school phobia, what can emerge is not a fear of school but a fear of leaving mummy or a fear that mummy will die if the child goes to school. I remember one situation where the child had a school phobia because he was afraid of mother stabbing herself while he was at school. This came as a great surprise to mother despite the fact that she had attempted suicide in the past.

In obsessive compulsive neurosis, the child is dominated by repetitive unwanted thoughts or actions or rituals, for example hand washing. These tend to occur in conscientious meticulous and hard working children. These children tend to have harsh super egos (consciences) and a very poor toleration of strong feelings. These neuroses are a pathological solution to strong sexual or aggressive impulses which are unconscious. In analysis, one becomes aware that these children have isolated thinking from feeling. They tend to intellectualise and the therapist is trying to help them to get in touch with their feelings and unconscious impulses. One can also analyse the defence mechanism of 'undoing' which attempts to ritualistically 'remove' the offensive act, for example, hand washing which attempts to 'undo' the guilt about masturbation.

Children also show 'conversion symptoms' where unacceptable mental content is changed into physical phenomena, for example headaches, were a child is unable to express anger at mother for being over controlling and, instead, develops a headache. Another example would be a child who develops abdominal pain because he is in conflict with someone in his environment. Children can also develop other conversion symptoms, for example, gait disturbances, tremors, convulsions and paralysis, because of stress in their environment. The development of the conversion symptom happens unconsciously.

Reaction formation is another defence mechanism were the child converts unacceptable feelings into acceptable ones and, in the process, keeps the unacceptable ones unconscious. For example, a child who has repressed feelings of hate for his mother can become over concerned for her welfare and over attentive to her.

Uncontrolled aggression in the classroom would be a common reason for referral for child psychotherapy. Such a child would tend to have a history of being in a family where there was considerable violence, or to have experienced violent attacks on himself outside the family. There would often be marital disharmony or alcoholism in the family. There may be a very large family where the parents are overwhelmed by the excessive caretaking needs and not able to meet them. These experiences can leave children feeling very angry and resentful. They then take these feelings out on other pupils or on the teacher in the classroom. In child psychotherapy, the child is helped to understand why he is so angry and aggressive and he is helped to see the origins of his symptoms. He is helped to see that the teachers and other pupils are not really the target of his aggression but persons in earlier childhood. The therapist helps the child to express feelings about experiences in earlier childhood and to understand them, and therefore to work throuqh them and resolve them by talking about them.

Another child may present with feelings of anxiety, nightmares, and fear of going out onto the street alone. This could be because he lives with extremely anxious, over-protective parents who are constantly anxious about his welfare and telling him that the world is full of dangers and that all kind of catastrophes could happen. It is hardly surprising, then, that he is having nightmares of catastrophes, is clinging to parents and is terrified of any separation from them. The child psychotherapist tries to help the child to see the world as a relatively safe place and that there is not 'a catastrophe around every corner'.

Another child may come for treatment because of an abnormal gait. The neurologist will have found nothing wrong with him from a physical point of view. During treatment, it emerges that the child has tremendous anger towards his father because of his constant criticism of him. The child cannot express his anger towards his father directly but instead expresses it indirectly through a physical symptom.

Another child will complain of pain in his tummy at 8 am each morning and may do so because he inappropriately fears criticism from a very sensitive teacher, or cannot face his own perfectionistic academic standards. He may see it as a total disaster if he is number two in the class, rather than number one where his standards are driving him. It is hardly surprising that this sends the child into conflict which is then expressed with abdominal pain. The child psychotherapist helps the child to understand his pain and helps him to modify his standards and to see the teacher as she is in reality.

Childhood depression is not an uncommon presenting symptom nowadays. The childhood depression could have a multitude of causes. An example would be a child of small stature whose father was tall and athletic and who had a very successful athletic career. This father was totally unaccepting of his son who was not athletic like himself. His father favoured another son who was athletic and fulfilled father's ideal for a son. Clearly, in this case, work is required with both father and child. The child in psychotherapy will have to be helped to come to terms with his small stature and not to be so angry about it.

In depressed children, anger is usually turned inwards and helping the child to express this anger outwards can partially relieve the depression. It can also be helpful for the child to have expressed this anger to his father who is behaving in such an inappropriate way. The child is also helped to value the assets that he has, as these can often get overlooked by the child when there is excessive focus on some negative issue like short stature. The therapist is trying to help the child to build up a positive self-image and increase his self-esteem. Low self- esteem is very much a feature of children coming for child psychotherapy. Low self-esteem is a particular feature of depressed children. The child psychotherapist is attempting to help other depressed children to come to terms with a loss in the family or with marital violence, something which can be so depressing to children.

In addition, children in families where there is marital violence blame themselves for this violence and feel inappropriately that it is caused by something in them that is 'bad'. The child psychotherapist helps the child to differentiate between that which they are responsible for and that which they are not responsible for.

Children from the age of about twelve years can commit, or attempt, suicide. For children who attempt suicide, child psychotherapy is required in addition to some other treatment like family therapy. These children will also often be depressed. The child psychotherapist has to explore the reason for the attempted suicide with the child. It may be because the child is being abused in some way, or they may feel that they are not being treated well in the family and that some other sibling is being favoured over them. They may then feel that life is not worth living. They may express their anger at someone close to them for not caring enough for them. The way they express this is through the attempted suicide. The attempted suicide is then a way of punishing this person. The child psychotherapist helps the child to see that this is not an appropriate way of communicating with this other person and helps them to communicate in a more direct verbal fashion. It is also clear that parents are often not aware that their child has suicidal ideas, and clearly the parents should consider this particularly when the child is depressed, and ask the child directly.

There can also be a role for the child psychotherapist with encopresis, that is when the child passes faeces in his pants. This child will also require other treatments, e.g. behavioural treatments which involve rewards for days without soiling, in addition to child psychotherapy. Again encopresis can be an expression of conflict between the child and the mother. The child who soils when he comes home from school is expressing anger at mother in this way. In one case, mother used to then rub the faeces onto the body of the child and make him more angry so that he soiled again the following afternoon to punish her. The child psychotherapist needs to discuss in detail with the child the factors surrounding the soiling and to help the child to communicate in a more appropriate way with the mother. The mother in this case needs psychotherapeutic help, in her own right, to come to terms with the critical punitive and over-controlling aspect of her personality which was causing the child so much anger.

Application of psychoanalytic psychotherapy

The basic technique of child analytic psychotherapy is a play technique. In play, children symbolise their conflicts and anxieties. Adult patients in analysis are able to free associate (i.e. to say freely what comes into their mind). Small children cannot do this so easily but play is their normal way of expressing themselves. The child psychotherapist treats the child's play and verbal discourse in the same way that the adult therapist treats the patients free association of ideas.

The child psychotherapy takes place in a room without dangerous objects. The surfaces are washable. This kind of room will allow the child the freedom to express himself. Each child will have a box of toys for his individual use. The box will usually contain bricks, toy cars, animals and figures of various sizes. It is also traditional to have paper, pencils, crayons, glue, scissors, string and running water. The aim is to have material that will allow the child to express herself as freely as possible. Children get quite attached to the room and insecure if they are changed. The change of room can be a reminder of many previous changes that may have occurred in their life and that may have been distressful. These events will need to be explored in detail.

The basic mode of communication is through interpretation, where the therapist tries to understand the patient's communications, make sense of them and communicate these insights to the child in a language that the child will understand. The therapist conveys to the child that she is interested in the child's worries and is there to help him understand them. The timing of interpretation is important and therefore an effort is made not to give an interpretation until the child is ready. For example, there may be evidence in a child's material that they have a death wish towards a parent or sibling, but the therapist initially will only focus on the anger and say something initially like 'some children can be very angry with their brothers and sisters or with their mother.' It can also be of considerable relief for children to realise that they are not the only ones who have these wishes. Before coming to treatment, children often feel they are the only ones in the world with these feelings, which greatly increases their suffering. Transference interpretations are among the most important, because they increase the child's self knowledge and help him to see the feelings he is transferring onto the therapist and people in the outside world that were originally felt towards parental figures. If a child felt that she was responsible for a parent's death then the experience of this would be highly significant and the unburdening would be of major importance. Psychosomatic symptoms may be interpreted, for example, as stemming from a conflict with a parental figure or sibling, or as a way of getting some love or care in a family where love is only available to someone who is sick.

It would be usual for a child, coming to a first session, to have fears or fantasies about the treatment. The child may feel that they are coming because they are 'naughty' and may see it as a punishment. If they have been mistreated for most of their life, they will have much mistrust and very little hope of help. They may expect to be let down again. Siblings may have mentioned the word 'mad' in relation to coming for therapy and this may cause the child great anxiety. Sometimes they will have been told that they are going to get their eyes tested and are therefore completely confused. These prior fantasies or explanations need to be explored by the therapist with the child or the child will feel totally confused. The major part of treatment is opening up clear lines of communication and openness, and dealing with fantasies so that the world makes sense to the child.

One of the other major tasks of the therapist is to overcome resistance, i.e. the resistance or reluctance of the child to communicate or cooperate with the therapist. He may not want to talk about something or may want to shut out something that makes him anxious or guilty.

The first visit to a child psychotherapist will involve a detailed history of the child and his or her family. The therapist will enquire about mother's pregnancy with the child, and developmental milestones, language development, feeding behaviour, experience of preschool and school. In addition, the child's temperament, which can have major effects on development, will be enquired about. Detailed histories would also be taken of the parents' life story and especially their marital relationship, as well as parental personality type and history of any mental illness. The family atmosphere in the earlier part of childhood, and currently, would also be of critical importance. The child would then be interviewed alone, using the play technique as well as verbal communication to assess suitability for child psychotherapy. If treatment was considered appropriate, the child would be seen one or more times per week and the sessions would last under one hour.

How change happens

When we talk about change in child psychoanalytic psychotherapy, we are referring to psychic change or emotional growth. This change is shown when the child displays clearer thinking, with insight into the causes of his / her problems and feelings.

The child can now put a meaning on his feelings and is not bewildered by them. An observer looking at the child has the sense of a more contained child, less at the mercy of instincts or feelings. I believe that the child identifies or models himself or herself on the calm, contained therapist. The good experience with the therapist is taken in by the child and strengthens the child's personality. The therapist's calm accepting voice becomes absorbed into the child's mind and laid down in memory traces. This voice counters critical parental voices from the past, and has the effect of boosting self esteem.

In the same way, good experience with the therapist increases the child's capacity to trust and form relationships with other children and people in general. This helps the child get back on the normal developmental course. One observes emotional growth happening again just as in non-disturbed children, and a smile coming on to the face of a child who previously had a frozen, frightened face. The child plays better and works better in school and relates better to peers. He is better able to cope with every day stresses. One also notices a softening of the super ego or conscience, and therefore less signs of inappropriate guilt.

Change is brought about by a good quality trusting therapeutic relationship and by the therapist making the unconscious conscious. The child is free to put the unspeakable into words and with that the burden on the child lightens – 'a problem shared is a problem halved'. Young children in particular have a tendency to blame themselves for everything that happens. For example, if a parent gets sick the child may believe that it was because that he/she was naughty. This fantasy can cause enormous distress and guilt, and be undetected for a long time by the parent. The child can feel that he or she is very 'bad' and that the expression of anger is both 'bad' and dangerous. The exploration by the therapist of these sort of fantasies is critical to the progress of therapy and to change.

Children will also have fantasies about the therapist and will transfer, or put onto the therapist, feelings, for example, that they had about a rejecting father or mother, and then perceive the therapist as rejecting. The therapist has to help the child to see that these fantasies are inappropriate and refer to powerful figures from outside the treatment. The resolution of these transferred feelings is very important for change to come about. In the process of resolution, it is important for the child to understand where these feelings have come from. Then they will be able to see the therapist and other adult figures in their life more realistically.

In the treatment, the child also has a corrective emotional experience, i.e. the therapist behaves differently from other figures in the child's life or in the child's past. With this experience the child can begin to see that not all adults are like their rejecting critical parents or other such figures. This development of trust and hope is absolutely critical for the child's future happiness and successful negotiation of life's hurdles.

Change is more likely to be maintained if the problems have been properly worked through in the psychoanalytic sense. This means covering the same ground many times and uncovering the many ramifications of conflict and fantasies as they appear in the child's clinical material with the therapist. There are many reasons why a child develops a particular symptom and all these need to be explored in so far as it is possible.

Work with parents is also important and can be a form of psychoanalytic child development education. It helps the parents to understand what the child has been through and emphasises the child's need for empathy, security and an accepting environment. The sessions with parents also have the role of protecting the child's treatment and supporting the parents in the demanding task of bringing the child for treatment. Some parents suffer very considerable guilt about having a disturbed child and others experience envy of the child's treatment and the attention that the child is receiving. These are matters that need to be attended to if the treatment is not to be prematurely terminated. The confidentiality of the child's material has to be respected, otherwise the child will mistrust the therapist. Some parents who have major psychological problems themselves will need formal psychotherapeutic help in their own right or they may need marital therapy .

In modern psychoanalysis, the importance of interpersonal factors has greatly increased. The earlier theories of psychoanalysis put major stress on factors within the child, such as instincts. While this still holds, the cause of psychological problems in childhood and adolescence are now perceived as being more complex and multifaceted. Nowadays crucial importance is given to the levels of empathy or sensitivity between the parents and the child.

To grow healthily a child needs parents who are good enough, who are sensitive enough to the needs of the child. This means that the child has more good experience with the parents than negative experience. The child's personality is built on this good experience. The child's personality is very much weakened if there is more negative experience than good experience. When the child is reared with sensitive parents, he lays down within himself or herself a strong foundation for personality. This makes him strong and more able to withstand the 'slings and arrows' of life. The child strengthens its personality by identifying with solid sensitive parents. There is major modelling on the parents' personality. What the child models on is not only the parents as they are, but the parents as the child perceives them. The small child will tend to project aggressive and other feelings onto the parents and will therefore perceive them as more threatening and dangerous than they are. It is this model of the parents that he or she will identify with. The child's superego or conscience is modelled on the parents and other significant figures in their environment.

In the past, conscience development tended to be very harsh in Irish children and adults and caused enormous guilt and anxiety when the standards of conscience were not met. Children who have parents with extremely high standards of behaviour will take these abnormally high standards into their super ego and then demand these inappropriate standards of themselves for the rest of their childhood, and indeed of their life if they are not modified.

There is substantial research evidence that psychotherapy is more effective than no treatment. Some of the positive effects of psychotherapy are not seen immediately and indeed some of the improvements continue to arise between eighteen months and three years after the children finish treatment with psychotherapy. For children, the overall improvement with psychotherapy has been put between 67% and 78%. The spontaneous improvement rate, that is the improvement rate without treatment, has been put at about 25%. It is likely that child psychotherapy considerably speeds up the rate of improvement. There is unfortunately much less research on child analytic psychotherapy as compared to adult analytic psychotherapy.

Selected Reading

1. Sandler J., Kennedy H., Tyson R., *The technique of child psychoanalysis* (London: The Hogarth Press, 1980).

2 Freud A., *Normality and pathology in childhood* (London: Penguin, 1973).

3. Segal H., *The work of Hanna Segal* (New York: Jason Aronson, 1981).

4. Kolvin I., Garside R., Nicol A., McMillian A., Wolstenholm F., Leitch I., *Help starts here* (London: Tavistock, 1981).

5. Freud A., *Introduction to psychoanalysis.* (London: The Hogarth Press, 1974).

CHAPTER 3

Jungian Analysis

Rita McCarthy and Patricia Skar

In embarking upon an introduction to analytical psychology, our aim is to describe the basic aspects of analytical methods whilst, at the same time, honouring the fact that the contents and practice of analysis varies considerably among practitioners. Analytical psychology, not unlike other schools of analysis, is very much undergoing its own process of modification and transformation, and the divergence between schools as to analytic practice is the subject of much lively debate. It is not felt to be within the scope of this introduction to explore these differences and we would refer those readers wishing to pursue this to Samuels (1985). Broadly speaking, contemporary Jungian psychology ranges from the Developmental (e.g. Fordham, Samuels) through the Classical (e.g. Adler, Woodman) to the Archetypal (e.g. Hillman) approach. The basic tenets of analytical psychology and its application as outlined here will very much reflect the practice and orientation of the authors.

Carl Gustav Jung (1875-1961) referred to his practice of psychological analysis as 'analytical psychology' to differentiate his work from the 'psychoanalysis' of the Freudian school. Jungian analysts today still refer to themselves as 'analytical psychologists' rather than 'psychoanalysts' to maintain this distinction. Jung's ideas range widely over many areas: from the practical aspects of psychotherapy to the psychological connotations of alchemy; from the psychology of religion to parapsychological phenomena. Jung's published works include some thirty books and ninety articles and essays of varying lengths. In popular bookstores, one often finds Jung's writings in the 'occult' or 'new age' sections, but Jung himself deplored being called a mystic and regarded his work as scientifically based. Since our purpose is to give a general introduction to Jungian analysis, we shall concentrate on Jung's most important theories concerning the structure of the psyche and the operation of psychic processes, with the aim of showing how these ideas are utilised in practice between analyst and analysand (client). In order to understand how Jung's thinking developed, it is first necessary to give a brief description of his personal development and the historical and philosophical factors that influenced him.

Growing up near Basel, Switzerland, Jung was the son of a Swiss Reformed pastor who was also an oriental and classical scholar. His childhood milieu gave Jung not only a familiarity with Protestant theology but also an interest in medicine, classical languages and the history of religion. Jung read extensively from the works of philosophers, theologians, mystics, orientalists, ethnologists, novelists and poets, but probably the most important sources for his ideas can be found in Romantic philosophy and the Philosophy of Nature.

Jung's original wish was to be an archaeologist, but his family were poor and he could only afford to go to the University of Basel, where there was no archaeology department. Jung chose medicine instead, and during his studies discovered a textbook on psychiatry by Krafft-Ebing. Since Jung was interested in natural science, while at the same time preoccupied with religious speculation, philosophy, and the search for value and meaning, the choice of psychiatry as a career seemed the perfect way to reconcile these opposites within himself. The Hegelian manner of organising thought into pairs of opposites which are capable of producing a new synthesis was a typical way of thinking at the time Jung's ideas developed. As we shall see, the theory of opposition became a fundamental theme of Jung's work and appears throughout his writings.

After qualification as a doctor, Jung became an assistant in the Burghölzli mental hospital in Zürich. Much of Jung's thought originates from his clinical experiences at the Burghölzli, where he worked from 1900-1909. For example, his hypothesis of a 'collective', as opposed to a merely 'personal', unconscious partially arose from his observation of schizophrenics' fantasies and delusions; Jung found that these contained many parallels with mythological material.

Jung had been familiar with Freud's ideas for a number of years, but their first meeting wasn't until 1907. An intense friendship between the two men developed: Jung became for Freud a kind of 'favourite-son' and Freud, for Jung, a 'father-figure.' But there were areas of disagreement from the beginning, and Jung slowly became aware that some of his ideas differed radically from those of Freud. For example, Freud tended to interpret emotionally significant experience as derived from, or as substitutes for, sex. Jung tended to see a search for meaning as man's motivating force, and primarily viewed sexuality as symbolic of a union of opposites toward the goal of a greater wholeness within the person.

Jung's break with Freud finally came in 1913. This had a profound effect on him, and directly preceded a period in his life which he referred to as one of 'inner uncertainty' and 'a state of disorientation'.[1] Jung writes that during this time (1913-1917) he retained his grip on reality only because he was anchored to the external world by his wife and five children and by the needs of his patients. The self-analysis which Jung then underwent was the foundation for his subsequent psychological theories, and also profoundly influenced his technique of psychotherapy. As he struggled to make conscious his inner images, Jung discovered the technique of 'active imagination', began using painting as a method of objectifying fantasies, and experienced the significance of mandala symbolism.[2] One of his major works, *The Psychological Types (Collected Works, Vol. 6),* was published directly after this period (1921) and greatly increased his reputation.

Jung's original methodological model was psychoanalysis, but after his break with Freud, he introduced changes in the structure and theories of analysis which reflected his own experience. As mentioned earlier, Jung couldn't agree with Freud's primarily sexual interpretation of human motivation and what he perceived as Freud's somewhat mechanistic and causal approach to the psyche. Freud had emphasised that the unconscious was a repository of repressed but once-conscious material. Jung divided the 'unconscious' into two areas: the 'personal unconscious' (more like Freud's 'unconscious') and the 'collective unconscious', whose contents had never been in consciousness and which reflected archetypal processes. Jung saw the collective unconscious as a substratum of mind, common to all men, which is the source of mythological and universal ideas. This mythological material has a positive function in giving meaning and significance to man's existence. A myth might not only have a compensatory, but also a prospective application: it could be seen as an attempt, on the part of the mind, at self-healing or creating a better adaptation in the future. This point of view implied that not all dreams and fantasies could be interpreted in terms of the subject's infantile past, as Freud maintained.

A core concept in Jungian thought, which one can trace back to Plato's 'Ideas' or more recently to Schopenhauer's prototypes, is the theory of the archetypes. Early in his career Jung had written about primordial images which he had recognised in the unconscious life of his patients, as well as in himself. These images were similar to motifs repeated everywhere and throughout history, forming the content of religions, mythologies, legends and folktales. Their main features were their numinosity (feelings of mystery and awe), unconsciousness and autonomy. Archetypal images tend to produce situations which have a considerable impact on the individual, seizing him and holding him in a grip. Jung saw archetypal images as transformers of psychic energy, as the 'instinct's perception of itself'.[3] The archetype itself is irrepresentable: it is a psychosomatic concept linking body and psyche, instinct and image.

Related to the archetype is the theory of complexes. A complex is a group of related images having a common emotional tone and formed around an archetypal core. Jung called the complex the 'via regia to the unconscious' and the 'architect of dreams and symptoms.' Actually, Jung admitted it wasn't such a 'royal road' but more like a 'rough and uncommonly devious footpath that often loses itself in the undergrowth and generally leads not into the heart of the unconscious but past it.'[4] For example, the 'mother archetype' is a predisposing instinctual form for 'mother.' It can be surrounded by a number of images, such as the personal mother, an older sister, a school teacher, etc., gradually shading into figures from the collective unconscious ranging from such figures as Cathleen Ni Houlihan as image of Mother Ireland to the Virgin Mary. Our own personal mother complex forms as experiences cluster around the archetypal determinant for mother. These can be both positive and negative: for example, in fairy tales the mother archetype can be represented by the helpful fairy godmother or the witch. Positive aspects of the mother complex frequently met in analysis in Ireland centre around the experience of mother as strong, nourishing, and self-sacrificing for her young. The mother complex in its negative aspects, however, shows mother as very powerful and dominant and mitigating against separation. For mother, the family is sacrosanct and the members must not stray too far beyond her world. In this regard, the Irish experience of mother and mothering finds a counterpart in the classic Jewish 'mama.'

Complexes are formed both around the emotional experiences of waking life and by the action of the unconscious, principally through dreams. In a dream, we see the complexes in personified form through the dream images. Jung also observed the action of complexes through his word-association experiments and other psychological testing procedures.[5]

The ego complex, our subjective sense of who we are, is different from the other complexes in that our consciousness is associated with it. The ego complex is based on the central archetype of order within the psyche, which Jung called the 'self.' As defined by Jung, the self is not only the centre of the psyche, but also the whole circumference: it includes both conscious and unconscious elements. The self and ego are in life-long interaction, since the self is attempting to be realised through the actions which are under the conscious control of the ego. This process of interaction between ego and self brings us to the core concept in Jungian psychology: the process of individuation. In Jung's words:

> ...it is the process by which individual beings are formed and differentiated; in particular, it is the development of the psychological *individual* (q.v.) as a being distinct from the general, collective psychology. Individuation, therefore, is a process of *differentiation* (q.v.), having for its goal the development of the individual personality.[6]

Both Plato and Aristotle had taught that to become your true self is to make explicit what implicitly you already are. Jung's individuation implied a process that is consciously lived and actively participated in by the ego. The main purpose of the individuation process is to achieve a conscious harmony with the forces in the unconscious that are seeking a centring of the whole personality.

These centring forces from the unconscious are structured by the self and are often manifested through symbols with a numinous element (the symbol of the self is often related to the God-image). The self initiates the 'transcendent function,' which is the capacity to go beyond the tension of the opposites through the creation of a symbolic form that transcends the level of the tension. The ego must sometimes hold the tension of the opposites, not putting either into action in the world. For example, a 30-year-old man entered analysis suffering from the inability to decide between two women (one was his wife and the other a colleague) with whom he was having a relationship. Initially, the man hoped that analysis would enable him to quickly make the 'right choice' between the two. However, as analysis proceeded, the man discovered that the problem lay not in choosing between two women, but in his own inability to be alone. The analysis centred on examining his fear of separation, and inevitably led back to his relationship with his mother. We could say that the tension of the opposites in this man's case was represented externally by his need to choose between two relationships (the women also were opposite personality types). By his *not* choosing between them, however, he was able to work on his real problem, found to be the inability to separate from his mother. Ultimately the man was able to see that he needed to experience a period of living on his own before he was ready to commit to a long-term relationship.

The process of individuation has often been described as a 'circumambulation of the self,' as the individual becomes conscious of how he / she is both a unique being and no more than a common man or woman. Jung saw the main function of analysis to be a furthering of the process of individuation in a person, not just curing neurotic symptoms or promoting better adjustment to social life. He thought that neurotic symptoms can be caused by the ego's attempt to hold back from the needed development in the individuation process. In this context, anxiety could be seen as an invitation to strengthen and extend the conscious attitude. Jung defined neurosis as disunion with oneself, or an unresolved expression of opposites: a misguided attempt to incorporate the unrecognised side of the total personality into conscious life.

Jung was less interested in the causes of neurosis than in its meaning and significance within the framework of the personality.

What was important to him was the hidden meaning of the symptom – the underlying archetypal process. For example, in the Jungian view, regression is not necessarily considered to be a pathological process; it is potentially positive, stimulating new values and a more productive attitude to life. Additionally, when a person's conscious attitude has become too one-sided, perhaps producing a sense of meaninglessness or lack of direction, a return to the inner world of the psyche and its tendencies toward self-realisation is needed. Regression can then also be seen as a goal-directed introversion of libido, which when balanced with conscious reflection, can result ultimately in a more balanced combination of unconscious and conscious forces in the life of the individual.

The process of individuation can often be seen through a series of dreams or in the life histories of persons who seem to outgrow their earlier problems. As complexes fluctuate and change throughout life, the self activates forces that attempt to counter pathological complexes while promoting growth and order within the psyche. To understand in more detail how this works, we must look at a few more of Jung' s archetypes.

Persona, a term which derived originally from the Latin word for the mask worn by actors in classical times, refers in Jungian psychology to the roles one plays in relation to other people.[7] The persona can be seen as the interface between the ego and the outside world, a kind of 'packaging' of the ego. If the persona is healthy, it facilitates the daily interactions of life, protecting the ego and enhancing its effectiveness in the world. However, if one is identified with the persona, things that threaten the persona feel like a threat to the ego itself, since the ego thinks it is nothing but the persona role.

As the persona mediates the ego to the external world, the *anima* or *animus* is the mediator of the unconscious to the ego in dreams and imagination. Anima is Latin for 'soul': Jung used the term to mean the unconscious, feminine side of a man's personality, which personifies his life and soul in a reflected form. The anima appears in dreams as images of women ranging from seductress to spiritual guide. Since anima connects to the *eros* principle, a man's anima development is reflected in how he relates to real women.

Animus is Latin for 'mind' or 'intellect,' what Jung termed the unconscious, masculine side of a woman's personality. The animus personifies the *logos* principle, the 'inner man' who acts as a bridge between the woman's ego and her creative resources in the unconscious. The kind of man to whom a woman is attracted could be seen as a portrait of her animus; this outer man often has qualities that she needs to integrate within herself for personal development.

Jung summarised both anima and animus as 'soul images,' calling each the 'not-I.' As the fundamental forms which underlie the 'feminine' aspects of man and the 'masculine' aspects of woman, they are seen as opposites. A state of possession by either the anima or the animus can transform the personality so that the person displays traits resembling the stereotyped deficiencies of the opposite sex: A man might become moody, lazy, irrational or effeminate, and a woman may seem over-assertive, obsessed by facts, literalness or insistence on what is correct.[8] However, anima and animus as archetypes are too wide to be contained in the notion of contrasexuality. For example, we encounter anima sentimentalities and inflations equally in both sexes. It is more useful to see animus and anima as related to unconscious potential or 'soul image'.

Jung speaks of soul as an inner personality or the true centre of the individual. Since anima and animus function from within the unconscious psyche, they act as 'guides of soul' and can become necessary links with creative possibilities and instruments of individuation. In projection, they have been represented in the form of gods and goddesses as well as public figures and movie stars, but they can also come in the form of friends, lovers and ordinary people. Often a person's motivation for entering analysis concerns the outer confrontation with the anima or animus in a love relationship. But whether we meet them as consorts in our dreams or as outer figures, the anima and animus connect and involve us with life, while linking us with the depths of the unconscious.

In analysis, separation of anima or animus is closely connected with the initial work of making conscious the shadow. Jung defined the shadow as everything the person has no wish to be – what he fears and despises in himself. It possesses qualities that are opposite to those of the persona, since it consists of the rejected aspects of the developing ego. The shadow can also represent what the collective (society or mankind as a whole) deems un-desirable. However, the shadow is not intrinsically a 'bad thing', as it links us to instinct and to a greater psychological wholeness. We encounter it in dreams as an individual of the same sex, but with opposite qualities and attributes; for example, he / she may be the enemy, the intruder, the treacherous 'dark' stranger, etc. In the conscious life, the shadow may be another person whom we may find intrinsically irritating or difficult to accept, provoking strong feeling. Assimilating the shadow and integrating this rejected side of the personality into consciousness is one of the main tasks of analysis.

If we sum up the archetypes we have examined so far, starting from the outside looking in, we begin with the persona, or the social roles with which we face the world. Often the first stage of analysis deals with the working through of persona issues. Continuing inwards, the next archetype is the shadow, which contains repressed qualities that need to be accepted for further growth of the personality. Since persona and shadow can largely be considered as extensions of the ego, they can both be integrated within the conscious personality to a considerable degree. The next inner layer contains the contrasexual archetype of anima or animus, which acts as a bridge between consciousness and the unconscious, a 'soul guide' connecting the person from who he is to what he may become. The innermost archetype is the self, which, as we have seen, is the central archetype of order within the individual. In Jung's conception, the self is in pursuit of the discovery of meaning and purpose in life, and involves the potent-ial of wholeness. The idea of having a centre, or being motivated or regulated by a centre, comes close to what most of us mean by a feeling of wholeness. While all the archetypes have a patterning function within the psyche, the self is the principle mediator of opposites, producing numinous symbols of a self-regulatory and healing nature.

To illustrate some of the concepts we have been discussing, a brief case illustration may be illuminating. A 38-year-old woman ('S') entered analysis wanting to, in her words, 'become more conscious, find security in myself, be able to act, and discover why I always feel so negative.' S was an only child from what she described as an unhappy marriage between her rather dominant mother and passive father. S had had various professional trainings and employment and was unhappy in her current job. She had also had a series of either negative or unfulfilling relationships with men, and was in the process of separating from her husband.

S had only a vague sense of personal identity and low self-esteem when she entered analysis. This was reflected in both the conscious and unconscious manifestations of her body-image. In reality, S was a good-looking woman with a pretty face and a strong, somewhat stocky body. But she constantly worried about being too fat, and perceived herself as ugly. It was apparent from the beginning of the analysis that S's body-image was tied up with her mother, who was slim, and who had criticised S in myriad ways since she was a small child. The process of analysis made it possible for S to get in touch with her painful early childhood memories concerning her mother, connecting her to the deep-seated sense of betrayal and abandonment that was being expressed today through her severe self-criticism and rejection of her body. S also slowly realised how she sometimes acted out her inner 'critical mother / tyrant' in relationships with others.

In addition to her struggle with her body-image, S's search for the right job was an external manifestation of her somewhat frantic search for her 'real self,' which had been abandoned so long ago. In Jungian terminology, S was suffering from a 'negative mother complex.' Her mother had rejected her archetypal need to be mothered so that the negative pole of the archetype – the image of the terrible mother or witch – had become established. As this negative complex grew stronger and became chronic, S eventually came to view the world with mistrust and anxiety, rejecting her own inner vitality and expecting to be rejected by those in her environment. Other people were typically experienced as parts of a rejecting or devouring archetypal Great Mother.

The progression of S's self-image in her dreams somewhat corresponded to her outer development during the analysis. In the early dreams, she would generally see herself only from the back, with all aspects of herself hazy or blurred. Later, dark clothes became visible, as she became a 'closed form.' Several months into the analysis, a focus on body parts began to emerge. For example, in one dream she saw only the 'cellulite skin' of her 'fat thighs' (which was a conscious concern as well). Around the same time, a more defined image of her body (mostly without a head) began to emerge. For example, S dreamed that a famous actor ('B') was in love with her. In the dream, she saw her body as being slim and attractive but having no head; at the same time she saw only the head and blonde hair of B. The narcissistic wounding S suffered in early childhood had cut her off from the ground of her being and therefore her 'body-self': her basic feelings and drives had been denied. In the dream, she regains a sense of her body through connection to a positive, although somewhat grandiose, animus figure: as she *sees* 'B's head, S. *feels* his 'warm, muscular body', and perceives her own headless body through sensual clothing. It is like a *coniunctio*,[9] but S has literally 'lost her head' to this ideal masculine figure. Continuing with the same dream, we see how her mother fits into the scenario:

> Behind us at the left a car stops at a crossing. Someone calls: 'Your mother is there.' I turn around, and B asks if I'll introduce him to my mother. Three women climb out of the car. My mother stands at the left near the car, dressed totally in black, as if she is in mourning (she is somewhat heavier than usual). Next to her stands a younger woman, also entirely in black. A beautiful young woman with long, wavy red hair comes toward me from this group. I think: 'She'll take B away from me.' In this moment, the woman becomes my mother, and her hair changes into a pinned-up style. All the people think, 'This is impossible: such a young mother with a type like that (B)!' But it is my mother.

It is hard to imagine a clearer picture of the mother-daughter constellation as it existed in S's psyche. The ideal fusion with B is stolen from S by her mother ('M'), just as by not being a 'good enough' mother, M never gave S the mirroring she needed to form an inner bond with the Self. With S, M behaved more like a sibling or peer, burdening her with her problems and complaining about her husband. In the dream, S is prevented from introducing her mother to B because M actually steals him from her. In real life, M's treatment of S had literally robbed her of her connection to the positive animus. M's unconscious envy of S had led her to openly disparage S's chances of ever attracting a 'good man'. In the dream, the juxtaposition of M with the younger woman, both in black, connect to a shadow aspect of S that often appeared as women dressed in black. It also points to ambiguous feelings S held toward her mother. The association with mourning dress could also connect to the real mourning that S had to do in order to integrate the lack of mothering she had received in childhood. The dream leaves us with a feeling of being robbed and shut out, quite a typical emotion for S.

S's sense of self-value was mostly unrealistic and distorted; we could say that the borders between her ego and self were not differentiated enough. Her ego had been forced into a defensive posture from the necessity to protect her primal self in infancy. Because of her disturbed relationship with her mother, S's ego had not become a relatively autonomous centre of consciousness. As Erich Neumann describes it, there was a deficient development of the ego-self axis, resulting in a 'negativistic narcissistic ego.'[10] This left her ego open to threats of identification with the negative aspects of the Self. One of the most obvious symptoms of this is what Marion Woodman aptly calls the 'addiction to perfection'.[11] This perfectionistic attitude was chronic in S.

As we have seen, Jung described the persona as the mediator between the ego and the external world. S's ego was more or less identified with her persona because social acceptability was so dominant a need. This 'persona-ego' with its external orientation demanded perfection according to collective values, not her own individual ones. S.s life had been a constant attempt to win self-esteem through achievement and physical appearance. Striving to meet these impossible demands, S would inevitably collapse under the strain and seek a less demanding environment. The endless quest for outer acceptance had left S little time to direct her energy toward her own inner being and its development. In analysis, S started to make contact, through memories and dreams, with the vulnerable child that was a vital part of her real self. She began allowing herself to 'be' rather than 'do' all the time. This connected her to the deep depression that surrounded the long denial of her true self, her basic feelings and drives. The rage at her parents also began to surface. S's own feelings had never been valued and therefore had been repressed. Her defensive persona facade was a survival strategy on the part of the ego, but suffering was locked in the shadow, or the personal unconscious containing her childhood history. S is a good example of someone whose being was actually *in* the shadow, along with the undeveloped archetypal positive mother. S had never had the chance to connect her feelings to actual experience, and therefore didn't know who she was.[12]

As S began to experience aspects of her past in the present, she began to feel more real. Along with this came depression and sadness, mostly over the realisation that she had denied her creative side. As she lived through the depression, the energy which had been inaccessible to her due to her repressed rage became gradually available, and her natural creativity began to flow. From the beginning, the most important thing analysis provided for S was a reliable setting where she could feel, share and be 'held': where she was taken seriously, and where her repressed real self would be encouraged to come out. After S had developed some trust that she would not be rejected or judged, she began associating more to body-feelings, which had so much to do with her rejected 'inner child', now starting to come to life. S's negative body-image tied in with an extremely negative animus, which could be seen clearly in the history of her relationships with men. As she discussed her rejected sexual feelings and fantasies, her vitality along with her self-respect visibly increased, and the split between body and mind started to heal. S's self-image in her dreams gradually became more positive and whole: she started to see herself from the front and, toward the end of the analysis, as a complete body. On termination of analysis, S remarked that the main difference she noticed in herself was that she was now able to *comprehend* her suffering and therefore bear it better. She also felt better at maintaining contact with her true feelings vis-a-vis others, and took it less personally when they criticised her. In broader terms, her focus had changed: from anxious watchfulness of others' reactions to a calmer concentration on the needs of her inner self.

Jung was interested in illustrating how consciousness works in different ways in different people. He noticed that some people were more excited or energised by the internal world and others by the external world. These attitudes he called introversion and extraversion respectively. In addition, Jung defined four functions or properties of consciousness: 1) Thinking: knowing what a thing is, naming it and linking it to other things; 2) Feeling: the consideration of the value of something; having a viewpoint or perspective on something; 3) Sensation: the perception of something, but not what it is; 4) Intuition: a sense of where something is going, what the possibilities are, without conscious proof or knowledge.

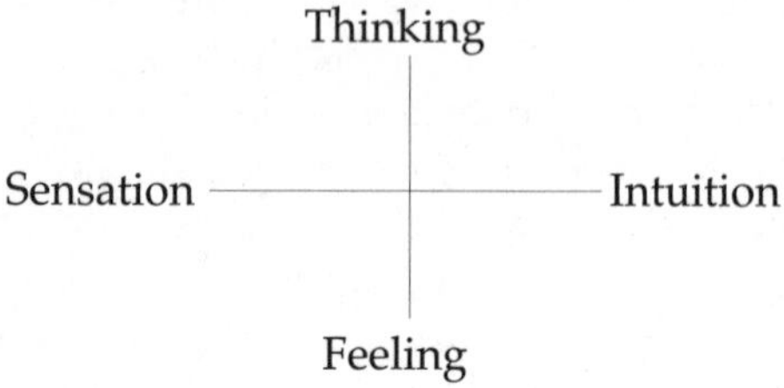

Jung divided these four functions into a rational (thinking and feeling) and irrational (sensation and intuition) pair. He found that a person will have a superior mode of functioning, such as thinking, and a second, auxiliary mode, usually from the opposite pair of rational or irrational functions, such as sensation. The function that is opposite to the superior function will often cause difficulty for the individual: for example, a thinking type may have difficulty with feeling. If we take the Irish as a collective, it could be said that the superior or primary function is intuition and the inferior function, sensation. Viewed from the outside, the 'Celtic twilight' could be seen to refer to the tremendous intuitive gift of the Irish to grasp the intangible: a gift of imagination and vision. The opposite of this intuitive inclination, however, shows in the difficulty often met in 'grounding' this vision and living in the concrete world of the here and now. In this regard, the sensation function as function of perception of what is tangible is a vital counterbalance. Jung termed this opposite area of consciousness the 'inferior function.' Although it may cause problems, the inferior function also contains great potential for change, if one attempts to integrate its contents into ego-consciousness. Realising one's inferior function is an important aspect of individuation and can be a significant part of analytic work.

Most people who undergo a Jungian analysis discover that they have been more highly influenced by unconscious assumptions and motivations than they had realised. As the specific forms of the persona, shadow and anima / animus are identified and integrated, the ego becomes stronger, more comprehensive and simultaneously more humble. But beyond all these inner figures lies the objective psyche or collective unconscious, which is the origin of the personal unconscious and also transcends it. The ego gradually learns that it is related to forces in the psyche which it can intuitively feel, or even respond to, but cannot grasp or control. As the analysand becomes more and more aware of the relation of the ego to the self, the centre of the personality shifts away from the tensions of the ego trying desperately to cling to an image of itself, while the psyche opens to a more profound participation in the world and with others. This leads to an increasing awareness of one's destiny, along with freedom to weave it in individual patterns.

We have seen how, in Jung's map of the psyche, the self re-presents the totality of the personality, and how the process of individuation is concerned with the unification of the personality. The analysand usually enters analysis having arrived at a stage in his developmental path where he is arrested. This may be des-cribed by the analysand as a feeling of being blocked or stuck in compulsive and projective repetitions of unresolved childhood and early relationships, most often with his parents or parental figures. Under these circumstances it is not at all surprising that the immediate aim of the analysand is relief from his symptoms or behaviour modification. However, as resistances are analysed, complexes named, and parental issues worked through in the analytic process, the way is slowly freed within the person for the natural process of individuation to take place. It must be stressed that the working through of issues in analysis forms an important part of the process. The identification of the root of the psychological problem is not sufficient to bring about change. It usually takes a considerable period of time of going over and over the same issues before integration can take place. This involves the analysand re-experiencing in a feeling way where he has become caught in certain repetitive patterns of behaviour and relating.

If we take the example of the analysand who feels stuck, we might be looking at someone, perhaps in his late thirties, who is outwardly very well adapted. He could have arrived at a place where he had achieved all he had hoped for in his work, found a partner, created a home and had children: many of the things which would have great value in the eyes of the collective. Such a person, however, may have begun to experience a growing sense of emptiness in his achievements – a feeling of no longer being able to find meaning and fulfilment in his life. The old direction he was moving in no longer satisfies. As his story unfolds in the analysis, it becomes clear that a shift of psychic balance from the area of consciousness (with the ego as its centre) to the totality of the conscious and unconscious psyche is necessary if his life is to take on a more meaningful tone. A dream in such an instance might show the dreamer as embarking on a voyage, perhaps to a place of antiquity, or with the purpose of retrieving some long-lost valuable object. The dream might portray the tasks he has to carry out on the journey, heroic tasks quite possibly – a modern-day Grail quest. In fact, the dream may point to the future course of the analytic process in charting unknown areas of the personality, in retrieving and making conscious previously repressed contents of the unconscious. Such a case might typify the process of individuation becoming activated in the analysis. The dream may also indicate the potential for psychic balance between consciousness and the unconscious. One of the outcomes of such a psychic shift would be the discovery of the Grail: the very meaning which his life had heretofore lacked.

Jung outlines three major attributes to the process of individuation:

1) the goal is the development of the personality;
2) it presupposes and includes collective relationship; i.e. it does not occur in a state of isolation;
3) it involves a degree of opposition to social norms which have no absolute validity: 'The more a man's life is shaped by the collective norm, the greater is his individual immorality.'[13]

From this it can be seen that for Jung the aim of analysis does not lie solely in finding a new adaptation to life (i.e., the capacity to work productively and enjoy life), but also in facilitating the analysand to withstand the inevitable tension that arises in forging a path of development and realisation which at times goes against the collective. Frequently it is the tension felt in trying to separate from the collective and find a satisfying individual standpoint that brings a person into analysis. Although issues around separation are inevitable in any analysis, the impact of loss which is indelibly stamped on the Irish psyche often provides the collective backdrop against which the individual struggles. Two famines and generations of emigration have reinforced the pain of loss, and naturally the collective unconscious will put up a resistance to further separation, as is often encountered in analysis.

It could be said that the process of individuation calls on the individual's capacity both for pleasure and for suffering. To become what one truly *is* involves a certain amount of pain, be it the pain of letting go of what has previously been maladaptively invested in, the dispelling of resistances, or the pain of allowing oneself to feel the conflict between ego needs and the demands of the self. When Jung speaks of suffering in this context, he is referring specifically to the analysand's capacity to sustain the conflict inherent in the opposites. As we have already seen, the theory of the opposites or the bipolarity inherent in all psychic functioning is fundamental to Jung's thought ('...the opposites are the ineradicable and indispensable preconditions of all psychic life '[14]) The movement of libido or psychic energy from one pole or end of the spectrum to another is what lends dynamism to psychic life. One way of describing these poles or ends of the spectrum might be to speak of instinct and symbol; whether a psychic content manifests itself in instinctual behaviour or in symbolic form. Thus the pairs of opposites might include: conscious / unconscious, progression / regression, ego / self, or in terms of typological functioning: feeling / thinking and intuition / sensation.

This fundamental approach to the psyche as bipolar is further reflected in Jung's view of the unconscious both as self-regulatory and compensatory. Jung observed a tendency in the unconscious to correct an overly one-sided conscious position. In fact, for him, psychic disturbance or imbalance was seen as too much emphasis or value being given to one or the other of these opposites. For instance, an overvaluing of conscious adaptation at the expense of the unconscious might manifest in a neurosis. The psychic disturbance caused by the activated complex would necessitate a restructuring of the conscious position in order that psychic equilibrium be restored. The neurosis in this respect was, for Jung, the psyche's compensatory and self-regulatory way of healing itself. Viewed in this light, Jung's concept of individuation as an instinct for wholeness becomes clearer.

It must be cautioned, however, that individuation as an aim of analysis may not be indicated in every case. It is a process which is dependent upon the unfolding of each individual analysand's potential for wholeness – a potential which may or may not unfold. Indeed, in borderline cases, where the ego is too weak and where consciousness is liable to flooding by the unconscious, individuation as an ultimate goal of analysis is contra-indicated.

The question of change in analysis is always dependent upon the individual case. For some it is symptom relief or behaviour modification. For others it is self-acceptance. Yet again for others, it is a new and more solid adaptation to life. Ultimately, the analyst follows the rhythm and dictates of the analysand's unconscious and where there is a repetitive need to continually work on the same material, the analyst follows the cue of the unconscious.

Technically, the analyst's job is to make sense of the analysand's unconscious and to make this sense known to the analysand. This the analyst might do through elucidating the developmental path of the analysand. Among the techniques employed for this elucidation are the use of the transference/countertransference and the interpretation of unconscious material: dreams and symbols which assist the analysand's ego in forming a creative dialogue with the unconscious and in providing an environment for the integration of unconscious material. When we speak of change or the facilitation of change within the analysis, we imply a certain context or environment in which this change takes place. The transference and counter-transference are of prime importance in providing the containment necessary for change. Within the relationship between the analysand and the analyst, much of what was problematic in the analysand's early relationships with significant others, primarily his parents, makes itself felt. The analyst is experienced and felt 'as if' he/she were the original mother/father/siblings. The original feelings toward the parental figures are unconsciously transferred into the analytic relationship, thus providing the opportunity to work through damaged primary relations and resolving infantile ties with the parents.

Jung identified two aspects of the transference: a personal transference as described above and an archetypal transference involving the projection of contents not in the analysand's own personal outer experience, an example of which might be the projection of the archetype of the healer onto the analyst. The main components of Jung's use of the transference might be best illustrated by the following diagram, adapted from Jung.[15]

This model was based on a series of alchemical illustrations which were originally meant to illustrate the equality between the male alchemist and his female co-worker, the *soror mystica* (mystical sister). When this diagram is applied to the transference/countertransference in the analytic relationship, it may seem that there is an exact symmetry between analyst and analysand. However, the boundary conditions, once agreed upon, become more the responsibility of the analyst's conscious ego, and the analyst assumes a larger responsibility for dealing with the activity of his or her own unconscious. In this way, a free and protected space (in alchemical terms, the 'vas') is created in which the analysand is safe to experience unconscious material that would ordinarily be repressed.

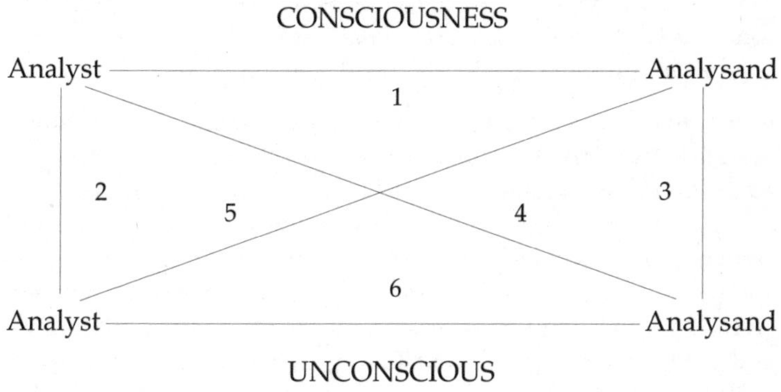

1. Designates the therapeutic alliance.
2. Refers to the active dialogue between the analyst's consciousness and unconscious. The analyst calls on her own former experience as an analysand and her relationship to the archetype of the wounded healer.
3. Shows the dialogue the analysand engages in with the unconscious, including any resistance he may have to the process.

4. Refers to the dialogue between the analyst's conscious position and the analysand's unconscious.
5. Refers to the reverse of 4, where the analysand speaks to the analyst's unconscious.
6. Relates to the immediate communication between both the analyst's and analysand's unconscious. This is a vital area of communication within the transference and would include both countertransferential and archetypal elements.

Freud thought that the basic purpose of the dream was to disguise a repressed or infantile wish, often sexual, in order to avoid arousing anxiety and thereby to preserve sleep. Jung, in contrast, saw the dream as a self-representation of the psyche, produced by the self as part of the self-regulation of psychological processes. Dreams produce a point of view in counterpoint or compensation to the stance of the conscious ego. The dream is to the psyche what the X-ray is to the body: it truthfully pictures the actual state of a portion of the whole organism / psyche. Just as the X-ray images are not the body itself, so dreams are not the actual psyche, but give images of its structure and dynamic movement. The dream can show what complexes are activated in the analysand's psyche, and what the unconscious is doing with the activated complexes. It can also point out what personality traits have been unconscious or not sufficiently noted in waking life.

Jung said that the correct way to approach a dream was to remind oneself at the start that one does not know its meaning. A Jungian analyst will generally work with a dream by obtaining the analysand's personal associations, while considering cultural associations and archetypal amplifications (from folklore, religion and mythology). The main purpose of analysing dreams in an analytic situation is to further the balance between the unconscious and conscious standpoints, facilitating the analysand's process of individuation.

Jung used the term 'active imagination' to describe a process of dreaming with open eyes.[16] It is a method for direct interaction with the unconscious through a controlled imaginal state. One first concentrates on a specific subject, mood, or event, and then allows a chain of associated fantasies to develop and take on a dramatic character. Active imagination is not conscious invention, but rather allows images to appear that want to compel the viewer's participation. A new situation is created in which unconscious contents are exposed in the waking state. As in the association process to the images of a dream, in active imagination previously unrelated contents may become more clear and articulate. The attitude of the ego in active imagination should remain the same as in a real situation, and imagined situations and persons should be permitted to act with no interference from the ego.

Many analysts recommend that one should not do active imagination involving real people. The practical reason for this is that the process may give only a symbolic solution to the problems with that person while inhibiting an actual solution in the real world.[17] When active imagination is used in analysis, the analysand might draw or paint the images that are produced. Some analytical music therapists are utilising music improvisation in a similar way. Jung did not recommend active imagination for everyone, finding it most useful in the later stages of an analysis. Although the process itself may stimulate the cure of a neurosis, Jung thought it achieves success only if it is integrated into the conscious standpoint, which demands the active and creative participation of the ego.

Thus far we have spoken about the content and process of analysis and now we might consider the first session. The initial interview is very important for both the analyst and the analysand, as invariably it is at this first meeting that it will be decided whether or not analysis is indicated. How the initial interview is conducted varies from analyst to analyst, but essentially the analyst will be looking at certain key issues, namely:

1) the presenting problem(s) and associated symptoms; what it is that has led the analysand into the analysis;
2) as thorough as possible a picture of the family background, including the analysand's relationship with his parents and siblings;
3) a history of the significant life events;
4) a description of the present life situation;
5) the analysand's capacity for insight, how he interprets his presenting problem;
6) how the analysand relates to any transference interpretations and possible indications of a therapeutic alliance.

An examination of these areas provides the basis for determining the suitability of the person for analysis. Where analysis is not indicated the initial interview affords an opportunity to explore other avenues open to the client. When it is decided by both analyst and client that the analysis should commence, the analyst might indicate something of the structure of the analysis: use of the couch or face-to-face; the place of dreams and associations in the analysis; the importance, where possible, of communicating to the analyst thoughts, associations, memories or feelings evoked during the session; the duration, usually fifty minutes; the frequency of sessions; and fee negotiation.

For the analysand, the initial interview provides him with the opportunity to see if he wishes to enter analysis. It is also an opportunity to ask questions concerning the analysis, since after analysis begins, many analysts will work with such questions in the context of the analysis.

Jung set out four stages of the analytic process which have come to be seen more as aspects of the content of analysis rather than stages, in that they do not necessarily appear in succession, but can overlap or be juxtaposed. Contemporary analysts tend to see the description as not being sufficiently expansive, most especially in that it does not take into account the analysis of the transference and counter-transference. Jung called the first stage 'catharsis,' this being the analysand's experience of relating or 'confessing' his personal story and the consequent feeling of relief at having his story witnessed. The second stage is one of 'elucidation', which involves interpretation of the unconscious motives behind the analysand's behaviour. The third stage could be described in analytic terms as a stage of 'working through' what has been elucidated. This is usually a lengthier stage in the analysis than the previous two, as it is at this time that much of the repressed aspects of the personality are integrated. The fourth stage Jung called 'transformation.' This is the stage which most clearly approximates the individuation process, in that it implies that the analysand becomes what he truly is.

Many people who come into analysis initially ask what analysis hopes to accomplish or what the goal of the process is. In summarising this short introduction to Jungian psychology, we can think of no better way to answer these questions than with Jung's own words:

> The goal is important only as an idea; the essential thing is the *opus* which leads to the goal: that is the goal of a lifetime.[18]

Notes

1. For Jung' s own description of this period in his life, see his *Memories, Dreams, Reflections,* Chapter Vl: 'Confrontation with the Unconscious.' (Recorded and edited by Aniela Jaffe, trans. by Richard and Clara Winston, originally published by Pantheon Books, 1963; New York: Vintage Books, 1989.)

2. Mandala, a Sanskrit word meaning 'magical circle', refers to a geometric figure with more or less regular sub-divisions, divided by four or multiples thereof. Jung felt the mandala expressed totality, radiating from the centre. Mandalas can serve as images of compensatory wholeness for people who are fragmented and contribute to the psyche's self-healing capacities.

3. Carl Gustav Jung, *The Collected Works of C. G. Jung,* ed. Sir Herbert Read, Michael Fordham, Gerhard Adler and William McGuire, trans. R:F.C. Hull (Bollingen Series XX; Princeton: Princeton University Press, 1960; 2nd ed. 1969), Vol. 8, para. 277.

4. Ibid., para. 210.

5. See Jung's 'Studies in Word Association,' *Collected Works,* Vol. 2, Part I .

6. Ibid., Vol. 6, para. 757.

7. Ibid., para. 800-801.

8. Ibid., Vol. 11, para. 48.

9. An important term for Jung (borrowed from alchemy), symbolising a pattern of relationships between two or more unconscious factors; a coming together of opposites which results in the birth of a new element.

10. Erich Neumann, 'Narcissism, normal self-formation and primary relation to the mother,' (New York: Analytical Psychology Club) *Spring* 26 (1966): 96.

11. Marion Woodman, *Addiction to Perfection The Still Unravished Bride* (Toronto: Inner City Books, 1982).

12. Kathrin Asper, 'Shadow Aspects of Narcissistic Disorders and Their Therapeutic Treatment', *Journal of Analytical Psychology* 32 (1987): 117-37.

13. Jung, *Collected Works*, Vol. 6, para. 757-62.

14. Ibid., Vol. 14, para. 206.

15. Ibid., Vol. 16, para. 422.

16. Ibid., Vol. 14, para. 706.

17. James Hall, *The Jungian Experience* (Toronto: Inner City Books, 1986), 105-6.

18. Jung, *Collected Works*, Vol. 16, para. 400.

Selected Reading

Bennet, E. A., *What Jung Really Said* (New York: Schocken, 1983).

Dieckmann, H., *Methods in Analytical Psychology: An Introduction* (Wilmette, Ill.: Chiron Publications, 1988).

Fordham, F., *An Introduction to Jung's Psychology* (London: Penguin, 1991)

Hall, J., *The Jungian Experience. Analysis and Individuation* (Toronto: Inner City Books, 1986)

Jacobi, J., *The Psychology of C G Jung* (New Haven: Yale U.P. 1973)

— *Complex/Archetype/Symbol in the Psychology of C G Jung* (Bollingen Series LVII. Princeton: Princeton U. P., 1959).

Jaffe, A., *The Myth of Meaning* (New York: Penguin, 1975).

Jung, C. G. (ed), *Man and His Symbols* (New York: Doubleday, 1964).

— *Memories, Dreams, Reflections* (New York: Vintage, 1989).

Samuels, A., *Jung and the Post-Jungians* (London: Tavistock, 1985).

—, Shorter, B., and Plaut, F. (eds), *A Critical Dictionary of Jungian Analysis* (London: Routledge, 1991).

Singer, J., *Boundaries of the Soul. The Practice of Jung's Psychology* (New York: Anchor Books, 1973).

Stein, M., *Jungian Analysis* (London: Open Court, 1982).

Storr, A., *Jung* (London: Fontana, 1973).

CHAPTER 4

Psychosynthesis and Transpersonal Theory

Miceal O'Regan

1. INTRODUCTION

History of the approach

Synthesis, whether it be of the psyche or of ideas, is a dangerous human project. It tends towards either tyranny and exclusion at one extreme, or an eclectic mishmash at the other. Assagioli, the founder of Psychosynthesis, was aware of this tendency. When asked by Sam Keen what he considered to be the shadow side of Psychosynthesis Assagioli replied 'It tries to do too much.' At the same time it attempts to answer the perennial human question concerning The One and the Many: In what sense is there unity and plurality in the world of ideas and things, in what sense am I as a person one and many? How do I live and describe this polarity of one and many within myself, between myself and others and between myself and the environment in which I live. A true synthesis has to hold the tension between oneness and plurality without collapsing one pole into the other. A true synthesis is a complexity that allows us to construe the whole in terms of the parts and the parts in terms of the whole.

Synthesis, as an explicit thrust of the psyche, is not an idea exclusive to Assagioli. Buber uses the word psychosynthesis in relation to the work of therapy. In fact it may have been used first by Buber in an essay in 1921: 'The more dissociated the soul, the more it is at the mercy of its sickness and attacks, the more concentrated it is, the more it is able to master them. It is not as if it conquered the body; for through its unity it ever again saves and protects the unity of the body.' According to Buber this process is effected 'through the psychosynthetic appearance of a whole, united soul laying hold of the dispersed soul, agitating it on all sides and demanding the event of crystallisation.'[1] In other words, a synthesis of the psyche proceeds by way of seeing the parts in terms of the whole as contrasted with building up the whole from isolated parts.

Until recently, synthesis as a means to construe the parts in terms of the whole, was more a religious and philosophical perspective than a scientific one. This is no longer true. It is now accepted within the positive sciences, especially in new physics.

Assagioli's religious sensibilities, his background in philosophy and culture, influenced him as much as his scientific studies in medicine, psychiatry and psychoanalysis.[2] Born in Venice in 1888, he was brought up in a cultured upper middle class Jewish family. He had a classical education in Greek and Latin and studied several languages including Russian and Sanscrit at the University of Florence. Through his Jewish background, he was introduced to the teachings of the Kabbala and the Hasidic tradition. From his Italian background, he was influenced by Plato, Dante and the Renaissance tradition. He studied medicine in Florence, psychiatry under Bleuler at the Burgholzi in Zurich and wrote a doctoral thesis on psychoanalysis.

While not jettisoning his scientific background in medicine or his Freudian studies, he pioneered a way of construing a person from the perspective of well being and spiritual experiences rather than from the mere perspective of pathology. In this way he was part of the humanistic movement in psychology – the third phase that included Rollo May, Fritz Perls and Carl Rogers. In so far as he included in his account of a person, experiences beyond the ordinary human well being or self actualisation, he is part of the fourth school of psychotherapy that included Jung, Maslow and Frankl. He served on the board of editors for both the Journal of Humanistic Psychology and the Journal of Transpersonal Psychology.

Perhaps it is more appropriate to speak of a transpersonal theory rather than a psychology, since many of its ideas and practices are taken from the religious and philosophical traditions rather than from scientific psychology. Assagioli, in touch with such men as Croce, Tagore and Inyat Khan, was also influenced by others like Suzuki, Ouspennsky, Jung and Buber. Therefore his synthesis of ideas (not withstanding its dangers) included those of psychoanalysis, humanistic psychology and transpersonal theory. Likewise his synthesis of the psyche drew on techniques and practices from the same disciplines and practices, i.e. from psychoanalysis, humanistic psychology and from the teachings and practices of the religious traditions. For this reason psychosynthesis as a theory and practice often has a different configuration or style in different institutes. As with the project of any synthesis, this too has its limitations and strengths. Without a strong psychoanalytic base, psychosynthesis may be presented as too speculative and disembodied, while without the insights of the Tradition and the Perenial Philosophy it tends to trivialise the spiritual dimension.

On the other hand, without a clear understanding of some original vision and axiol theses, it becomes an eclectic mishmash. Ken Wilber suggests Assagioli himself avoided these tendencies.[3]

2. PHILOSOPHY OF THE PERSON

Assumptions
There are many ways of telling the story of the Self – of what it means to be a person. As in any story, the starting point and context are important. For example within the Buddhist tradition the starting point, the assumptions and the elements of the story of the self are different from the account within the Judeo-Christian-Greek Western tradition. In the former, one speaks of the self in terms of no self, emptiness, void etc while, in the latter, one speaks of the self in terms of body, feelings, mind, soul spirit, conscious, unconscious etc. How one tells and shapes the story of the self within each tradition gives rise to different accounts. Therefore within the Western tradition there are stories of the self different from that told in psychosynthesis. In our Institute we teach the story of the self as complex, dynamic, embodied and relational. To construe every self in this way is to assume an account of the self that essentially includes these perspectives.

The Self as Complex
Psychosynthesis is probably best known for Assagiol's egg diagram.[4] The diagram (overleaf) may be considered as a map for construing especially the inner territory or geography of a person:

1. The lower Unconscious.
2. The Middle Unconscious.
3. The Higher Unconscious (Superconscious)
4. The Field of Consciousness.
5. The Conscious Self ('I').

6. The Higher Self.
7. The Collective Unconscious.

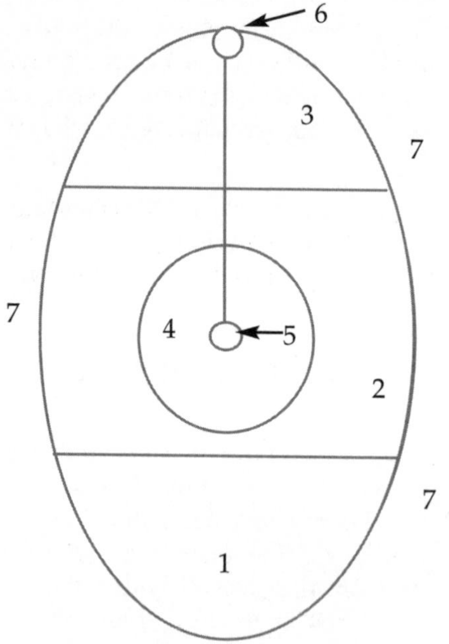

1. *The Lower Unconscious:* This is the territory of life's fundamental energies, shaped and sculpted by genes and early learning experiences.
2. *The Middle Unconscious:* This represents psychological processes and events accessible to conscious awareness by a small trigger. It is Freud's ante-room of consciousness.
3. *The Higher Unconscious or Superconscious:* This is the territory of a person's aspirations or thrust to express love, creativity, beauty, justice, music, etc. According to Assagioli, it is the region from which we receive 'our higher intuitions and inspirations, artistic and philosophical or scientific, ethical imperatives and urges to humanitarian and heroic action.'
4. *The Field of Consciousness:* Assagioli describes this as the part of our personality of which we are directly aware, i.e. the incessant flow of sensations,images, thoughts, feelings, desires and impulses which we can observe, analyse and judge. We receive such awareness in our bodies, feelings and mind.

5. *The Conscious Self or I:* This represents the distinction between the contents of awareness and the one who is aware. It points to our capacity not to identify with the contents of our awareness and to open to the reality that no experience exhausts all the possibility of experience.
6. *Higher Self:* This is the deeper Subject or Source of inner processes and outer actions. It is beyond and within the conscious self as ground and figure. In the map, as it points downwards, the star represents that because of which a person is related to as a unified whole not withstanding fragmentation. In Greek philosophy it was referred to as soul – the principle of life.
7. *Collective Unconscious:* The outer line of the diagram delineates but does not divide. For Assagioli it is analogous to the membrane delineating a cell which permits a constant and active interchange with the whole body to which the cell belongs.

Properly understood, this diagram is extremely useful as 'a crude and elementary picture that can give only a structural, static, almost "anatomical" representation of our inner constitutions.'[5] It is especially useful as distinguishing different levels of a person which are distinct though not separate. 'All the lines are dotted to indicate that a continuous exchange of elements and energies – a 'psychic osmosis', one might say – is taking place between any and all of these psychic areas.'[6] This comment helps correct the two dimensional distortion of one level being seen as more or less important than another. For example, the processes and energies of the higher unconscious, such as the desire for justice and peace, are inextricably bound up with less differentiated and less well organised energies of the lower unconscious. A person's capacities to bond, touch, withdraw and self delineate, essential for embodying justice and peace, are largely determined by early learning experiences of saying yes and no. However, while being intimately and inseparably linked, the levels are nevertheless distinct. 'The different levels of the unconscious — higher, middle and lower – may be thought of as comprising a spectrum of different potential types of experience or states of consciousness. They are termed 'unconscious' because during the normal course of daily living they most often remain only potentially available to awareness.'[7]

The most serious difficulty with the egg diagram is the ease with which it can be reified. The diagram becomes a model of a person somewhat along the lines of a Russian doll. To describe a person in spatial metaphor has limited use. This is especially so when the spatial metaphor is linked with an energetic metaphor. The hermeneutic critique of psychoanalysis in general, namely its tendency towards reification of the psyche, is equally valid of psychosynthesis and maybe more so. It is tempting from the egg diagram to construe a person as a cauldron of hydraulics rather than a speaking subject in a dialogue. At the same time, to point to the limitations and possible distortions, when speaking of a person in terms of energy metaphors and transformation of energy, is not to jettison them altogether. Even the most trenchant hermeneutic approach finally requires some glancing at energetics to account fully for itself.[8] Properly understood, there is a dehiscent quality about the egg diagram. It explodes with meaning. Simple and elegant, it holds together a description of a person as one, singular and at the same time many and plural. A person speaks with many voices even if it is not always easy to distinguish them. The movement and direction of a life, a psychosynthesis, is towards a polyphony rather than a single monotheistic note.

The Self as Dynamic

To construe the self as dynamic is to account for the self in terms of desire proceeding or stretching. That is to say, an account of the life of a person stretching and responding to the call of a greater life. It is to tell the story of a person in terms of the many shapings and sculpting of desire through different phases and stages.

The sculpted desire of an adult in terms of:

body
feelings mind
soul
spirit

is different from, but essentially connected to, the shaped desire of an infant. One strand or note of desire might be more or less dominant through the different stages of evolution. For example, at certain stages or moments of life the voice of the feelings or of the mind might dominate and throw the sense of harmony into disarray. Such disarray might not be pathological but rather part of the ongoing orchestration of life.

A pathology, however, might arise when one note or one stage oppresses or acts unduly on another. For example, the voice of the mind might drown out or oppress the feelings, just as the feelings might oppress the body by acting out in and through the body. Likewise the voice of the mind and feelings might be so loud that the whisperings of the soul and spirit are unheard. Each voice has its part to play in the whole symphony. The language of the feelings is the particular shaping or organisation of the body in terms of its basic pulsations and rhythms. The pulsations and rhythms themselves are the basic phonemes of the language. The variations of emotion and feelings is the spectrum of experience between the contracting pole of the pulsation and its expanding pole. Thus we distinguish a cluster of feelings that are close to one pole rather than those that cluster closer to the other pole. For example, each of us tends to organise fear and shame by contracting, and to organise joy and gratitude by expanding. How each of us personally does this gives rise to our particular and concrete story.

The story or language of the feelings is taken up and included in the language of the mind. The mind as understood in the context of this story of the self, speaks through concepts, division and analysis. It is the human capacity to observe, gather data, form hypotheses and test them. The emergence of this capacity for analytical thinking was a significant moment in the life of the species as it is in the life of an individual. It is a movement away from embeddedness in the body and feelings. Nevertheless it remains a limited value in so far as it is not the whole story.

It too is transcended by, or taken up in, creative imagination and language of the soul. The soul speaks through the making of images, the telling of the stories and the doing of the rituals. It is not a thing, a substance, and its language is focally an activity, not a product. The language of the soul is not the story, symbol or ritual as an object of analysis but rather the telling of the story and the making of the ritual. Soul-making focuses not on poems or paintings but rather on their making. The myth itself is more than mythology. The darkness of mythos recedes before the light of the logos.

Soul healing, whether of an individual or a people, focuses on evoking the symbol making faculty rather than on its products. It is this activity of soul that creates a sense of unity within a person, a unity that is not monotheistic and tyrannical but rather polytheistic and tolerant. The language of the spirit transcends not only feelings and analytical thoughts but also creative imagination. It is a speaking by not speaking – a silence that is not a vacuum – a space or emptiness that is brimful of life. In so far as it speaks at all, it does so by way of mirroring and reflecting in the soul. In that sense it speaks in stories and paradoxes: e.g. gospel parables, zen koans and the lived life of individuals.

The story of the self as body, feelings, mind, soul and spirit embodying desire may be told from the perspective of the whole as well as from that of the parts. We can distinguish three main stages in its evolution: Prepersonal, Personal and Transpersonal.

The prepersonal phase is characterised by radical uncoordination and fear of disintegration, together with the desire for coordination, control and management of life. A human infant, because of the prematurity of birth, is to all intents and purposes a body in bits and pieces. The parts are there but their functions are unco-ordinated. One of the first projects of an infant is to unify and integrate its chaotic life and bodily functions through fascination with its care giver. Its energy is towards building up the necessary structures and functions required for life.

The personal phase is characterised by the capacity to achieve and work in society. Its energy is achievement oriented, a desire to acquire whatever is necessary for the well being of the life of a person in terms of security, meaning and relationships. Its energy and *amour propre* is narcissistic. It is self-referential and always curves in upon itself. To this extent the self in its personal phase, sometimes referred to as egoic stage, is always anxious and fearful of its own demise. This is so notwithstanding its worldly success or achievements. The ego never fully encapsulates the fullness of life or desire. There is always more desiring. The successful person at a personal or egoic level is always restless, accompanied by feelings of despair and a desire for more. If construed only at its own level, this desire for more becomes a manic pursuit in a never ending spiral for more of the same experiences that are thought to bring contentment. These 'objects' of egoic desire, whether they be people, money or more abstract objects like virtues or even God, are pursued with the same achievement oriented energy required to build up the self as ego in the first instance. What is required, however, is not a calcification of desire sculpted as ego but rather the emergence of the self in its transpersonal stage.

The Transpersonal stage involves the freedom of desire from its egoic attachments to allow the self proceed towards new shapings. It is the quality of desire itself or the desiring self rather than the objects of desire that seeks to move forward. This occurs not through manic pursuit but rather through stilling the ego so that other voices might be heard and other colours seen. The babbling of the ego gives way to the voice of the self that does not negate the ego but goes beyond it. These experiences come along in the manner of a gift or grace and cannot be willed or made to happen any more than we can will sleep or relaxation. They come without any apparent usefulness attached to them. Music in itself is delightful and has no other use unless perverted. These transpersonal experiences, constituents of being a person, may be prepared for and waited upon by an act of recollection – what Heiddegger refers to as the 'gathering of thought' or an act of making still, quietening or attending to. There are, however, other experiences that are initiated in a totally gratuitous movement from the Divine or Ultimate Ground of Being. To quote Goethe 'This I have finally obtained from you by waiting/God's presence in all elements.' This brings to mind Goethe's contemporary, Blake, who wrote:

> To see a world in a Grain of Sand
> And a Heaven in a Wild Flower,
> Hold Infinity in the palm of your hand
> And Eternity in an Hour.

However, wherever the source or origin of these experiences, the dynamic assumption of the self suggests they are always embodied. Transcendence is by way of inclusion rather than exclusion. Therefore all human experiences are embodied.

The Self as Embodied

To construe the self as complex and dynamic is to focus on the inner processes and events of the self. To construe the self as embodied is to focus on the outer expressive aspect of the self. In some traditions the relationship between the two is seen as container and contained. In these traditions the real self is inner and is contained within the body. The true self is hidden and only glimpsed at inwardly. The body is like a veil concealing it. True self realisation implies transcending the body and leaving it behind like the bird flying from its gilded cage. This is a distorted view of the relationship between the body and the real self as we understand it.

We speak of the body in two ways: the body as object, i.e. the body I have, and the body as subject, i.e. the body I am.[9] The body as object is the body I'm given in my genetic patterns. It is the body that has its own laws and fluctuations; the body that is acted on by the surgeon. As already seen, the mind and feelings can act on this body in an unjust way. The mind can ignore it and a person can try to live as though disembodied. At other times, the body is used as a means to discharge feelings and act them out. In both instances, the body is related to as an object to be used.

The body as subject, or the body I am, is the living shaping organism in action. To say it is non-reflexive is not to say it is mindless but rather that it cannot be grasped by the mind alone. The notion of self as somatic is as elusive from the mind as self as spiritual. The complex and dynamic self has the possibility to sculpt and shape how it is in the world of people and objects. Its outer gesture or posture reflects its inner stance. As well as embodying the inner stance, the gesture or posture creates it. This sacramental way of being is well known in the religious traditions. The joined hands or clenched fist not only express but also create that which is expressed. This is also well known to therapists who work somatically and to those who design sacred and healing space.

To construe the self as embodied is also to construe it as expressive. Inner and outer are essentially related. The self seeks continuously to express itself in the way a fountain overflows. The embodied self as expressive is in the mode of the artist rather than the autocrat. The medium or form of the art, together with the artist, determine the final outcome. No artist rides roughshod over the medium of the art. Rather he enters into dialogue with it and through it some new being is made. Similarly, a person enters into dialogue with the stuff of life i.e. the body as given and through it a 'some body', the person. The body as subject is made and received. The self creates and shapes itself and the world around it. This capacity of the self to express and create is sometimes referred to as will.

The ego image or disembodied mind, in so far as it uses the body simply as an instrument of action, confuses effort with will. This is easy to see when we recall the delusion of the ego that everything is possible if sufficient effort is applied. We may say then that failure in life is more often failure of creative imagination in somatic knowing rather than failure of effort. Failure and suffering in life are frequently caused by lack of insight into the failure of the ego to create all human experiences. Pain and suffering flow from a lack of recognition and understanding of the essentially narcissistic aspects of the ego and its failure to accept the self as essentially relational.

The Self as Relational

The self, (complex, dynamic, and embodied) is a network of relationships. Therefore a person is essentially in relationship both inner and outer. To say the self is relational is to say it is in a constant process of give and take with its environment within, around and between. To say the relationship between people is essential is to say it is more than useful or a good thing. It is more than social contract. It implies that a self or person is not a monad or self-contained system but rather, in its very essential structures, calls out for, and to, the other. Relationship requires some sense of separation and boundaries as well as contact and completion. The self is experienced as delineated from the other at the same time as confirming and engaging the other.

Mutual relationships require mutual confirmation and engagement. These come about through an act of distance and through an act of creative imagination. In the act of distancing, a person can receive how the inner life may be distorting and affecting the relationship. Through the act of creative imagination, the other is perceived as truly other yet essentially connected to oneself. In this way the other is not the mirror in which one sees oneself reflected as one might desire to seem, but rather in the act of imagination itself, or the flow between, a new kind of knowing emerges. This knowing is such that it is neither of oneself alone or of the other as an object of knowledge, but rather as a knowing that occurs between persons.[10] Because the focus is not on one person alone, or the other person alone, but rather on both together, i.e. on what is between, the relationship avoids being narcissistic. Just as there is the self-staring of narcissism, there is also a kind of dual-staring – a staring at the starer. A true dialogue is palpably different from dual or collective monologue.

What happens between two people in a true dialogue transcends the here and now to include historical time. Some of the processes and events that occur between two people can only be understood in the wider context of history. Over and above the dialogue of two people, there is also the meta-dialogue of the ancestors. Our ancestors speak not only through the genes and the rhythms of our blood but also in the collective stories, myths and belief systems we inherit or that are given to us.

We need to distinguish the different whisperings heard within which might prevent us from hearing fully in the here and now. Nevertheless, these intrusive voices of our ancestors need to be included in the meeting. For not all voices of our ancestors are intrusive in a negative way. Their cumulative wisdom is handed down in the living traditions of literature and rituals, as for example in the great human existential themes embodied in Shakespeare's Hamlet or Lear. A true conversation – a flowing with – in the here and now – has to include a conversation with tradition. In the act of self-delineation, a person learns to listen not only to the voices of the ancestors but also to the more immediate tribal voices of the father, mother and siblings. Early learning experiences are the basic patterns of our relationships. In fact, present patterns of relationships often simply mirror earlier patterns.

However, to construe the self as relational implies more than a valid analysis of interactions between people. Such an analysis can be done by the mind alone. There is, as already suggested, a meeting at soul level – a sympathetic imagination that transcends though includes body, feelings and mind. Can we speak of a meeting at spirit level – a meeting that transcends soul level? Such a meeting would be beyond words and symbols, a meeting at the level of mystery that is unknowable wherein deep calls to deep. It is a meeting with the other that is unutterable. Unutterable, not because of the failure of language, but because it transcends all language as positive statement. At the same time, the meeting echoes or rinses through soul, mind, feelings and body and so its unutterability is uttered.

To construe the self as relational is to give it its deepest and most fundamental description. It follows that self-realisation does not occur within a person but rather between persons. It follows that spirit realisation, or God realisation, does not occur within a person but between persons. A person is fully a person only in relationship – a relationship that includes solitude. A community, therefore, is more than a collection of individuals thrown together. There is some seamless garment or pattern that connects all people, past, present and future, with one another, with the envir-onment around them and with God.

3. HOW DOES THIS APPROACH UNDERSTAND AND CONCEPTUALISE HUMAN PROBLEMS AND DISORDERS?

The story of the self as desire (complex, dynamic, embodied and relational) proceeding, stretching and evolving, is not necessarily a smooth one. It has its own knots and kuffufles. Any strand, whether of the body, feelings, mind, soul or spirit, might be knotted and in need of untying at any of its different stages, prepersonal, personal or transpersonal. Likewise, the absence or diminishment of any thread affects the overall weave of the story. Therefore it is important to place the human problem or disorder in its proper place; to decide where in the story the knot occurs. Problems at prepersonal levels require some reparative work. Indeed many forms of bizarre behaviour might be construed as the self attempting to repair itself and succeeding only in maintaining the problem.

Many forms of human suffering are more usefully construed as solutions to a problem rather than the problem itself. The self tells or expresses its own story of desire in its own particular way. Many seemingly odd shapings of desire in the body, feelings or mind, might be seen as the flow of desire finding its best expression. For that reason it is not always useful to take away a person's defence, whether of feelings or belief system, without understanding the purpose it serves in that person's story. Only then might that person be helped to tell his story in another way which might involve experiencing some of it in a different way or even finding the language in words and gestures. For example, a person's adult difficulties with sexuality may have their origins in a diminished capacity to bond from a prepersonal level. Similarly a person's adult difficulty in self delineating might originate in a prepersonal inability to create boundaries and separate from the environment.

Human problems at a personal level usually have to do with the inability of the ego, i.e. the self at personal level, to accept its inherent limitations. As already suggested, the amour propre of ego is achievement oriented and narcissistic. Its focus is always on the 'objects' of desire construed as essential to its own maintenance. Nevertheless, notwithstanding its apparent success, it fails to recognise its inherent anxiety and restlessness – its inability to satisfy the whole person and embody all of desire. Indeed it must learn painfully to withdraw attention from the objects of its desire to include the subject of desire. There is a movement away from, (while not denying or excluding) the many objects of desire, e.g. achievement and success, and a movement towards the emergence of a sense of the one who desires. This liberation of desire, born through insight into the failure of the ego, opens up the possibility of moving to a new level of personhood.

This part of the story of a self is sometimes referred to as the time of existential crisis, a time when the ego, sufficiently well integrated to cope and survive with a sense of well being, becomes acutely aware of its own nervousness and possibility of disintegration. To continue to build up the ego at this point, and to continue repeating the same paragraphs of the story, is to miss the opportunity to move forward and write another chapter.

Disorders at the transpersonal level have to do mainly with the inflation of the ego. These occur when the self in its personal stage collapses authentic and genuine transpersonal experiences into itself and lives as if it is the source of these experiences. This gives rise to the illusion that the ego can will all and every human experience. Anxiety, from this perspective, might be construed as the attempt to will the unwillable. It is this same illusory attitude that lends to addiction. Addiction is sometimes referred to as the modern sacred disease, in so far as it continuously points up the inherent failure of the ego in its superwill projects. On the other hand, without a well-enough integrated ego, such transpersonal experiences, even when authentic and genuine, may further destabilise the ego and lead to breakdown. A person affected in this way could become less and less capable of living an ordinary human life of give and take with the world within, about and between.

To misplace a human problem is to create category error.[11] Some experiences and suffering, that properly belong to a prepersonal phase, might be construed as transpersonal experience. For example, the desire for and experience of love, peace and security might be nothing more than a regression to an earlier phase of non-separation. On the other hand, it might indeed be a response to the call and promise of a greater and fuller life. It is the art of the clinician, in dialogue with the person, to decide which is which.

Is This Approach For Everyone?
While it is useful to construe the story of the self in terms of its prepersonal, personal and transpersonal stages, lived life is not so neat and tidy. At any given moment, a person's knots and kuffufles might echo in all three phases. Nevertheless, in so far as one always needs a thread to lead out of the labyrinth of confusion, it is important to decide what thread to take hold of. For some it might be, focally, issues at one level, and for others it might be, focally, at another level. Eventually all the threads weave the whole story. In general, the thread at personal or transpersonal levels is the one taken hold of in the psychosynthesis approach. This is not to imply that the same thread does not lead to prepersonal issues but rather that they are construed in the light of personal and transpersonal ones. In this way, the focus is more on what is emerging, developing and proceeding for the person rather than what focally needs repair. Inevitably, repair occurs in so far as the whole story is seen as essentially one, even though it includes many sub-stories.

4.PHILOSOPHY OF CHANGE

What is understood by change?
If synthesis, whether of ideas or of the psyche, is a dangerous human project, so also is change when used in relation to psychotherapy. Every therapist needs to keep in mind Rilke's determination not to be psychoanalysed lest, if his demons were to depart, his angels might leave as well. The charlatan, who promises more than he can deliver, accompanies every therapist, especially in relation to change.[12] Usually the promise, perhaps only implied by the therapeutic situation, is that change is not only possible but desirable. And the change promised is usually some form of wholeness, perfection or holiness: some ideal abstract model of a self. This implied promise, if not openly dealt with in the begin-

ning of therapy by the therapist, is oftentimes the client's desired response. Usually the change asked for by the client is the absence of pain or the erasing of history – 'make my past never to have happened.' 'Change me so that I no longer bear the wounds of my personal history.' To collude in any way with such a project is not only dangerous, it is wrong. At most, one can point to other strands in the story and lead the person to experience that every wound implies someone who is wounded. The very fact of sitting in a therapist's room recounting the horrors of childhood or adolescence implies that someone has survived, come through, and lived to tell the story though wounded. That someone is not the wound itself but the one who bears it. In this way someone may be led from the manic pursuit of certainty – whether of being loved, understood, healthy or holy – to a more compassionate understanding of ambivalence. The pursuit of certainty leads to tension, intolerance, violence and finally breakdown. A compassionate acceptance of ambivalence leads to relaxation, humility, tolerance and a joy of living. It is an experience of living from a position of plenitude and fullness rather than from a position of scarcity and emptiness. It is a focus on the one who suffers and is wounded without denying either the suffering or wound. It is a befriending of the multiplicity of the psyche.

How does change occur?

Change, understood as the move from the manic pursuit of certainty and the illusion of the ego to achieve certainty, occurs through a healing dialogue or presence to self as complex, dynamic, embodied and relational. All healing and transformation occurs in meeting.[13] In this sense, pathology might be construed as the absence of relationship, and healing as a turning to the other – a metanoia. There is nothing more frightening than the vacant staring of despair in a patient locked up within himself or herself. It is a looking without seeing. Dante's description of hell is of a place full of noise and effort but without relationship. Healing is the opening up to the grace or presence of the other. It is to feel oneself spoken to and addressed as a subject. It is to know there is a hand outstretched to help and hold on to. A healing dialogue or presence is more than a mere use of technical, skillful or abstract knowledge. It is more in line with Yeat's understanding of knowledge:

> God guard me from those thoughts men think
> In the mind alone;

He that sings a lasting song
Thinks in a marrow bone.

The dialogue and presence occurs through 'thinking in a marrow bone.' One could have much training, many skills and conceptual clarity and yet lack the art of 'thinking in a marrow bone.' It comes only through practice, a practice of attention to what is happening within and between, a practice of mindfulness that is from the heart, rather than an abstract staring from the mind alone or the feelings alone. Within the temenos, or sanctuary of the healing dialogue, a greater life appears and manifests itself to both client and therapist. A transparency occurs within and between so that the deep inner life reveals itself even in the apparent ruins of the ego and its inability to function as it would like. The process continues outside the therapeutic session as the client learns to live daily life by witnessing to this deeper life, i.e. by remembering things through attending to and expressing the greater life that enfolds each individual life as the ocean enfolds the wave and the tree the leaf. Such a transparency for, and surrender to, a deeper life may not get rid of the painful symptom or erase painful memories, but it does allow for the possibility of an experience of oneself as greater, deeper, beyond, unfathomable and mysterious. The client comes to live daily life in gracious co-operation with the inevitable.

5.APPLICATION

It is easy to read Part II of Assagioli's book *Psychosynthesis* as a recipe of techniques for manipulating the psyche.[14] This is especially so if his introduction is not carefully read and reflected on. His book, *Act of Will,* reads like a series of simple and naïve steps for willing whatever one wants, unless one understands its underlying philosophical assumptions.[15] In his book, *The Future of the Body,* Michael Murphy carefully contextualises Assagioli's approach. He writes, 'Many therapists with a transpersonal orientation have been influenced by the Italian psychiatrist, Roberto Assagioli, who from the 1920s until he died in 1974 developed a comprehensive discipline for healing and growth which he called Psychosynthesis.

Assagioli's approach draws upon psychoanalysis and the work of therapists such as Desoille, Leurner and Jung and it employs meditative techniques from both Eastern and Western contemplative traditions. It aims to shift the centre of personality from normal consciousness to its fundamental core which Assagioli sometimes called the true or Higher Self. The methods used in Psychosynthesis include symbolic visualisation and guided day dreams to illuminate unconscious issues and open up new dimensions of consciousness; active imagination to establish contact with the psyche's purpose and dynamics; and concentration upon positive symbols to reinforce desirable capacities.'[16] As already suggested, Assagioli draws on the insights of many different schools – psychiatric and religious. He describes a wide range of capacities and is insightful about contemporary forms of pathology in relation to the spiritual quest.

More than most therapies, as Murphy suggests, Psychosynthesis aims at facilitating the growth of consciousness and moral sensibility beyond the healing of personal conflict; and more than most religious disciplines, it incorporates the discoveries of modern psychology and psychiatry. However, notwithstanding these more obvious strengths, it does not typically involve the systematic cultivation of kinaesthetic or movement abilities. Assagioli drew little from the martial arts or other somatic disciplines and most Psychosynthesis practitioners have not emphasised enough the body's potential for dynamic activity and restructuring. The insights of Assagioli into methods and techniques, so carefully contextualised by Michael Murphy, need to be completed and grounded by the insights of Karlfried Von Durckheim in the Initiation therapy developed in his centre in Germany and by those of his student, Stanley Keleman, in somatic knowledge.[17] It is the art of the therapist to choose which approach to take with any particular client.

One of the functions of initial sessions is not only to decide whether or not the client is in the right territory in terms of general approach, but also to decide what particular approach is most suitable and whether or not that approach is available. However, whatever approach is taken, it is always within the sanctuary of a healing dialogue. The dialogue itself is the healing sanctuary. How long it needs to continue varies from person to person and is usually decided on by both client and therapist.

In general, the life of any therapy has a beginning, middle and

→ 4 years to accredited.
=
turning pt. what course would?

23 Crofton Rd. Dun L.

Dublin.

General
Ph: 01 280 7888.

training dep. tel 2801603

www.turningpoint.ie

3 year graduate diploma course.

MSc Year 4.

accredited by UCD.

end. One can predict classical issues that emerge at each stage. In the beginning, issues arise in relation to inclusion, exclusion, building up trust and the first telling of story, usually well edited. The story is told many times over until it sounds and reads right to the storyteller; until it reaches some gestalt and closure that makes sense. The safety of the therapeutic sanctuary allows the telling of the story to echo and re-echo in the many chambers of the storyteller. The events of the story may remain the same, the words and images used may sound the same as in the beginning, but eventually it echoes, resonates and sounds complete. There are no new pieces of information but the voice of the one telling the story has changed. Perhaps only the tone is different or the hues of description different but, nevertheless, the one who tells the story hears it differently and begins to tell and write the story forward. In this process the therapist is no passive or silent element but becomes another character in the story. He or she may embody not only roles from the past but also be something of an icon that embodies, opens up and points forward to a deeper life beyond and between. This iconic quality is not primarily encapsulated within the therapist but rather the dialogue in, and commitment between client and therapist. The therapeutic situation itself is the icon of the larger and deeper life. As the client writes and moves the story forward, he moves towards the end of the therapy contract. In so doing, he / she implicitly, even if not explicitly, is confronted with the question: is death the end and completion of the story or yet another event to be lived through? The implied answer to that question affects the quality of lived life. 'If someday I must die, how shall I live?' is a question about endings as completion or as experiences to be lived through, included and transcended. For that reason, the quality of the ending in therapy may take a long time in the working through, with all the attendant feelings of mourning, grief, acceptance, and the temptation of denial.

5. TRAINING

As suggested, Psychosynthesis is essentially a perspective a way of construing a person. Assagioli writes, 'If we now consider psychosynthesis as a whole, with all its implications and developments, we see that it should not be looked upon as a particular psychological doctrine, nor as a single technical procedure. It is first and foremost a dynamic, even a dramatic conception of our psychological life.'[18] This perspective on the drama of human life can be applied to many different fields including medicine, education, psychology, business and spiritual life. In this sense there is no practitioner of Psychosynthesis as such. Rather there are men and women practitioners who express this perspective in their work, whether as doctors, teachers or psychotherapists. Eckhart House offers a four-year training for those who wish to use this perspective in their work or as psychotherapists. The programme is in two parts. Part I focuses primarily on the personal and interpersonal processes of participants from a psychosynthesis perspective, whilst Part II allows participants to deepen their study of Psychosynthesis as a transpersonal theory and learn the methodology to practice it in their work or as psychotherapists.

SUMMARY

1. Psychosynthesis is a way of construing a person as complex, dynamic, embodied and relational.
2. The self as a complex, dynamic, embodied and relational person moves through three stages: Prepersonal, Personal and Transpersonal.
3. The self narrates or tells its own story of its desire on each stage of its evolution.
4. Movement forward or evolution from stage to stage is by way of transcendence through inclusion rather than negation.
5. Each stage has its own pathologies and appropriate healing interventions.
6. Change occurs in the healing dialogue.
7. Psychosynthesis is a perspective, or a construing, rather than a series of techniques.
8. As a transpersonal theory, Psychosynthesis 'does not aim to give a metaphysical nor a theological explanation of the great Mystery. It leads to the door but stops there.'[19]

Notes

1. Buber, M., *The Origin and Meaninq of Hasidism* (New Jersey: Humanities Press International Inc., 1988)142.

2. Hardy, J., *A Psychology with a Soul* (Arcana 1986).

3. Wilber, K., *Eye to Eye: the Quest for a New Paradigm* (Anchor Books, 1983).

4. Assagioli, R., *Psychosynthesis: A manual of Principles and Techniques* (Turnstone Books, 1980) Ch.l.

5. Assagioli: op.cit., 16

6. Firman, J., and Russell, A., *What is Psychosynthesis?* (459 Hawthorne Ave. Palo Alto California 94301) 4.

7. Firman and Russell: op.cit.,4

8. Ricoeur, P., *Freud and Philosophy: An Essay on Interpretation* (Yale University Press, 1970).

9. Von Durckheim:, K., *Our Twofold Origin* (George Allen and Unwin, 1983).

10. Buber, M., *The Knowledge of Man* (Humanities Press International, USA, 1988).

11. Wilber, K., op.cit.,209

12. Guggenbuhl-Craig, A., *Power in the Helping Professions* (Zurich: Spring Publications, 1971).

13. Friedman, M., *The Healing Dialogue in Psychotherapy* (New York: Jason Aronson, 1985).

14. Assagioli: op.cit.

15. Assagioli: *Act of Will* (London: Wildwood House, 1974).

16. Murphy:, M., *The Future of the Body* (Los Angeles: Jeremy P. Tarcher Inc., 1992) 384

17. Von Durckheim, K., op.cit.; *The Way of Transformation* (Allen and Unwin, 1971). Stanley Keleman: *Emotional Anatomy* (Berkeley, CA: Center Press, 1985).

18. Assagioli: *Psychosynthesis* 30

19. Assagioli: *Psychosynthesis* 6-7

CHAPTER 5

Constructivist Psychotherapy

Bernadette O'Sullivan and Dorothy Gunne

> '... the task of psychotherapy is not to produce behaviour, but rather to enable the client as well as the therapist to utilise behaviour for asking important questions. In fact, the task of psychotherapy is to get the human process going again so that life may go on and on from where psychotherapy left off.' (Kelly, 1969, p.223).

This chapter is a distillation of a number of conversations we had together in late summer 1992. In these discussions we endeavoured to:
(i) briefly outline some of the philosophical and theoretical ideas that inform us in our work as constructivist psychotherapists;
(ii) to look at some of the ways in which these ideas are translated into therapeutic practice, and
(iii) to make some reference as to why it makes sense to each of us to choose to work from this theoretical context.

The Beginnings

In 1955 *The Psychology of Personal Constructs* was published. It was as George Kelly, its American author, said 'a two volume, twenty-year collection of impacted ideas about a new theory of personality and its application in a clinical setting'. He could claim it as a new theory of personality because it was 'a psychology concerned with what we do and why we do it, rather than one that attempts to pinpoint the events that compel others to do what they do not choose to do,' (Kelly, 1969, p.49).

This was the first published account of a psychological clinical practice which was consciously informed by the epistemological perspective of *Constructivism*. In the very first paragraph of Volume 1, Kelly stated that his philosophical starting point was that of *Constructive Alternativism*. His premise was that 'all of our present interpretations of the universe are subject to revision or replacement' so that 'there are always some alternative constructions available to choose among in dealing with the world.' (Kelly,

1955, p.15). Along with Kelly (who died in 1967) many other academicians and practitioners have continued to elaborate and explore the usefulness of Personal Construct Psychology and its particular form of Constructivism.

Resonating with developments in scientific thinking, especially in the area of New Physics, a constructivist understanding of knowledge has gradually come to inform a much broader group of psychological workers and clinical practitioners than those of us working within the frame of Kelly's Personal Construct Theory. The influence of constructivist ideas is especially evident in the systemic-therapy field where the writings of the anthropologist Gregory Bateson and biologist Humberto Maturana have been instrumental in providing a number of systemic (family therapy) clinicians with theoretical constructivist explanations for therapeutic possibilities. So today, Personal Construct Psychotherapists are by no means alone in favouring a constructivist perspective on the human venture.

What do we mean by constructivism?

By Constructivism we mean that epistemological perspective which views:

(i) knowledge as actively built up – indeed invented – by the person but in a social context. The recognition of the importance of the cultural and linguistic milieu within which people build up their understanding cannot be stressed enough. Such a context and network of conversations is seen as forever embedded in individual understanding and it, in turn, embeds that experience. Thus, a constructivist psychology is not a psychology of the individual but of the individual within society and about societies of individuals;

(ii) Secondly, constructivism views invented knowledge as the reality one lives. It is argued that one lives through the understanding one has of the world. Such an understanding or knowledge cannot be proven to be a true representation of the 'real world' (of an objective ontological reality), but it is decidedly the understanding we draw on to negotiate – our way around the world we inhabit. Within this view we cannot use objects to validate our truths because it is the understanding and viewpoints we have which is being validated, and can only be validated. We can never suspend our meaning-making faculties, so it is always within their terms that we are operating.

Wallace Stevens (1879-1955), the American poet, put this position most succinctly:

> Description is revelation. It is neither
> The thing described, nor false facsimile.
> It is an artificial thing that exists
> In its own seeming, plainly visible.
> Yet not too closely the double of our lives
> Intenser than any actual life could be.

When clients come to therapy with a problem to be resolved the starting point will be a description of the problem, for whom it is a problem, and how life may have been organised around it. In other words, the material used in therapy will be understanding, and the relationship between what is done and that understanding. Therapy is situated within a forum of conversation because, from a constructivist perspective, understanding is the centre of action. This is not to say that to think differently about something is necessarily the primary source of change, but it is to recognise that thinking and understanding indeed mediate and are mediated by human action. They are connected recursively and are entirely interdependent. 'Behaviour,' Kelly has frequently pointed out, 'is the experiment'. In other words behaviour is the way we have of living out our truths.

There are, of course, many differences within such a broad view of invented human knowledge. But for now it is probably sufficient to say that two widely held assumptions within construct-ivism would be that:
(i) Human beings together invent (verbally and non-verbally) the knowledge and the particular ways, meanings and distinctions etc. through which they come to know, or indeed, to notice (as Maturana says 'bring forth') the world;
(ii) Such an invented world in turn influences that particular knowing. This would imply that we cannot see that for which we are not looking or are not in a state of readiness to see. As Einstein has been reported as saying 'it is the theory which decides what we can observe' (Landfield, 1982). It is recognised, therefore, that there is a constant recursive relationship between knowing and

what is known. Much more comprehensive discussions on this view of knowledge can be found elsewhere (e.g. Watzlawick, 1984; Von Glaserfeld, 1988).

What Does a Constructivist Philosophy, and Psychology Assume about the Nature of the Human Person?

The fundamental postulate or central principle of Personal Construct Psychology is that 'a person's processes are psychologically channelised by the ways in which she anticipates events'. Personal Construct Psychology recognises the person as always in the business of negotiating the future and, therefore, places an explicit emphasis on anticipation in the business of living. By anticipation here we mean the way in which our past experiences, and understandings of them, influences the ways in which we bring forth our futures. It is in this sense that PCP describes the person as a maker of meaning. This happens most often at a non-verbal level, part of which can be accessible to a person through language.

Person as maker of meaning

We have already intimated what could be described as a fundamental tenet of a constructivist psychology when we said that persons are inventors of the world in which they live. From this perspective, it is considered to be in the nature of the human person to *make meaning, to define, to construe.* In no sense is this understood to be a solely cognitive act, nor is meaning equated with verbalised statements or 'common-sense' deductions. Indeed, very frequently what is meaningful (full of meaning) is neither sensible nor logical or even rational. In discussing the creation of meaning that we human beings undertake, Kelly comments that the person 'understands (the) world by finding out what (he/she) can do with it' (Kelly, 1973, p.398). He argues that we come to understand ourselves in the same say 'by finding out what' we can make of ourselves. Such a comment does not suggest that construing is synonymous with cognition but rather that it is a recursive bodily, emotional and cognitive engagement. It is a way of anticipating one's world and living in it, constantly turned towards the future and making sense of that in terms of past positions, construings or distinctions drawn.

Capacity to live within a network of meaning and to create a consensual domain

It is emphasised that language and the capacity to live within a network of meaning both for oneself and with others is central to human nature. It is part of what we have become and something from which we cannot escape. 'We must,' says Shotter (1975, p.134) 'make and continually remake our own nature, we must constantly be in search of ourselves.' He goes on to say that this can only be done 'by people in dialogue, as the product of a social act, in continual mutual interrogation and reply.' We are born into a world of language. That world implies shared meanings and therefore it is very difficult to live outside this cultural consensus, or to move from it to another culture / family / grouping. It awaits us and indeed influences both the way we meet the world and how we are met by it.

Being born female into an Irish rural Catholic society will lead us into quite different beliefs and understandings of ourselves than if we were born into e.g. an Irish Muslim urban family. The world we are born into implies shared meanings and a capacity to establish common belief systems and norms through which to grasp and actually perceive and work in the world about us. It is therefore difficult to live outside this cultural consensus or to move from it to another culture or family or grouping. For example, there is hardly anyone amongst us who has not had the experience of returning to visit a parental home and of finding ourselves reacting and being treated, against our will and better judgement, in exactly the manner that occurred when we were young. The norms set, the belief systems operating, and the roles allowed do not easily change.

Another example is how when two people set up home together, they inevitably run into strong differences about quite small things, differences which derive from their particular families of origin. Joining another family or culture is rarely without difficulty. These are quite mundane examples of the extent to which we live out our lives within networks of meaning. We would say that in therapy we can never forget this even if we are working with the individual client. The client(s) and the therapist both come holding innumerable positions within many other networks and together they also establish another within the context of therapy, which itself is situated within a professional and cultural network.

The Autonomy of the Living System

It is further understood within a constructivist perspective that the nature of the human person is that of a *Living Autonomous System*. By this we mean that it is a self-generating system which is not capable of being changed in any deliberate way by its environment (or other organisms within its environment). For example, I can insist, by force of authority or physical superiority, that another 'do my will', but I can never directly change anothers attitude, belief or understanding. I can help it along the way, I can persuade, but ultimately the other will be the one to change and even then, not necessarily in the manner I may have intended. Rather, a person (as an autonomous living system) may be perturbed by outside events but will change according to her/his own structures.

In the human person there are the bodily struct-ures and also the meaning-system structure. This meaning-system is comprised of both verbal and non-verbal, (cognitive. physical and emotional) elements which have been built up over time. Indeed it would be argued that the non-verbal elements are of immensely greater importance and often covering a wider span of experience than anything that can be verbalised.

Change as a human characteristic

Another characteristic of living-systems is that of *change* but it is change of a particular kind i.e. it is in terms of renewing oneself and in ensuring a continuation of the self. One could say therefore, that there is a fundamental challenge to all living-systems of how to change and yet remain stable or apparently the same, of how to ensure predictability and the certainty of a continuing existence in the terms one has come to value or sense as central to one's meaningfulness or survival. George Kelly describes the human person as a 'process in motion' which probably captures as well as anything might the exciting but perhaps at times alarming sense of a continuously enactive being, caught up in the flux of life.

Such a perspective leads one to assume that change is idiosyncratic and not under the control of another or at least not unless one recognises or senses (as an infant may do, for example) that it seems to be in the interests of one's own survival to admit the greater power of another and to 'co-operate'. In other words, undoubtedly, constraints on change are very real. A constructivist perspective does not deny the reality of constraints. It simply invites us to recognise them as constructed, invented, within a consensual domain of meaning. So what we make can be unmade, although often with the greatest difficulty. 'Nobody,' says Kelly, 'need be a victim of their own biography.' That is the optimistic theme within constructivism, but it would be utterly foolhardy and naïve to underestimate the power of the inventions, truths, and worlds, which we have heretofore constructed and that cannot be changed simply by logically deciding to do so.

We might well ask however, if we can say what constitutes change. In view of all that has been said about the person as an enactive, cognising, inventing and anticipating being ('a process in motion'), and of difference only occurring within the terms defined by the person themselves (who *is* a construing-system rather than he *has* one), it will not be surprising to note that Kelly talks primarily of *movement* rather than *change.* The movement being sought through therapy is a new or different way of construing i.e. a new way of living and acting towards something, some person, some experience, some feeling etc. But such new construings must be developed 'out of the materials that the client is able to furnish' (Kelly, 1955, p.1089). Any other solutions proposed by the therapist, may well be for the therapist alone, and may not feel relevant to the client. We mention this, because all too often, we therapists find that our clients do not change in the manner in which we would envisage they should. An interpretation or movement by the therapist is not of itself useful to the client and says nothing about change for the client.

Movement is considered to occur through the process of reconstruing. For example, it was when one of our clients decided that her 'overeating' was a 'pandering to a starving Mary' who could not 'voice' her needs in a way that they were recognised by another, that she began to act on 'voicing' and found that eating diminished as an issue for her. Indeed her 'voicing' of needs also was reconstrued, in that it now included inquiries and changes in her work activities, as well as in the actual verbal articulation of her needs as she saw them. She started a process of negotiation with herself, the world and her relationships which continues two years later.

A Therapeutic approach which embraces these ideas of the nature of the human person

An understanding of the human venture drawn from a constructivist perspective leads to a 'psychology for getting along with the unknown' (1977, p.19), the uncertainty within which we are destined to live. The psychotherapeutic conversation related to that is about attempting to enable the participants to risk striking out into the unknown. Without seeking predictability, the therapist attempts to encourage the client to engage in anticipatory actions as if they were true, whilst retaining all the time, a realisation that one's action may be more appropriately and usefully understood as an enquiry, rather than a guarantee of predictable outcomes.

It is possible to summarise the main features of a constructivist psychotherapy conversation as follows:

(i) It is *A Collaborative Inquiry* between two (or more) experts. One participant (the client) is seen as an expert on themselves, even though they may not feel this to be the case, and the other (the therapist) is seen as bringing an expertise in ways of exploring, of setting up ultimately helpful inquiries, and in drawing on psychological theories;

(ii) It is *An Experimental and Invitational Venture* with the aim of facilitating the client(s) to try out alternative possibilities rather than seeking to 'get it right'. In looking for ways of 'transcending the obvious', there is a constant dependence on using an approach of exploration such as 'if this were so/true ... what then?' This allows the possibility for the client to arrive at previously unthought of or unknown ways of going on;

(iii) It involves the *creation of an emerging reality through a conversational dialogue* which gives as much and often more weight to unverbalised and non-verbal construing as to the verbalised labels;

(iv) It requires an *attending to the recursive relationship between doing and knowing* so that the invitation is to revise one's anticipations in the light of engagements.

There will always be an emphasis on living, and on our daily and even banal acts of living, as acts of inquiry, as ways of establishing, revealing and confirming our understandings. Bringing a glass of water to one's bedroom every night may, for example, now carry for you many more meanings than it did at the outset when you simply were following your grandmother's example.

APPLICATION

An understanding of human problems and disorders from a constructivist perspective

Within Personal Construct Psychology, disorder can be looked on as having two aspects:

(i) It is a feeling or experience of not coming up with solutions, of being stuck, trapped, either by one's own sense of inability to *do* anything which changes the situation, or brings about change *or* being trapped by somebody else's apparent inability or unwillingness to change themselves or change the situation;

(ii) it is that continued use of a solution or perspective even though it does not actually work to relieve or un-stick the situation. An example of this would be always trying harder although we know that trying harder is not actually bringing about the results we want. This is where the solution or the attempted solution becomes a problem in its own right.

Disorder is 'any personal construction that is used repeatedly, in spite of consistent invalidation' (Kelly, 1955, p.831). It is really a failure of learning from experience and a failure to reconstrue or revise on the basis of an experience of something not working. We would argue that this happens because the implication of reconstruing for that person appears to be too threatening, to imply the loss of their essential familiar identity, an identity which we strive all the time to maintain. Conversely, it is presumed that human 'order' is about continuously changing, although not necessarily always cataclysmically, on the basis of past information and future anticipations, rather than on habitual patterns. It is indeed premised on the understanding that, as previously mentioned, change is central to human nature and that our challenge is not so much to achieve stability without change but rather one of changing in such a manner as to ensure a continuing stable sense of the self.

Such a view is not an attempt to minimise the distress, the terror even, and the anger, the utter inability to sense alternatives and the most usual experience of being trapped in or hounded by psychological ill-health or disorder. It is however a clear statement that a constructivist perspective leads one to understand that what is happening in psychological disorder (and in experiencing all the concomitant distress) is the only possible solution at that point in time.

Psychotherapy as a collaborative venture

Therapy, said Kelly 'takes place when one person makes constructive use of another' and the process gets under way when someone 'sets out to be what (they) are not'. It is for the therapist a 'commitment to joining (the client) in a common undertaking' as one involves oneself 'deeply with a person whose life is at a turning point' (1977, p.12). The collaborative venture suggested here, the theme of experimental inquiry that is hinted at, and the goal of therapy as a 'transcending of the obvious' alternatives, all contrast sharply with a position on therapy as a treatment process where the aim may be the alleviation or cure of symptoms and the process may be prescriptively organised.

There is never an attempt to eschew the responsibility and expertise of the professional but there is within constructivist psychotherapy an invitation to consider the expertise of the therapist as something other than that of privileged observer. In the client–therapist venture we would propose that it is as if 'we create our understanding in relationship, between us, rather than as separated scientist constructing an edifice of specialist knowledge in terms only accepted by his fraternity' (Mair, 1979, p.46). The 'expertise' is believed to be that of listening 'to people in trouble' and 'trying to help them figure out what they could do about it' (Kelly, 1969, p.50). Such a simple description cannot hide the complexity and demands of the task that any therapist sets themselves – 'the heart-breaking tasks of the psychotherapist.' says Kelly (1969, p.49).

Psychotherapy – An enquiry for whom?

When we come to talk about the application of constructivist psychotherapy, we should be very clear that it's important to be aware of the psychotherapeutic venture as being a very personal one not only for the client, but also a very personal one for the therapist. However, the enquiry is of a differing sort for all participants. While we sense the importance of mentioning the personal nature of the work for the therapist, it seems necessary to make reference to the primacy of the client and the centrality of their venture in the whole endeavour. The constructivist psychotherapist will see therapy as an invitation to see, feel and hear the world from the perspective of each particular client i.e. to subsume in so far as possible the verbal and non-verbal patterns of meanings of the other. In endeavouring to come to know the client it is the task of the therapist to try to come to know the client in a very personal way, 'I will have to enter your world, breathe your air, feel something about the shape of your living, share something of your pain and your passion, meet the world through your eyes, with the armaments of your hopes and longings' (Mair, 1980, p.123).

So we might say that the process of psychotherapy is a constant negotiation of realities between client and therapist. Thus, a constructivist psychotherapist will pay particular attention to the language of the client, and will constantly come as near as possible to the meaning that the client uses when he speaks. In the initial session(s) a person who decides to attend a constructivist psychotherapist could expect to be invited to pay a lot of attention to what it was that led them to pursue the venture of psychotherapy in the first place. The therapist will want to explore with a client why it makes sense to enter this kind of relationship at this point in time, and what 'psychotherapy' means to them. She will also wish to understand in what way the client is experiencing their dilemma or questioning their personal or social world. We are making an assumption here that a person who enters therapy comes to it with a number of questions about themselves in a personal or social context, while we accept that it may take a number of sessions to frame these questions in a mutually recognisable way.

Very often a person will speak about some way they have of 'being in the world' that doesn't seem to be working for them. It might also be that what is problematic for them, is that in some way, they do not find a 'fit' with 'conversations' that go on in say, their family, with their friends, or even in society as a whole. Yet they may be aware that they don't seem to be able to be or do or understand or feel in any other way, despite the fact that they identify this way as being very problematic for them. In a strange way the therapist enters a paradoxical world, where on the one hand, she tries to understand how this way of being is troublesome for the client, and at the same time tries to understand why this particular way of being or doing makes the best possible sense for that person at this time. A therapist may be slow to start recommending 'solutions' to the client. What we are trying to touch on here is a sense that a client will have spent many years living life and negotiating their existence in the world about them. Whatever that negotiation has been about, is the very best solution that the client has come up with to-date in the endeavour of living. One might say that a client may have become unable to:

> 'decisively test out and elaborate their personal theories, their understanding of themselves and their interpersonal world. Their construing may have become circular, so that they are endlessly testing and retesting the same hypotheses and are unable to accept the implications of the data which they collect. They may have. moved into the kind of chaos where constructions are so vague and loose that they cannot provide expectations clear enough to be tested and they simply flow back and forth around the same issue. Whatever the specific difficulty, the psychotherapist would never set out to sell a particular construct system to the client; they would seek to help the client to test the validity of the client's own construct system. If they are successful, in that the system once again begins to move and elaborate, then the direction in which it goes and the issues which it pursues are, in a very definite sense, no longer the psychotherapist's business.' (Bannister & Francella, 1986, p.116)

For example, if a client comes with some kind of understanding of therapy as say, that they are sick and that the therapist is in the business of providing some kind of cure, then this will be their expectation of the therapist. Rather than saying 'I am not willing to have this kind of conversation with you because you have unreal expectations of me' (e.g. meaning system of therapist), a constructivist psychotherapist might not see that this in any way diminishes her ability to work with that particular client, but might keep an eye out for what anticipations the client has around this conversation. The therapist will be aware that whatever responses she provides must in some way fit with the client, or else she is talking in a language that is inappropriate, and the client will (wisely) opt out of the therapeutic venture with this therapist. This challenges the creativity of the therapist, to find ways of usefully fitting with the clients ways of being in the world, in such a way as to invite the client to be different.

In listening to a person's 'story' a therapist will (sometimes unknowingly) pick up the major ways of positioning and anticipating the world used by the client. This can be described as an inquiry, as if she and the client are co-experimenters in the client's venture. She will begin to pick up on recurring themes of the client. At this point the client(s) and the therapist are speaking and listening and devising inquiries and experiments within a discourse space which is fundamentally about life, and how it can be lived within that person's cultural, social, emotional, political and economic milieu.

It is vital that what is happening in the therapy conversation must be understood in terms of the client's own system. The effort is not only to achieve empathy with the client but to, as it were, stand in the other(s)' shoes. This is a recognition that dilemmas experienced and solutions which may result in a sense of change or difference must ultimately emerge out of that person's position rather than from the perspective of the therapist. We do not need to be professional therapists to know well that arriving at, and indeed, creating new possibilities from within our old positions can be blindingly difficult. The task is as Millar Mair says, about 'drawing meaning and possible meaning (possibilities of intention) from the silent world beyond our ordinary attending'. It is for the therapist and the client(s) about finding ways and the courage to throw out a different line, to *experimentally venture* with a difference. Enabling this may require of the therapist not only to be a conversationalist, alert to the many levels of unspoken meaning, but also to become an expert at detecting the possible indications of the style of knowing that another may have. It demands of the therapist to be involved in an 'ethical project aimed at human emancipation' (Mair, 1989, p.215). This 'emancipation' will necessarily involve a negotiation around the possible ways of accessing the webs of meanings of the client 'wherein I, for instance, sense and engage with you behind and through your various masks and roles' (Mair, 1980, p 114).

Language can be seen as centrally important in the invention of sense (of the emerging reality in therapy). Once one takes that view there is no way now to avoid the experience of the impermanence and uncertainty of patterns, distinctions made, differences or similarities that are punctuated. For 'in coming to know ourselves or others personally we will need to find ways to realise the invisible, to enter private worlds and get close enough to touch what hitherto we have refused to feel' (Mair, 1980, p 113), It must also be said that language can be as much imprisoning as emancipating. In therapy sessions use might be made of the richness of metaphor or storytelling as a means of getting in touch with what may as yet have not or never been articulated in language, as many of our constructs would have been developed before we would have had language that could express them. It would be seen as important to help a client to articulate these different layers of knowing throughout the process of therapy. Thus, sessions could be very verbal. Some sessions might vary between the verbal and the non-verbal. The emphasis on non-verbal might be through art work or body work, or some other negotiated form of pre-verbal work. Whatever mode predominates, the sessions will weave back and forth between what is easily identified for the client, to what is as yet un-verbalised. An example of this would be the sessions one of us had with a client a few years ago. This client frequently brought to sessions parts of a journal which she was keeping during the series of conversations. The parts she brought were almost always samples of the way she painted and coloured through times of great pain and deep inarticulacy. She commented on the paintings (which to her sophisticated eye were very childlike) and through this process found herself coming to a much firmer understanding of where she wanted to go and what was holding her back. We never actually pushed ourselves to interpret the paintings but they were a rich source personal and fruitful elaboration that could be acted on.

When a therapist feels that she has been able to 'subsume' the most important parts of the client's 'construing system' within her own, she may feel ready to make some kind of diagnosis i.e. begin to identify with the client possible pathways of movement which may be available to him. Movement here would be understood to occur through the process of reconstruing. This is rarely confined to or always evidenced in the therapeutic session. 'Much of what takes place to help the client reconstrue life takes place outside the interview-room,' points out Kelly (1955, p.1092). Reconstruing, within Personal Construct Psychology terms, refers to the act of living out, dealing with something or somebody or some experience or event differently, with the belief that this is, at least for now, a preferable alternative until the evidence suggests otherwise. This latter can of course happen at a very low level of cognitive awareness indeed, so that the client may be quite unable to articulate logical or apparently rational reasons for the change. Reconstruction then is understood to occur only as the end product of an enquiry which, as in a series of therapy conversations, is often deliberately evoked. This inquiry is described as the 'Cycle of Experience' in Personal Construct Psychology. Sometimes such reconstruction could be described as taking a contrasting position to that previously engaged in e.g. being an 'outsider' might now be sensed as not always desirable but as potentially fruitful and even exciting where as previously, it may have been experienced solely as a negative and rejecting experience. Reconstruction can be a consequence of elaborating and living out a new way truly unexpected by this person. This possibility is surely the most unusual because it is the most difficult. The degree to which the therapy sessions are experienced by the client as a jumping-off ground for careful experimentation with difference, will serve here more than anything else perhaps to facilitate novel reconstruing.

How can movement (reconstruing) be recognised?

It frequently takes a long time for somebody to be able to articulate the changes they are engaged in, and most particularly to elaborate and be easy with the implications of such movement when movement can be argued as occurring over time. As one of our clients put it when she wrote (one year after a series of therapy conversations) 'I think that now I feel the benefit of all those agonising sessions ... it's as if it's taken a long while to shed the skin ... and though the prospect ... might seem fairly daunting, it's amazing how positive I am ...'.

How does change happen. What is necessary in the therapeutic relationship in order to facilitate movement?

Since within a constructivist perspective, it is considered that movement may happen through the process of an experiential and experimental enquiry, the therapist is asked especially to encourage and enable the client(s) to set up constructive experiments, at a time and within a context, which is most likely to be informative and useful for them.

We already mentioned the need for the therapist to be forever listening, often more to what is not said than to what is said. Such a therapist, if she is to be a trustworthy supervisor of the client(s)' enquiries, must consciously find ways to time and time again suspend her own projects and aims for those of the client. Being alert to the 'kind of transference the client places on the therapist' is also considered to be an essential aspect of therapy if only to invite the client to experience alternative perspectives on old assumptions.

The therapist herself can never be released from the consideration of the perspectives she may be bringing to the sessions. Along with Kelly we would argue that psychotherapy is a 'basic science in which the scientists are the client and therapist' (Kelly, 1969, p.220). The more accurate the therapist can be in understanding the outlook and projects of the client, the more useful to the client will be their interaction. A 'good relationship' in this setting might be one which lays emphasis on a deeper familiarisation with the clients' networks of meaning, construing, anticipations of the world. It is hypothesised that it is this that facilitates movement and change. We would suggest that in such therapy one almost always comes to love one's clients although you and they might not at all like each other in the ordinary course of events. Coming to know another as intimately as one does in therapy, even for such a brief period of time, is a humbling experience. It is truly about the human story.

How can/is change sustained?

It is recognised that change or movement in a particular direction will not be maintained if it is found or sensed by the client to imply a degree of change in e.g. their sense of identity, in their position within their relationship context, which feels centrally important; or to be likely to lead them into an experience of the world which seems too foreign and unpredictable. From a constructivist perspective, all of these experiences are ones which we might expect in exploring alternative pathways or positions to the solutions we have previously arrived at, and which now serve to create a 'stuck' feeling. But it is very explicitly the task of the therapist to facilitate, in so far as she can, the client(s) during their exploration with alternatives. This is specifically to enable them to come to a degree of ease with, and a differing set of anticipations about, the pathways finally chosen as most consonant with a sense of movement and difference. In other words, when a client chooses not to pursue the alternatives arrived at in therapy, it may be because the therapist has not been sufficiently engaged in enabling a helpful anticipation about all the implications of change for that person. But it has also to be recognised that the client(s) may choose not to pursue difference out of a sense that they could not sustain themselves in the changes implied. However, the very act of engaging in the experimental enquiry can of itself be expected to bring about difference even if that difference is only described in words such as 'I knew before that nothing could be different and now I'm certain of it! It is not at all unusual to work with a couple, for example, and for them to decide that it is more constructive to separate although the declared aim at the outset was of staying together.

For whom will Constructivist Psychotherapy be useful?

The largest body of literature discussing the applications of constructivist ideas in therapy emanates primarily from Personal Construct Theorists (e.g. Button 1985; Fransella & Thomas 1988; Neimeyer & Neimeyer 1987; Winter 1992). Such accounts give much weight to the suggestion that Personal Construct Therapy is usefully able to 'subsume the diverse multitude of personal concerns which people in therapy will present and reasonably hope to have understood' (Bannister & Fransella, 1971, p.159).

Personal Construct Therapists, and constructivist therapists in general will, like all other therapists, often experience difficulty in being useful to the clients that consult them. But the explanation for lack of success can be more usefully be recognised perhaps, as related to e.g. the therapist's difficulty in listening etc. at that time or to that particular issue or client; to the client(s)' uncertainty about change and its implications; to the therapist's difficulty in creating a helpful relationship and ambience for this client at this time; or to a lack of support within the social context if this client changes etc. It is often the people around one who feel most perturbed when someone whom they have previously believed to be e.g. shy begins to behave differently. Often it will seem easier to go back to being the way one was, despite the drawbacks, than to tackle the 'fall-out' of change with the people closest to one.

We would also like to say here that we are of the opinion that the therapist's choice of a therapeutic perspective is a consequence of a fit with *their* personal world view. It is this that makes it possible for that therapist to be potentially useful to the client who in turn may have a very different perspective. It is for this reason perhaps that outcome research on psychotherapy is able to point to the general usefulness of therapies rather than to the efficacy of one approach over another. The degree of comfort which the therapist experiences must be at least as important in being free to be helpful to the client, as hearing well the particular language and sense-making of that client. Equally important will obviously be the clients fit with the perspective utilised by the therapist. We would argue that while there are particular ways, for all therapists, of behaving ethically, there is no end to the variation between styles of therapy and therapists that can be useful.

Evaluation and research in this method

As Winter (1992) reports, 'Numerous single case reports have now appeared which indicate positive changes on various measures during Personal Construct Psychotherapy.' These are accounts of work on a very broad range of problematic issues with individual clients, couples, families and in group settings. There is only a limited number of reports which employ adequate comparison groups but this is a shortcoming of research design that is shared by the great body of work emanating from the therapy field and in no way specific to the constructivists. Indeed because constructivists give such attention to ideas regarding the creation of knowledge, the review of the work going on in the therapy field is of constant concern to them.

Some final remarks

We are acutely aware that even a well-constructed narrative of what therapy is about, or how it is understood, stands for nothing if, in an actual series of therapy-conversations, the experience of being known and knowing another eludes us. It is that we struggle for, because, like Millar Mair, we believe that 'we create realities by and through the conversational practices we are involved within and undertake' (1989, p.272). Thus we must be 'attentive to our ways of speaking together', realising that much of that speaking can never be accurately verbalised ... and still we go on!

References:

Bannister, D., & Franseila, F., (1971) *Inquiring Man* (London: Penguin).

Button, E., (1985) *Personal Construct Therapy and Mental Health* (London: Croom Helm).

Fransella, F., & Thomas, L., (1988) *Experimenting with Personal Construct Psychology* (London: Routledge Kegan Paul).

Kelly, G., (1955) *The Psychology of Personal Constructs* Vols 1 & 11 (New York: Norton).

Kelly, G., (1969) *The Autobiography of a Theory* in Brendan Maher (ed.) *Kelly Papers* (New York: Wiley).

Kelly, G., (1969) *The Psychotherapeutic Relationship* (Maher c.f. above)

Kelly, G., (1980) *The Psychology of the Optimal Man Landfield,* in A & Leitner, L., (eds.) *PCP: Psychotherapy & Personality.* (New York: Wiley).

Kelly, G., (1969) *The Language of Hypothesis* (Maher c.f. above).

Kelly, G., (1977) *The Psychology of the Unknown* in Bannister, D., (ed.) *New Perspectives in PCT* (London: Academic Press).

Landfield, A., (1982) *A Construction of Fragmentation and Unity* in Mancuso, J., & Adams-Weber, J., (eds.) *The Construing Person* (N.Y.: Praeger).

Mair, M., (1979) *The Personal Venture* in Stringer & Bannister (eds.) *Constructs of Sociality & Individuality* (London: Academic Press).

Mair, M., (1980) *Feeling and Knowing* in Salmon P (ed.) *Coming to Know* (London: Routledge Kegan Paul).

Neimeyer, R., & Neimeyer, G., (1987) *Personal Construct Therapy Casebook* (N.Y.: Harper & Row)

Patterson, C., (1980) *Theories of Counselling & Psychotherapy* (N.Y.: Harper & Row)

Shotter, J., (1975) *Images of Man in Psychological Research* (London: Methuen)

Von Glaserfeld, E., (1988) 'The Reluctance to Change a Way of Thinking' in *Irish Journal of Psychology* (Special Issue) 9, i. pp 83 - 90)

Watzlawick, P., (1984) *The Invented Reality* (New York: Norton)

Useful Reading List For Interested Beginners

Banninster, D., & Fransella, F., (1988 3rd ed.) *Inquiring Man* (Penguin).

Dunnett, G., (1988) *Working with People: Clinical Uses of Personal Construct Psychology* (Routledge)

Efran, J., Lukens, M.D., & Lukens, R.J., (1990) *Language, Structure and Change* (New York: Norton)

Fransella, F. & Dalton, P., (1990) *Personal Construct Counselling in Action* (Sage)

Mair, Millar., (1989) *Between Psychology and Psychotherapy* (Routledge)

CHAPTER 6

Family Therapy

Edmund McHale

The term Family Therapy is both appealingly obvious and hopelessly misleading as a description of an approach to psychotherapy. The obvious appeal is that the word 'family' identifies one characteristic of this approach insofar as the family therapist does not usually focus on the individual client's experience alone, but views problems in context and frequently the significant context will include other people, often other members of the client's family. However, this is not necessarily always the case and family therapy or systems theory can also apply to therapy with individuals. In addition, the use of the term 'family therapy' in the singular implies that the approach is a unified one, whereas in fact there are many 'schools' of family therapy with their own distinct theoretical principles and their differing styles of practice. Amidst lively international debate innovations and developments have swept through the field incorporating the influence of feminism, deconstructionism and social constructionism providing an approach consistent with current post-modern thinking.

Origins and History

In the early 1950s in the United States of America, a number of psychotherapists and clinicians began to innovate by including members of their client's family in their therapy or treatment programmes. This happened spontaneously in a number of centres throughout the country indicating possibly that conditions in the field were suitable to this departure from what was accepted practice. Most practitioners described their work as research to ensure acceptance by their colleagues and employers, and they carried it out quietly and independently. Articles began to be published towards the end of the fifties and practitioners began to correspond with each other. The first meeting or conference took place in 1961 which led to the publication of a journal in 1962 called 'Family Process', which continues as one of the leading journals in the Family Therapy field today.

The explanation of the simultaneous multiple emergence of interest in the family as the unit of study and therapy lies partly in the trends which were taking place within the psychoanalytic field, and with the development of clinical/social services. Freud's enormous contribution to psychotherapy had been restrained from further growth by his uncovering of the first indications of child sexual abuse in his work with 'hysterical' women patients. The enormity of this discovery could be said to have pushed him back to an intrapsychic exploration of the past and a denial of the interpersonal implications of the present, resulting in his Oedipal theory based on a dynamic principle of an instinctual, libidinal drive. Subsequently, building on Freud's new paradigm, Adler and Jung offered more socially-based, psychodynamic theories addressing the child-parent relationship and the influence of parental conflict. With the Nazi rise to power in Germany many analysts left Europe and travelled to America where they came into closer contact with the research work of anthropologists and social psychologists. A greater social emphasis emerged in the work and writings of a number of these analysts giving rise to a new movement within the field. The work of Harry Stack Sullivan, Erich Fromm and Karen Horney in particular led to greater emphasis on the relationship between a patient's behaviour and his or her experiences and interactions within the family. Coinciding with these developments the social work and marriage counselling movements were firmly taking root providing a clearer focus on the significance of family relationships.

In the 1 950's in Britain the early object-relations therapists, Henry Dicks and WRD Fairbairn of the Tavistock Clinic identified significant couples relationship dynamics which they initially regarded as collusive neuroses or *Folie a deux.* They in turn had been influenced by the relationship based theory of Melanie Klein and presumably by the work of earlier psychoanalysts such as Clarence Obendorf in New York, who published a paper on the psychoanalysis of married couples in 1938, entitled 'Folie a Deux', and Bella Mittleman who elaborated the concept and published a further account of concurrent marital therapy in 1948.

However, the qualitative shift which occured in the psychotherapy field in the US was not sustained with similar momentum in Britain. The brilliant and incisive writings of R. D. Laing were theoretically significant but his innovations in practice were limited to the establishment of group therapy communities without the inclusion of family members in the treatment. Laing's anti-psychiatry and essentially anti-family view makes sense when we consider the nature of his social and professional context, which was markedly different from that experienced by his contemporaries in the U.S. Europe was recovering from the Second World War and going through a period of consolidation. Laing was probably faced with a professional establishment and wider society invested in reconstituting and consolidating itself, creating the foundations necessary for continued development and research. He in turn presented his ideas in a fiercely challenging and critical way and I assume this style was influenced by his experience of a lack of receptivity to his new ideas. By comparison most of the innovators in the US were grant funded to develop innovative forms of treatment and they did so quietly initially, without offering much criticism of the accepted beliefs and practices of the time. Laing's perspective of the schizophenic person victimised by their families might be viewed as reflecting his own professional experience.

Milton Erickson and Gregory Bateson stand out as two significant influences in the birth and growth of family therapy. The lifetime of each may be viewed as a crucible of thought and practice providing the foundations which inspired so many others.

Their complementary styles have left a rich and significant legacy which continues to inform developments within the family therapy field. They were both people whose thinking and practice transcended the contextual limitations of their time. Erickson, a psychiatrist, was a gifted practitioner who developed a range of direct and indirect hypnotic techniques and worked with individuals, couples and families in what was and continues to be a very innovative, effective and extraordinarily efficient style of therapy. Bateson, by contrast, was a thinker and theorist, an anthropologist and philosopher who was initially influenced by his father's contribution to the field of genetics, and later by developments in mathematics, by the new science of cybernetics, by his own field work in social anthropology, and by the emerging scientific and philosophical concepts related to energy, knowledge and cognition. His field of interest could not be contained by any of these disciplines and he sought to provide a scientific explanation for that pattern in which all things are immanent, referred to as Mind in the title of his first collection of essays (Bateson, 1972).

The founding decade from 1952 on was characterised by the innovations of a number of other individuals who developed their own style of practice and their unique theoretical contributions. They included John Bell, Nathan Ackerman, Lyman Wynne, Theodore Lidz, Murray Bowen, Carl Whitaker, James Framo, Virginia Satir and Ivan Boszormenyi-Nagy.

In 1952, Bateson, who had previously moved from England to assist American intelligence in the Second World war, succeeded in getting a grant to pursue his studies in the general area of communication. He was interested in the nature of paradox and in the related distinction of logical types proposed by Whitehead and Russell. Consonant with his interest in the evolution and harmony of nature and mind he studied the communication and play of animals such as otters, chimpanzees and later dolphins, always with the widest possible breadth of vision identifying the patterns which connect. With the grant funding he engaged two people from disparate backgrounds and both having a common interest in the broad field of communication. They were Jay Haley and John Weakland. Bateson had made the acquaintance of Milton Erickson in the 1930's having consulted him to study films he had made of ritual tribal ceremonies in the South Pacific where dances appeared to have been performed in a hypnotic trance. Haley attended a workshop of Erickson's and developed a keen interest in his therapy which was radically different from any form of psychotherapy identified at that time. He met with Erickson on many subsequent occasions to interview him regarding his work and the underlying principles. Bateson and Weakland accompanied him participating in many of the conversations. Haley later published these conversations (Haley, J 1985) and an intriguing anecdotal account of Erickson's work (Haley, J 1973). Erickson's influence in family therapy and beyond has steadily grown since this time, and his influence within the field as a brilliant practitioner has complemented Bateson's intellectual breadth of vision. Their style also differed and complemented one another, Bateson being cautious of any form of influence and rejecting totally the use of force and the concept of power, while Erickson engaged with people and exercised considerable influence and power with his patients and those who met with him to learn from him. This difference was in fact, expressed in more extreme form between Haley and Bateson and their diverging views of power have continued in twin strands through the development of family therapy to the present time.

The initial project of Bateson, Haley and Weakland concluded in 1954 and the group applied for and successfully obtained another grant, on this occasion limiting their field of study to schizophrenia. This disorder was receiving a lot of attention in the health field and in fact many of the other pioneers of family therapy also pursued research in this subject. Don Jackson, a psychiatrist, and the only member with a clinical background was engaged as a clinical consultant to the team. This project produced the double bind theory explaining the apparently illogical behaviour and communication of schizophrenia as an understandable response in a conflictual or impossible context.

Their report published in 1956 was significant as the first theoretical explanation of 'pathological' behaviour in terms of the individual's social context or network of intimate relationships, in which all participating members are stuck. The report has one significant shortcoming however, insofar as it tended to describe the schizophrenic condition as caused by another person, inevitably the patient's mother, despite Bateson's attempt to transcend simple cause and effect explanations. He later attempted to redress this anomaly but the inequality of power or influence between parent and child presents a dynamic which does not lend itself to a systemic explanation which views all participants as contributing equally. This anomaly within system's theory, which is essentially a scientific explanation from an observer's perspective, was to surface later with feminist criticisms of the tendency of systemic practitioners to dilute individual differences relating to power and responsibility.

Jackson, Haley and Weakland later established a Brief Therapy Centre to continue their work which they called the Mental Research Institute (M.R.I.) and they were joined by Paul Watzlawick, a psychologist from Vienna and Richard Fish. Virginia Satir also joined this group for a period. Haley then moved to Philadelphia in 1967 and joined Salvador Minuchin, an

Argentinian psychiatrist who worked in the deprived ghetto areas of New York. Haley and Minuchin both took an interest in the distribution of power within families. Minuchin later became director of the Philadelphia Child Guidance Clinic where he established a training programme in his style of family therapy known as structural family therapy.

The period encompassing the 60s and 70s was characterised by the development of two somewhat distinct models of family therapy. One was influenced by social psychiatry and object-relations and placed emphases upon trans-generational themes. The individual was seen to be part of a family emotional system or a network of interlocking relationships. Individual development or maturing was described as 'individuation' or becoming better defined as an individual within one's evolving context. This process was facilitated in therapy by enabling clients to acknowledge or become aware of the themes which influenced them and their families, and to become less emotionally reactive to these influences, thus exercising greater degrees of choice in their lives.

Not only was the family conceptualised as a system with a life of its own which organised itself in its own characteristic fashion but this system was part of a larger one which transcended generations. Some factors influencing the life of this system may be fairly readily recognised such as tragic losses including fatal illness, suicide, or early death. Wider socio-political events like war, famine or economic depression may also be apparent but other factors may be less obvious and may not have been acknowledged or discussed, including feelings of shame, or fear related to how families or family members become identified in their community. Debts of loyalty or a mission to lead, save or sacrifice, may also evolve in the next generation or subsequent ones following a significant event or life experience.

The forces which develop within families are frequently complex and may be extremely difficult to identify or unravel by family members in pain or distress. Ivan Boszormenyi-Nagy and Geraldine Spark comment in the preface to their book (1973), 'The real forces of bondage or freedom are beyond observable power games or manipulative tactics. Invisible loyalty commitments to one's family follow paradoxical laws: The martyr who doesn't let other family members 'work off' their guilt is a far more powerfully controlling force than the loud, demanding 'bully'. The manifestly rebellious or delinquent child may actually be the most loyal member of the family'.

Murray Bowen, James Framo and Carl Whittaker have contributed significantly to this style of family therapy. Virginia Satir who was primarily influenced by the humanistic movement incorporated and developed psychodrama techniques in her work and explored influences across generations in a powerful experiential manner.

The other stream evolving in the 60s and 70s developed very much in reaction to the prevalent psychiatric and clinical practices of the time and to psychoanalytic theory. These included M.R.I.'s *Brief Therapy*, Jay Haley's *Strategic Therapy* and Salvador Minuchin's *Structural Therapy*. Each incorporated the concept of power in their understanding of human problems and they aspired to provide models of therapy free from what they viewed as the mystification and elaborate indoctrination training process of the then prevalent style of psychotherapy. They sought to develop models of therapy which would be easily understood, easily learned and easily evaluated. Their style of intervention was weighted more towards the pragmatic effective use of skills, in which the therapist took responsibility as expert, strongly determining the course and outcome of therapy, either through direct or indirect means.

Second Order Cybernetics

In 1982 a number of younger family therapists published articles in the journal Family Process, critiquing the pragmatic approach and proposing the application of Batesons's principles with which Haley had taken issue. This debate heralded a new stage in the development of the field now identified as that of second order cybernetics. Cybernetics refers to the understanding of biological, mechanical and human systems in terms of communication theory, adaption, self-regulation and self-reproduction. Bateson had emphasised the importance of this theory in understanding complex human relationships. It provided an understanding of how families and other intimate groups functioned, having as it were a life of their own. The first order stage encompassed this view of the client/family. The therapist stood apart and viewed the system from without, then determined how s/he might correct the problem and intervened accordingly. Second order cybernetics in contrast placed emphasis upon the subjective nature not only of the client family's experience but of the therapist's also, and widened the concept of system to encompass the therapist. In this client-therapist system not only is the family seen to be influenced by the exchanges and interactions but the therapist is also.

This of course had never been denied by the more strategic theorists, but the second stage was characterised by a distinct change in emphasis and a swing from Haley's instrumental end of the spectrum to Bateson's more ecological co-evolutionary model.

Milan Team Approach

During the early 1970s a group of psychoanalysts with an interest in a family approach were convened by Mara Selvini Palazzoli in Milan. Their original intention was to attempt to integrate a family approach within psychoanalytic practice. When this proved impossible, they divided with a smaller group of four members combining to develop a family therapy approach. They initially engaged the services of Paul Watzlawick from M.R.I. as their consultant. M.R.I. used one-way mirrors and video-relay to observe therapy sessions for training and consultation, always with the permission of clients of course. The Milan group incorporated the observation as an additional dimension of the therapy, with two observers viewing and commenting upon the noteworthy aspects of the client / therapist system. Their method included discussion between all four members of the team before, during and after the session. A characteristic feature of this approach is the emphasis placed on hypothesising. The team share all their observations and consider all possible explanation of the family's dilemma. These hypothetical explanations provide the basis for further exploration leading to the rejection or modification of the hypothesis. The questioning involves everyone considered to be significant in contributing to beliefs about the problem. This may include, for instance, other professionals involved with the family, school staff and relatives or friends of the family. When the hypothesis is sufficiently fitting for all involved the exploratory process will lead to new understanding, and to significant shifts in the way they relate and manage what had been their problem.

In 1980 the incompatibility of views regarding the concept of power between Bateson and Haley again made itself felt as views within the team diverged, resulting in their parting, with the two men establishing a training institute and the two women setting up a separate research centre. A rich stream of theory and clinical practice continues to flow from both groups.

In recent years the pendulum has swung again in dialectic fashion, with emphasis in the field returning to the instrumental side, with the identification of problems to which a pure systemic approach is inadequate. Because a systems view enables a therapist to view problems without attributing blame to any one individual it can be very helpful to families or couples in helping them to disengage from the recursive cycle of blame, or attack and counter-attack. When a couple in conflict attend therapy and the woman is hurt and critical of the man's coldness and the man is hurt and withdrawn because of his perception of the woman's criticism, a neutral third party can introduce the view of each of them coping in their characteristically different ways: the woman by pursuing and the man by withdrawing and the more one pursues the more the other withdraws, the more he withdraws the more she pursues and so on. The therapist's acknowledgement of different 'styles', can result in each feeling less defensive and less angry, contributing to a reduction in anxiety and conflict. If however there is a significant imbalance of power between two people, as can occur between a husband and wife or even more evidently between a parent and child then a neutral stance may be inadequate and inappropriate. In the case of child abuse for instance the child does not contribute to the problem in a comparable way to the adult, and there may be a need for the therapist to ensure that the child is adequately protected from future abuse. In this case the therapist is required to evaluate or make a judgement and to intervene on behalf of one member in a very instrumental manner. Feminist family therapists have been calling for greater awareness of gender political issues and a more informed stance by therapists in redressing imbalances of power.

Philosophy of the Person and Theoretical Influences

The two principle theories which underpin family therapy are constructivism and systems theory. Their combined influence has resulted in the development of an understanding of the person as:

1. one who by nature experiences the world meaningfully, or imposes meaning on his or her experiences, and is disposed to exploring or searching for better ways of understanding and finding correspondingly better ways of engaging with life;
2. one whose search is enacted in the context of others engaged in essentially the same pursuit. Meaning is largely conveyed through language, and language is socially constructed. The focus of family therapy is therefore very much on the person in transition, influenced by and influencing the transition of those around her or him;
3 . one who is constantly becoming) influenced by her or his changing context and influencing that context. This life cycle perspective of the family and wider systems and not just of the individual provides the essential backdrop to the therapy process.

1. Reality is brought forth by the individual

Constructivism implies that we can never know reality other than through the biological 'instrumentation' of our senses, and in terms of the personal construct system which we develop and modify constantly through our lifetime. Hence each person's reality is unique. This is not to say that we simply invent our own reality or that 'anything goes'. The understanding most conson-ant with the way in which I make sense of my experience is that there is an external reality which constrains us in certain ways. We learn to avoid injury and hurt by respecting such constraints as the inability of fast moving vehicles to stop instantly, or the inability of other drivers to predict our movements. It usually takes us a little longer to recognise the inability of our partners to read our minds if we have been initially impressed by their apparent skill in doing so. We constantly fine-tune our experience and our understanding. Beliefs are modified as they are tested in action. and the modified understanding informs our subsequent action and the cycle continues through our lives. This continuous active process of construing is a more useful concept than the static state implied by the term 'personality'. The essential difference in our subjective experiences or our realities has also been emphasised by Bateson in suggesting that the word 'multiverse' is a more appropriate descriptive term than 'universe'.

The complexity of our subjective and consensual realities has been explored and elucidated by two Chilean biologists, Humberto Maturana and Francesco Varela (Maturana & Varela,

1987) in terms of structural determinism. They describe with well defined and precisely integrated terms the continuity between observer and observed and the consequential impossibility of attaining total objectivity. The insight that cognition is not a representation of the world 'out there', but rather a bringing forth of a world through the process of living itself, leads to the further exploration of the nature of living. They say that all doing is knowing and all knowing doing. Every reflection takes place in language which is a distinctive form of human action.

The fact that we impose meaning on our experience is easily demonstrated by optical illusions and the study of perception. A one-to-one correspondence does not exist between what is out there, and what we receive in our sense organs. We fill in the gaps, or read between the lines as it were, as for instance the rapid series of still pictures on the screen become moving animated people.

Likewise the many optical illusions such as the Mueller-Lyer figures and the Ponzo illusion, below, demonstrate that our way of imposing meaning on the world can sometimes lead us into error. In this instance segments of lives appear longer and shorter than they are, straight lines appear curved, and our judgement of size is distorted. We do not perceive a one-to-one representation of the external object but we bring to bear our dynamic way of 'seeing' objects and images influenced by our physiological structure and our learnt way of making sense of reality from previous experiences. This is also illustrated by the fact that our name may 'stand out' in a page or in other people's conversation.

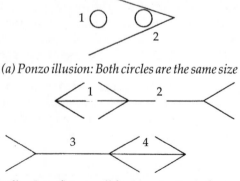

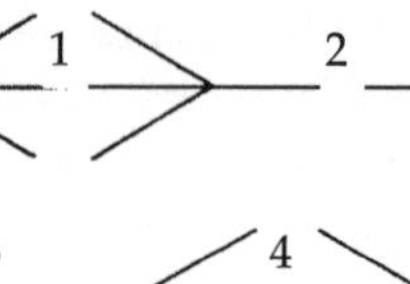

(a) Ponzo illusion: Both circles are the same size

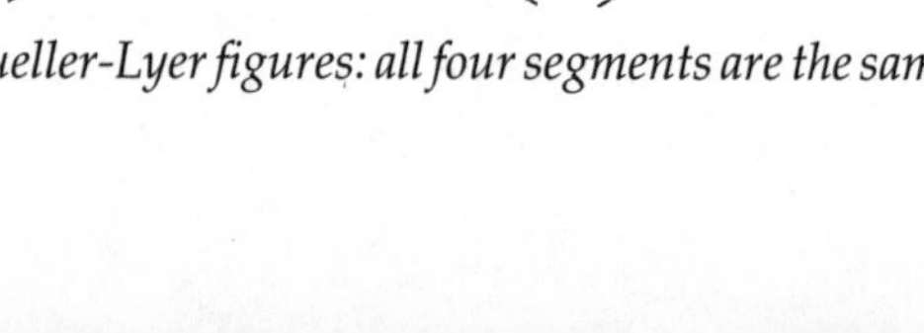

(b) Mueller-Lyer figures: all four segments are the same size

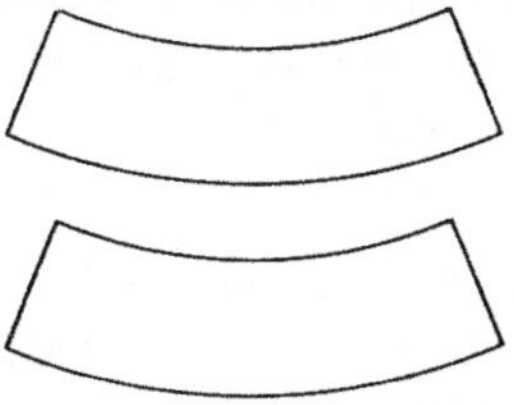

(c) Jastrow illusion: both crescents are the same size

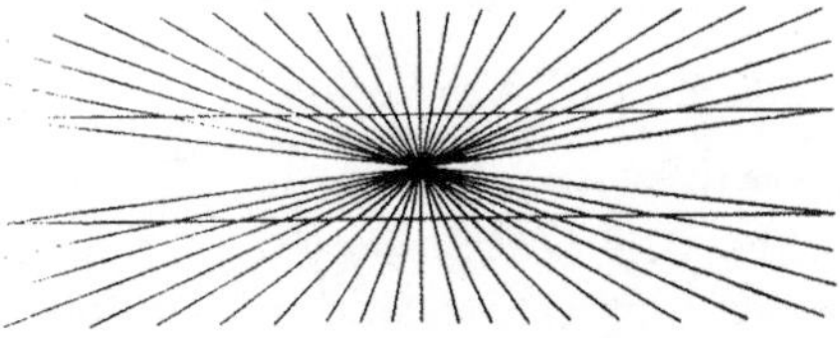

(d) Hering illusion: horizontal lines are parallel

Another visuo-perceptual phenomenon which illustrates the subjectivity of our knowledge is the figure / ground images, the most common being a picture which represents an old woman and a young woman simultaneously or another which can represent two facial profiles facing one another and which can also be seen as a vase. The striking aspect of these pictures is that we cannot perceive both figures simultaneously. We can only perceive one as figure in which case the other becomes background. We cannot see what is there, we can only perceive one part at a time.

We do not passively register information like a tape recorder or camera. We screen what comes to our awareness, and we order and interpret the sounds and symbols. Neither is remembering like replaying a tape or film but it is more a process of re-producing or recreating an experience in terms of how that experience makes sense to us at the time of recall. Though we constantly strive to improve our understanding of reality and hence to engage better with 'reality', including ourselves and others, we can never achieve a direct or complete knowledge or understanding. As George Kelly, the founder of Personal Construct Theory* has stated we are constantly engaged in a process of formulating explanations or hypotheses, testing them in action, and modifying

* *See chapter 5, 'Constructivist Psychotheraphy' by Bernadette O'Sullivan and Dorothy Gunne.*

them. We do this at the micro-level of sensory perception and at the macro level of searching for meaning in our behaviour and the behaviour of others, and in creating purpose and meaning in our lives.

This dynamic imposition of meaning and our tendency to seek to understand better and to engage more effectively with ourselves, others and the world at large is a human characteristic which invites further explanation and calls into question the limits of a purely biological explanation of the person.

2. Each system calls forth a Shared Reality

However successful we may be in acquiring a shared understanding of the world of objects, it is many times more difficult to get a good enough common understanding with others of the more abstract aspects of our lives such as love, commitment, responsibility, intimacy and individuality.

Systems theory concerns itself with the study of mechanical, biological and living systems, and has direct relevance to engineering, computer design, artificial intelligence, biology, social anthropology and the understanding of human experience. In its most easily recognised application, systems principles can be seen to operate in ecological systems. Water is redistributed and recycled through a process of condensation and cloud formation by the heat of the sun, carried by wind and conveyed back to earth at other locations by reduction in temperature. This process contributes to the replenishment of springs', and reservoirs, to irrigation and the maintenance of life for plants, animals and humans. Vast quantities of water are contained in the oceans and the ice caps, and relatively minor fluctuations in the ecological balance of the planet can result in very significant consequences. A reduction in the ozone layer can result in an increase in temperature of the atmosphere which in turn could cause an increase in water level in the seas and oceans of the world causing widespread flooding and coastal erosion. James Lovelock was so impressed by the fine balances maintained by the many interrelated natural elements that he came to regard the world as a living organism, and coined a new term, Gaia to denote this concept, in essence a stable system.

The central heating system in a home may be understood as a simple system. On a winter's day, if the thermostat is set at 70 and the system switched on, the boiler will operate until the temperature within the house in the vicinity of the thermostat rises to 70 or a degree or two above. At this temperature a switch will be triggered which will switch off the boiler. The temperature will gradually reduce within a predetermined range of perhaps three or four degrees. As it drops to the lower end of this range the switch will again be activated and the boiler switched on. This feedback process between thermostat and boiler can continue indefinitely, maintaining the temperature in the house constant within a few degrees of the set temperature.

If someone who did not understand the interrelationship of these factors, sought to reduce the temperature of the house by opening the doors and windows rather than altering the thermostat setting, the boiler would continue operating or it would work harder as it were, to compensate for the heat loss. This process is referred to as the system maintaining 'homeostasis'.

This example illustrates what sometimes happens in human systems. Within a family, enormous effort is sometimes expended by one or more members to compensate for the failure of another to adjust to changing circumstances. So an overprotective mother may work harder at protecting a son she perceives as vulnerable and deny him the opporunities he needs to learn to take care of himself. His increasing vulnerability then elicits a greater level of protection, further inhibiting the development of independence. Likewise an insecure father may feel threatened by the strength of his teenage daughter's expression of opinion and he may attempt to restrict her resulting in her even more forceful expression of opinion as she seeks to establish her autonomy, and the cycle continues.

The early work of Don Jackson in M.R.I. focussed on these ways of understanding problems. Like mechanical systems, human systems also seek to maintain a balance within a certain range. Unlike mechanical systems, the homeostatic function in a family and other human systems is not a simple static process. Human systems are influenced by changing circumstances without, and by developmental change of its members within. A family is faced with the task of maintaining appropriate relationships to meet all the needs of its members and to support their individual functioning. The nature of this balance has to change to accommodate the changing needs of children for instance, as they move from the dependency of infancy to childhood, or from childhood to the accelerated identity development of adolescence. So two systemic forces can explain human systems: homeostasis which refers to the maintenance of balance and stability and morphogenesis which is the force to change. All organisations have to maintain this balance between forces of stability and change.

Other early contributions from systems theory include the concepts of symmetry and complementarity. Relationship patterns based on difference are said to be complementary, whereas those patterns identified in terms of similarity are symmetrical. Couple relationships may be seen to include symmetrical and complementary dimensions. While people usually have similar interests and socio-cultural values, they are often quite different in personality or personal styles. So a very outgoing gregarious person may be found in a relationship with a more reflective quieter person, or a creative expressive person with a more methodical rational one. Sometimes these styles may become engaged in a runaway or escalating cycle.

At a socio-political level the pre-Glasnost arms race between the so called superpower nations illustrates a symmetrical escalation with movement on the part of one superpower to acquire strategic advantage eliciting a similar and greater reaction from the other. A common scenario in couple relationships is that of one partner, often the woman in heterosexual relationships, initiating the closeness and intimacy. The man may put greater emphasis on autonomy and separateness in the relationship. Every relationship has to maintain a balance, incorporating both autonomy and intimacy. The relationship may develop a complementary escalation with the woman pursuing closeness more vigorously and the man withdrawing and seeking greater separateness. The increased tendency of one partner results in the greater effort of the other partner to behave in the opposite way. At some point the woman may give up this pursuit and decide that she will attend to her own life and expect less of her partner. If he does not respond to these changed events, but continues to distance while she does likewise then the relationship pattern may be described as in escalating symmetry. Likewise if he were to become critical and blaming, and she responded with retaliatory criticism and blame, they would be engaged in another form of escalating symmetry.

Systems theory provided a lens with which to view human experience as an alternative to those psychological approaches which sought explanations in terms of internal drives and social theory, explaining behaviour in terms of the goals and functions of social groups. It usefully lends itself to an understanding of how people get stuck in relationship problems or in attempting to resolve personal dilemmas without attributing a primary causal effect or blame to any one individual. When we experience a problem and have difficulty resolving it we often feel inadequate and tend to blame ourselves or someone else. A systems view can provide therapist and clients with an explanation which enables them to engage in a process of exploration and change, disengaging from the attribution of blame to self or others.

The systemic perspective also calls into question the boundary of self, if that boundary is assumed to coincide with our outer layer of skin. Systems exist as supraordinate systems and subsystems of other systems. So the autonomic nervous system or cardiovascular system are physiological subsystems of the individual and the individual may be a subsystem of the family system. Explanations may be sought at many different levels.

In the previous example the tendency of women to take greater responsibility for the quality of closeness or intimacy in a relationship and the subsequent tendency of women to pursue and men to distance, reflects the wider social distribution of power. As women become more financially autonomous and more involved in the male dominated professions and business world, a growing tendency may be observed of women refusing to carry more than their fair share of responsibility for maintaining intimacy and expecting a more equal agreement in terms of having different values and lifestyles respected. This is I believe, contributing to more rounded roles for men also, with less stark contrast between the gender types.

A further dimension of family therapy is that the principles which apply to any system also apply to the client/therapist system. Gregory Bateson has referred to two basic epistemological errors, one active and one passive. The active one is attempting to bring about change by force. This error may operate between nations, in organisations or in a couple relationship. Essentially we cannot force another to change, and attempting to do so is often counter-productive. The passive error to which he referred was not accepting that what is, is. We often reject information which does not suit us and we can build further distortions and defenses to avoid accepting the obvious. Therapists too, can fall into the error of attempting to force change in clients and may sometimes not attend sufficiently to what is, in this case the clients reality.

In the therapy process, the therapist's usefulness is greatly influenced by her ability to understand the complexity of the client system's reality. Her greatest contribution in fact, may be her ability to engage with the client in seeking clarification and exploring understanding. In this process the therapist is influenced by the clients and their process, as the clients are influenced by the therapist's enquiries and changing views.

Gianfranco Cecchin, one of the original Milan team in a fascinating brief review (1992) of their history, refers to three stages of development. The first represented a transition from energy to communication. The early family therapy movement understood human dilemmas in terms of the relationships between people and networks of relationships rather than in terms of drives or psychic energy within the individual. The simplest manner to study relationships was in terms of communication. People living in close relationships live in constant communication. Words, inflexions, behaviour, all become forms of communication, as does silence and absence. Cybernetics, which developed from the study of artificiai intelligence provided a model for understanding the nature of relationships within and between mechanical, biological and social systems. However the language and early examples tended to be mechanistic and lent themselves to narrow focussed explanations and fairly mechanical interventions, leading to some discomfort with the prevalent style of therapy.

The Milan team then entered a second phase moving from entities to social constructions. In keeping with Bateson's view of power, which he described as a concept, an arbitrary way of making sense of people's behaviour they reviewed earlier way of explaining family tensions in terms of power struggles and games. Instead, they viewed tensions in relationships as people's attempts to make sense of their relationships with one another. In this shift they moved closer to the transgenerational family therapists who sought explanations in the wider networks of relationship and in the struggle to find and express meaning in those relationships.

This in turn enabled them to review the nature of their hypothesising, which for many was the most impressive aspect of their work and also the aspect which seemed least amenable to explanation or clarification. Cecchin explains the hypothesis as a manner of contributing to the formation of a therapeutic relationship, of engaging with the clients in a way which resonates for all participants. This resonance becomes the medium for evolving a new system of beliefs and understanding. The value of the hypothesis is not in its 'objective truth' but in its relevance to the understanding and disposition of the people involved.

The therapist does not have access to any touchstone of truth or any more objective standard of values. The therapy process is a co-construction and hopefully one that provides the opportunity for unintended consequences to materialise. However, the therapist as a co-contributor brings her values, opinions, knowlecige and disposition to the therapy context. She cannot take a stand and Cecchin advocates that she maintains an appropriate balance by keeping a healthy state of mild irreverence towards her own truths no matter how much hardship it took to conquer them. Therefore, a therapist with a social construction perspective takes responsibility for his or her convictions and declares them as personal and not universal truths, and may develop hypotheses at any one moment from any theory, system of explanation or body of information, but never subscribe to it as the only body of truth. In Cecchin's words, 'it is exactly this reflexive loop between our taking a stand and immediately thereafter putting this stand in a larger context that creates the 'becoming' and not the 'being' of a therapist.'

The social constructionist perspective brings our cultural embeddedness into relief and highlights the role of language in influencing the decisions which we make in day-to-day living which in turn have a major influence in channeling our experience and in organising our behaviour. (Tomm, 1992). In this sense thinking is understood as internalised language, of talking to oneself. While this is thought of as an individual personal experience, it is enbedded within the social interaction of the family and cultural systems within which we live. Language evolves within and is sustained by these coordinated social interactions. Language is not our only way of interacting, but it is much richer and more involved than any other because of its recursive nature and in Maturana's terms 'it's expansion is multiplicative' (Maturana, 1988). So, even though we may consider our thoughts and distinctions to be personal and private, they are rooted in and are given further expression and elaboration in the social context, or the social process.

Human Problems

Family therapists do not use classifications of pathology. Human problems are understood, not as a deficit or pathology of the individual, but as a consequence of an inappropriate attempt by the individual, couple, family or wider system, to make sense of their situation or dilemma. Problems may also be understood as an inappropriate way of attempting to negotiate change or transitions whether that change occurs within the system or from without. The changes occurring within any system will include developmental or life cycle changes and the changes without may include natural disaster, adverse economic developments or political upheaval.

Again, ecological solutions provide an appropriate analogy. Problems are maintained and unnecessary hardships are incurred by either over-reacting or under-reacting to these events. So we may ignore changes taking place which require our acceptance and accommodation and this may lead to problems for the individual or system. This was exemplified by a family whose twelve year old daughter, the youngest of three, became 'difficult' and school phobic four years after the sudden death of her father. The well intentioned failure of the mother to express her grief with the children had resulted in the family as a group not acknowledging sufficiently the loss of the dead parent. The need to do so became more pressing with the passage of time as mother remarried and the family attempted to integrate her new husband and subsequently their child. The transitions to a new family composition could not be adequately completed without first grieving the loss of the dead father and husband, and the youngest child's 'problematic' behaviour was the call to do so, expressed on behalf of the entire family.

Problems may also be overestimated, and people may over-react amplifying their concern and distress as they attempt to control using unnecessary force. Forced solutions such as the use of DDT as a pesticide produce other problems often greater than the original.

Clients and client systems are recognised as having adequate powers of self-direction and self-healing, and therapy seeks to provide the context in which these capacities may be utilised and in which complexity may be appreciated and conflict resolved. Another way in which problems are maintained is in the repeated application of inappropriate solutions. A fairly common tendency is to repeat solutions which worked in the past and if they do not work again we may fall into the active and passive errors of attempting to force the solution by doing more of the same. So the manner of directing and guiding a child of six may be quite inappropriate with a twelve year old, and likewise a deep rooted bond of loyalty or debt to a member of a previous generation may find expression in ways which can give rise to concern and conflict if not adequately understood.

Proof of Change

The therapist's or client's satisfaction with progress, may be an adequate measure of beneficial change. In fact it is ultimately the only measure, as we can never get beyond our own personal and subjective interpretation of reality although we may use scales of quantification or measurement as an attempt to acquire greater standardisation or consensus. Attempts to apply the principles of the physical sciences to our understanding of human nature have had limited success and the limitations of this approach have been most dramatically exposed by the understanding of corres-ponding limitations in quantum physics and with the formulation of Einstein's theory of relativity. Ultimately, we cannot stand outside our personal subjective view. However measures and scales of behaviour change may be useful to clients and therapist if the agreed problem is presented in behavioural or symptomatic terms. Such measures are less useful if the client is confused about the nature of the problem, if there are many interrelated aspects to their difficulties, or if they are interested in personality development, or identity issues which do not lend themselves to quantification without reducing or trivialising the issues.

Another difficulty is that the problem as described by clients may differ with regard to what constitutes progress. This is frequentiy seen to be the case with relationship difficulties. Interpersonal conflict may be resolved but an outcome which leads to marital separation, or a young adult child leaving home, may not be welcomed by all concerned at that time. Approaches which focus on behaviour or symptoms lend themselves to easy evaluation of success whereas those which focus on the family's belief systems, or influences transmitted from previous generations may facilitate changes which are more fundamental and which in turn enable the clients to understand and manage their 'problems' in different ways. In these circumstances clients may not identify their experience in therapy as a contributing factor.

Consequently progress may be difficult for a therapist to quantify and the client's evaluation may not appropriately reflect the significance of the therapy process. This remains one of the aspects of therapy which family therapists continuously strive to address. The therapist who completely ignores the pragmatic effects of therapy and who is disinterested in any measure of usefulness or benefit, is at risk of getting lost in the client's dilemmas and upholding social belief systems which do not benefit client's longer term interests. A therapist who attempts to quantify all aspects of therapy is in danger of oversimplifying the process and reducing it to the level of trivial advice and formulistic problem solving. Somewhere in between lies the development of a useful service which acknowledges the complexity and the potential of human existence.

Application

The many schools of family therapy share the common theoretical foundation of constructivist and systems theory. The therapy process occurs in a context of cooperative exploration, in which the therapist facilitates the client's process of clarification and change, and the 'client' may be a couple or members of a family. The areas of exploration may vary in emphasis between *beliefs, behaviour* and *structure.* Exploration of beliefs may cover myths, rules and the many distinctions of understanding between individuals; behaviour can include communication and interaction patterns in addition to individual behaviour patterns; structure refers to the distribution of power in an organisation. People in any organisation including a family, will introduce a certain amount of order and predictability to their interactions and this order may be conceptualised as hierarchy or structure. These three levels are of course all interrelated and they will reciprocally influence one another as the individuals and their relationships change.

The process of therapy begins with the first contact with the therapist or agency, and this is usually a phone call requesting an appointment. The family therapist may then consider who s/he would like to invite to attend and would then negotiate this with the contact person. Family therapists sometimes work conjointly or in pairs and even as a team, with three or more working together. This practice was developed by the innovative Milan team, as an integral part of their approach. Two therapists interviewed the family and the other two observed from an adjoining room by means of video relay and one-way mirror, with the prior knowledge and permission of the family. The team meets prior to the session and discusses the information presented over the phone. They meet again during the session when the therapists who are with the family will withdraw temporarily either at their own initiative or in response to a request from their observing colleagues, and finally they meet after the session.

First sessions may vary considerably in respect of the number of people invited to attend and the focus of exploration, which may be narrowly restricted to what actually happens and how the problem is managed or it may focus more widely on the views and opinions of many people and their ways of understanding the problem, relationships and other events which might be relevant. Sometimes suggestions and opinions are requested and offered, and at other times the process of questioning-as-explor-ation provides the clients with sufficient food for thought. Couples and families in crisis or conflict often benefit by clarifying some structure or understanding within which they may continue their process of exploration and change in therapy. However, a first session will generally unfold in the following way. After initially facilitating the clients to feel at ease, the therapist may enquire about the problem of each person present. This in itself can be a very beneficial exercise as it makes explicit the therapist's assumption that they are not dealing with an objective quantifiable reality but with a number of people's interpretations of separate and diverse realities. If the problem is concisely stated the therapist will seek to clarify that her understanding is correct and agreed by the clients. If not, then the therapist and clients may be immediately engaged in the process of therapeutic exploration, seeking to disentangle the web of their shared reality, introducing distinctions and alternative views and facilitating understanding, acceptance, resolution of conflict, (possibly first expression of conflict) and increase in trust and respect.

If therapist and clients have a clear understanding of the nature of the problem, the therapist may then begin to clarify the goals of therapy, to ensure that there is a common understanding of what changes are desired and considered appropriate. Finally, agreement may be sought on the therapy 'contract' the timing of the next and subsequent appointments, the cost, if not clarified previously, and who will attend.

One consultation can produce significant change and may be sufficient. A short number of sessions such as five or six is frequently sufficient in facilitating key changes which enable individual clients, couples and families to get unstuck, to negotiate life cycle transitions and to proceed with managing their lives and relationships with a renewed sense of confidence. Sometimes longer term therapy may be appropriate.

Case Example

'Just Metaphors'
Marginal Illuminations in a Colonial Retreat.

This case history is a synopsised account of an article written by Philip A Kearney, Nollaig O'Reilly-Byrne and Imelda Colgan McCarthy and published in Family Therapy Case Studies *1989, 4 (1), 17-31, an Australian publication. The three authors work together as a team in Dublin, under the descriptive title 'Fifth Province Associates'. The title derives from the metaphorical fifth province, the 'place' where the inhabitants of ancient Ireland's four provinces might transcend their differences and conflicts.*

Reflecting on the nature of their relationship with many so-called multi-problem families and the tendency of 'helping' agencies to invade, label and disempower already disadvantaged families under the benevolent banner of care and treatment, the authors propose the analogy of colonisation. The families maintain an uncomfortable and appreciative attitude with felt dependancy and expected gratitude oscillating with 'uncontrolled' revolt and rejection, thus maintaining their autonomy and congruence. The language of the social and health care services is replete with descriptions of families as helpless and dependant in stark contrast with the view of the family defined in article 41 of our constitution: 'The State recognises the Family as the natural primary and fundamental unit group of Society, and as a moral institution possessing inalienable and imprescriptible rights, antecedent and superior to all positive law' (*Government Publications* 1937). Seduced by diagnostic metaphors, professionals may consolidate distinctions of social hierarchy and impose policies of social control. 'For if another can control me, that other has usurped me, and how terrible I seem diminished by this seeming addition' (Stephens, J, 1978).

The following case description illustrates an alternative approach to work with a socially disadvantaged family, in which the professional team respect the self-healing and self-directing capacity of the family. They invite the family to join with them in an exploration which will elicit an understanding of their relationships and their current dilemma, enabling them to transcend their present sense of futility and to again exercise meaningful choice in their lives.

The Bard family live in a public housing area in Dublin. The community live in very impoverished circumstances, alienated from the wider society, and yet their existence is characterised by passion, individuality and great cohesiveness.

The parents of the family, Jerry and Eileen are members of old established families within the community. They have been living apart for seven years. Jerry, the eldest of his family of origin, became leader of the extended family following the death of his father eleven years previously. Jerry has spent considerable time in prison and has achieved considerable status in the community for having done so, and even more for the occasions in which he evaded doing so. He and Eileen, both in their late thirties, have six children ranging in age from ten years to twenty-one. Kevin, aged twelve, the second youngest is brain damaged from a fall from a third story window eight years previously, while he was in the care of his older sister and brothers. The three oldest children Annie, Ernie and Tommie abuse pills, solvents and alcohol in whatever combination and quantity they can obtain them. Paddy, aged ten has been out of school for a year, and Peggy, aged fourteen no longer attends school. The children reside mostly with their mother, but frequently stay overnight with other relatives in the flats. Sheila, the paternal grandmother, having borne twenty children is a matriarchal institution.

More recently, Ernie and Annie's aggressive behaviour have become an increasing cause of concern to the family and community. They have not responded to their mother's helpless rem-onstrations nor has their father's threats and authority proved capable of restraining their escalating excessive behaviour.

The Professionals

The fifth province team had been meeting with a community based pastoral worker and family therapist, Eugene. He brought his interest in the family to the attention of the team and they proposed a meeting to include Eileen and the children, Eugene and the three team members, and also other professional workers involved with the family including the probation officer and the school attendance officer. All workers wished to avoid the continuation of the history of statutory interventions and incarcerations with which the family was familiar.

The meeting provided the family with the opportunity to narrate their story. The telling and retelling of such stories is it's own goal (Wilden 1980). Narration is not simply a representation, rather a reproduction. We recreate our image of the past from the vantage of our current perspective. Each re-telling is a reorganising, a reframing, and a redefinition of identity.

In the first session, Philip met with the family and professionals whilst Imelda and Nollaig participated from behind a one-way screen. Annie, the oldest child, opens with 'things are going very badly in the family, we are giving my mother a hard time'. In this double description she articulated the team's perception of the juxtaposed relationship of 'control' and 'waywardness' between mother and children, and between statutory workers and family/Eugene. Philip follows the family narrative helping them to elaborate and to make imagined extremes explicit. They speak of drug overdoses, attempted suicides by drowning and hanging and a recurring disposition to fight, and to kill, their father being an identified protagonist. Annie then mentions Kevin.

Annie: I would say my mother would have taken her life long ago if my brother wasn't the way he is today, she knows he is depending on her, you know.
Philip: Which brother? Kevin?
Annie: Kevin, yeh, Kevin is brain damaged too.
Philip: Yes.
Annie: He can't walk or anything.
Philip: So you think if it weren't for him, your mother would have killed herself a long time ago?
Annie: Ah yes, it is weren't for him, she wouldn't be here today or neither would we, you know.
Phi lip: I see, what would have happened?
Annie: She would either have killed herself or left us.
Philip: I see, yeah.
Annie: And we would be after driving her to it.
Paddy: And if she had died, we would have killed ourselves.
Ernie: Then if she died we would have killed ourselves and if she went everything would have been worse and worse and worse.
Tommie: And we would probably have followed her.
Philip: Yes, O.K.
Paddy: If she left us there would be nothing left of the family.

The theme is elegaic and is developed in accounts of father's desertion, mother's heroic abandonment to Kevin and her tenuous hold on life. Without regret or rancour the lived experience is narrated. Extreme events, described as casual, paradoxically heighten the portrayal of a heroic tone.

When the conversation ended, the team proposed to Eileen and to Eugene that an invitation be extended to Jerry and his mother Sheila to attend the next session. All, including the children readily agreed.

At the next session, Jerry talks of his father's death, from a heart attack following an altercation with a neighbour. Jerry and his brother were imprisoned to prevent them from retaliating, but when released they did retaliate and the aggressor himself subsequently died of 'a heart attack'.

As the head of the clan and keeper of tradition since his father's death Jerry is locked into the 'old world' view. In this position he expresses his loyalty to his mother, Sheila and to his father's values, represented by strength of purpose, physical power, and control by domination. Jerry is confused by the counter balanced 'new world' views expressed by Eileen, where even a crippled child is valued. The children's views fluctuate in confusion between these worlds and Jerry himself may be viewed as struggling to reconcile the values of clan leader with the rewards of family membership.

Philip: What was the impact of your Da's death on the family, Jerry?
Jerry: Ah, I think it broke us all up.
Sheila: A pushed heart attack, oh what happened?
Philip: Yeah, in the family, I mean ...
Jerry: How did the family ...
Sheila: They all scattered.
Philip: Did they?
Jerry: The whole family broke up.
Philip: And was there a gap in the family after that?
Jerry: When my father left, yeah there was, the gap that he left is still there.
Philip: Did anyone move into it ... fill that gap.
Jerry: Well I more or less went in and took over from him.
Philip: We talked the two previous times with your wife and children about other major events like Kevin's accident. ...
Jerry: (*voice breaking*) That was just ... that was ... I wouldn't even go into that now, you know what I mean.
Philip: It is too upsetting?
Jerry: I think I would still be at home to-day if that had not happened to Kevin, you know.
Philip: Oh.
Jerry: Because I know for a fact and she (Eileen) knows as well if I was to stay in that house for three days with that young fellow, I would smother him.
Philip: I didn't know that (*To Eileen*) did you know that?

Eileen: He did, he came in one night ... he had left. He came in one night and (*to Jerry*) you were drunk and I was putting him (*Kevin*) to bed and you came up and you did say that to me ...

Jerry: I had the pillow and I was going to do it and I was crying and I said to her the only way I can ...

Eileen: And I nearly lost my reason ... I have never really forgotten that, you know ...

Jerry: I mean you are looking at a child who was perfect and running around and like this .... It was unfortunate that it had to be him that it happened to, you know.

Eileen: But he is so lovable.

Philip: Did you hear what Eileen has just said, that he could be so lovable. Because I was very struck by your kids talk about how important Kevin is in the family.

Jerry: I mean Kevin is everything, I mean if anything happened to him now, I don't know, like but there is no way could I live with the guy, you know. I couldn't live in the same house as him or I can't even bear to look at him the way ... not ... not bear to look at him. Don't get me wrong ... everytime I go up there and I see Kevin, I think of the way he was, you know what I mean. I cannot accept what happened to him.

Philip: And you are saying that that is the reason why you are not in the house, that is why you left?

Jerry: Well that was ... that was really the breaking point between me and her then, you know. She took a nervous breakdown. I was running to the hospital to her, I was running to the hospital in the morning, at dinner time and in the evening to Kevin and she was in hospital six or seven months, whatever it was and I was trying to manage the kids on my own, by myself. It was just too much. I just couldn't cope and that was it. I ended up cracking up myself then as well.

Philip: What happened?

Jerry: Ah well, I took a couple of overdoses (*voice trembles*) and that myself, you know. And then I said to myself I would be better off getting rid of him (*Kevin*) rather than getting rid of myself. Do you know that sort of way?

Philip? Ah hah, yeah.
Jerry: And I think I would have 'n' anyway.
Philip: And is it still the same for you?
Jerry: Oh yeah, I still feel the same way about it, yeah, even to the present day. I mean I have talked to her of this before.
Eileen: No, I never heard those points so much before, I really didn't. I didn't think you felt that strongly. I thought it was due to the ... you were just drunk that night.
Jerry: It was just like having a building and you going away on holidays for a week and just looking and your building is just condemned. I mean it is the same way with Kevin, I mean, Kevin is going to need to be lifted around for the rest of his life. I mean there is no way he is ever going to be able to live a life.
Philip: Who gets blamed for Kevin's accident?
Jerry: Well I always blame Ernie for Kevin's accident.
Philip: Uh huh.
Jerry: And I always will.
Philip: And how does that effect your relationship with Ernie?
Jerry: Ah it doesn't effect my relationship with Ernie now because I mean he was only a child himself.

Reeling with the force of this violent account the team struggled to find a frame of inclusion and tenderness. The spirit of Kevin presents itself as the unifying force, the medium by which a positively connoted (Palazzoli et al, 1978) more encompassing frame of meaning develops.

Philip: It has been very helpful that you came to-day. It has really helped to clarify things for us. We were very struck by speaking with your children, that they were in a dilemma. They could not decide which way to go. It seemed that if they went one way and were loyal to their father and the Bards (Tribe) they would end up being disloyal to their mother.
Jerry: (*nods*) Yeah.
Philip: And the other way around, if they stayed and were good kids with their mother, they would be disloyal to their father and the Bards. But now we realise that there

is much more to it than that. It goes much deeper than that and the story that you have told us about Kevin is absolutely central .... that it seems that the family's possibilities ... in a sense stopped with Kevin's accident. That the possibilities of people in this family, going on to a life of happiness and fulfilment stopped because of Kevin's injury and his handicap. It is as if when you look into his face you say something like, 'I cannot enjoy my wife, my kids, my family because of what happened to you'. It almost comes across that way and that everybody in the family is under a spell. That because this child was injured and handicapped you tell yourselves you are not free. In a sense it is as if he has all the innocence ...

Jerry: (*nods*) Yeah.

Philip: And everybody else has all the guilt. So that is what we now see as the spell that this family is under and that it is for you people (father, mother and grandmother) to decide whether that is going to continue or not. Because if you don't, there is no doubt but that the outside (*pointing to the professionals*) society will intervene...

Jerry: Um

Philip: And they will come and place your kids in care and they will be doing it for the best reasons in the world. But somewhere in there, there is the possibility to change that for yourselves. We imagine that if we could see the world, see the family through Kevin's eyes, we would see only the good side, of being taken care of, of people smiling at him, people doing things for him. I would say he would see an awful lot of good about the people in this family.

Jerry: I would agree with that alright, like if I was Kevin looking out and like the way he is, yeah.

Philip: Yeah.

Jerry: Of course he would, yeah.

Philip: He has had an extraordinarily powerful influence in this family. It is as if everyone is going around under a spell since his accident, really.

Jerry: Well that is what the priest said to us, the priest in the hospital. 'This is going to change your lives, completely.

When you walk outside the door now, after you know the news, you know how hard things are, it is going to be a completely different world out there. Even the road you walk on is going to seem different, walking back down.'

Philip: O.K. well we are saying that we believe it doesn't have to be like that always, but that has something to do with the attitude that the adults in the family have about Kevin and his handicap, like it seems to us that you have made a huge sacrifice since then, you gave up a lot.

Jerry: I gave up everything that meant anything to me.

Philip: Yeah, and Eileen gave up a lot too.

Jerry: She did of course, yeah.

Philip: Maybe you have paid whatever dues (debts) have to be paid and maybe for your kids' sake you need perhaps to stop paying them. I don't know, it is just a thought. Because otherwise the kids may think they have to go on paying them for ever ...

Jerry: I know yeah. (*rubbing his eyes*)

Philip: And that is the way they are behaving.

Jerry: I know what you mean, like they feel guilty as well.

Philip: Yeah and they maybe think that the only way that they can be in the world is to continue to pay those dues (debts) and they don't have to.

Jerry: (*nods*)

Philip: Because Kevin is not asking it of them.

Jerry: I know that, yeah.

In the eight years following this meeting, Eugene reports that no one has died, been jailed or hospitalised. The family remains intact and respected in the community. In fact, they have become a more respected resource to the community and an authority maintaining the local identity and integrity. The other professionals reported a dramatic decrease in tension and welcomed the clarification of their relationship with the community, in reducing their emphasis on constraint and imposition of values, allowing the people to identify and express their responsibility for themselves. This shift may be quantitative rather than qualitative but it has been sufficient to change a pattern of escalating control, disempowerment and recursive alienation and rebellion, to one of acknowledgement, empowerment and reciprocating cooperative responsible self-direction. Professional intervention is not viewed as fixing, correcting or controlling but helping families to find meaning to become unstuck, and enabling systemic processes to function more freely between workers and clients.

The reader is recommended to read the article from which this synopsised account is extracted for a more complete and eloquent commentary and description of the case.

Limitations of Therapy

There are situations when such neutrality is not appropriate, as when one person is more powerful and uses this power abusively, as is the case with child sexual abuse or physical abuse of a partner. In such situations an important aspect of the process is that the therapist ensure that the power imbalance be redressed to protect the person at risk before proceeding. Also therapy may not be an adequate response to all situations. A number of clients may have to have recourse to legal or statutory services if they cannot succeed in the voluntary context of therapy.

Given the difficulty, if not the impossibility of assessing outcome in therapy, and of making comparative evaluations between therapies, it is difficult to enumerate the areas of application of family therapy. As stated at the outset, family therapy is more a way of conceptualising problems than it is a separate and cohesive way of doing therapy. Practioners would therefore see family therapy as having an appropriate application to the full range of human problems. However because of the emphasis upon context and relationships it does have a very obvious application to relationship difficulties including the enhancement of couples relationships, resolution of conflict, psychosexual difficulties, child and adolescent problems, and family therapists are uniquely advantaged in practising mediation with couples separating and their children. Other obvious applications include, the treatment of drug addiction and alcohol abuse, and eating disorders, often in conjunction with group therapy.

The therapist's ability to join with each client and to understand the dynamics of the client system is essential to enable him or her to broaden the focus of enquiry and to engage the clients in the exploratory process of therapy.

References

Bateson, G. , *Steps to an Ecology of Mind* (N.Y.: Ballantine, 1972).

Bateson, G., *Mind and Nature* (N.Y.: E.P. Dutto, 1979).

Boscolo, L., Cecchin, G. Hoffman, L., Penn, P., *Milan Systemic Family Therapy* (N.Y.: Basic Books, 1987).

Boszormenyi-Nagy, I. and Sparks, G., *Invisible Loyalties* (Harper & Row, 1973).

Byrne, N. OR. & McCarthy J. C., 'Moving Status: Re-Questing Ambivalence through Ambiguous Discourse' in V. Kenny (ed) 'Radical Constructivism, Autopoieisis and Psychotherapy' *Irish Journal of Psychology* 9.1. 1988.

Cecchin, 'Constructing Therapeutic Possibilities' in *Therapy as Social Construction,* S. McNamee and K. Gergen(eds) (Sage, 1992).

Dicks, H., *Marital Tensions* (N.Y.: Basic Books, 1967).

Fairbairn, W., *An Object Relations Theory of the Personality* (N.Y.: Basic Books, 1954).

Government Publications, *Bunreacht na hÉireann* (Dublin, 1 937).

Haley, J., *Reflections on Therapy* (Washington D.C.: F. T. Inst. 1981).

McCarthy, J. C. & Byrne,N. OR., 'Mis-taken Love: Conversations on the Problem of Incest' in *Irish Journal of Psychology* 1988. v.9. No.l.

Maturana, H., An Interview with Humberto Maturana in *Family Therapy Networker,* May-June 1 985.

Maturana, H., and Varela, F., The Tree of Knowledge (Shambhala: New Science Library).

Maturana, H. , Reality: 'The Search for Objectivity or The Quest for a Compelling Argument' in the *Irish Journal of Psychology,* v 9. No.l, 1988. *Radical Constructivism, Autopoiesis & Psychotherapy,* Vincent Kenny (ed).

Stephens, J., *The Crock of Gold* (London: Pan Books, 1978).

Tomm, K., (1992) 'Therapeutic Distinctions in an Ongoing Therapy', by Karl, Cynthia, Andrew & Vanessa in *Therapy as Social Construction* Ed.

Wilden, A., (1980), *System and Structure* (London:Tavistock).

CHAPTER 7

Cognitive-Behavioural Therapy

Anthony Bates

We are disturbed not by events,
but by how we interpret events.
Epictetus

One Sunday, an hour after returning from coaching the junior football team, Tom had his 'heart attack'. His GP was summoned and, finding him collapsed on the dining-room floor with an alarmingly low pulse, despatched him by ambulance to the local Accident and Emergency. Relatives were contacted 'just in case', and gathered around the cardiac monitor. Their respectful silence and concerned faces spoke volumes. Tom got the message: he was forty-three, happily married with four children, had a good job, but his number was up. How would they cope after he was gone?

It was no solace to Tom when the suspected heart attack was ruled out and the much more benign condition of Pericarditis diagnosed. In five days he was treated and discharged but what followed was six years of chronic depression. Two ten-week psychiatric admissions, ECT, and drug treatment did little to help. When he eventually was referred for cognitive therapy, those years of relentless misery had taken their toll. He didn't feel much like talking.

As trust developed between us, we relived in detail the events of that Sunday afternoon. I began to understand what had made him so upset. It was not the imagined cardiac arrest, the imminent threat of death, or the potential loss of his family. Rather, it was a nagging fear, a quiet whisper from a grim childhood that had been awoken and had seized him with total conviction. As he lay there in those moments waiting for the ambulance to arrive, he heard clearly the cutting voice of his father when he was a youngster, saying, 'You're a loser, you can never be counted on, you just don't have what it takes to make it.' Tom interpreted this crisis as proof that his dad was right. Clearly he was unreliable, and his family should never count on him to provide for them. His self-esteem was completely undermined as he surrendered to this verdict.

As he told his story, Tom began to see how this negative view of himself was at the root of his depression. Deep down he had, in fact, always feared his dad was right and had overworked to compensate for his imagined deficiency. His coping was by any standard impressive, but he was overtaken by the crisis of that Sunday afternoon and had relived since, with complete conviction, the shameful self-image he had formed as a boy. For the past six years, since his suspected 'heart attack' he had lived out this belief, adopting a passive and ineffectual role at home, as though to prove to his family he should not be relied upon. In Tom's mind this was the best he could do to avoid further experiences of failure which he believed would be more than he could bear.

Together we brought his pain out into the open and questioned this childhood image of himself. Despair slowly gave way to anger as he struggled against that negative inner voice that drained his energy and his will to live. Tom's early attempts to refute this mental 'bully', with the evidence of a life lived out steadily, faithfully, and successfully, were timid at best. Gradually he got stronger and acknowledged the pain of his childhood. He also gave recognition to the strength of the bullied child within him, who had survived, grown into an adult and had given a good life to others. He recognised too that his dad's behaviour reflected specific problems that afflicted his dad, rather than anything he, Tom, had provoked or deserved.

A sense of hope began to take root in a relatively short time. We worked out practical ways of expressing his recovered self-esteem in his relationships with each member of his family. As his mood lifted, his behaviour at home and at work changed noticeably. In the eyes of others he seemed to wake out of a sleep and become present and available to them after years of morbid self-centredness.

****

Life can present each of us with painful realities such as sudden bereavement, break-down of a close relationship, failure to achieve some valued goal, poverty or medical illness. Therapy is concerned with helping individuals confront difficult situations such as these without becoming engulfed by them. Growth – or recovery from distress – happens when people transcend negative, habitual, self-defeating coping strategies in favour of new ways of thinking and acting which work better for them. At the heart of such change is a recovery of self-esteem which gives renewed energy and the confidence to engage in life.

Cognitive-Behavioural Therapy is particularly concerned with how an individual interprets events and how this might help or hinder his or her attempt to respond to a crisis. As can be seen in the case of 'Tom', it is not events as much as the 'meaning' we give them, that explains our emotional and behavioural responses. Based on this premise, Cognitive-Behavioural Therapy seeks to carefully reveal the meaning a particular event holds for someone, and how their thinking in response to that event may be creating a mood of fear and despair, and paralysing them in their attempt to cope. It's goal is to help people identify and challenge their negative thinking so they become free to see themselves clearly and honestly for who they are, and respond creatively to the particular crisis that has overwhelmed them.

The Historical Roots of Cognitive-Behavioural Therapy

Cognitive-Behavioural Therapy has evolved, as its name suggests, from two strands of psychology: cognitive therapy and behaviour therapy. Cognitive therapy is based on a principal elucidated by the Greek stoic philosopher, Epictetus, that we are upset not by what happens but by *the way we look at things*, i.e. our *cognitions*. Albert Ellis (1962, 1975) and Aaron Beck (1976, 1979), both originally practising psychoanalysts, are credited with devising a therapeutic system based on this premise, which they have developed as a brief, structured, solution-oriented approach.

Ellis, a psychologist in New York, devised his approach, called 'Rational Emotive Therapy' (RET), after noticing how his patients were unable to maintain benefits of psychoanalysis over the long term. By the mid-fifties he had become increasingly disillusioned by analysis, finding it to be unscientific and dogmatic (Dryden, 1984). Aaron Beck, a psychiatrist by training, based at the University of Pennsylvania in Philadelphia, practised psychoanalysis until he found, also in the mid-fifties, that the approach did not seem to work for his depressed patients. He began to test the psychoanalytic explanation for depression (i.e., depression is an expression of inverted anger) and found it simply didn't bear up. While giving credit to both psychoanalysis and client-centred therapy as foremost among his own influences, he found the unstructured nature of these approaches to be unhelpful for depressed people and so set about devising a briefer, more focused approach which he called 'Cognitive Therapy'. While developed and researched initially with depressed patients, cognitive therapy has since incorporated a wide range of behavioural and interpersonal interventions, so that its application has broadened to include most clinical conditions.

The other root of Cognitive-Behavioural Therapy is the tradition of behaviour therapy which developed structured treatments for a wide range of problems, including phobias, sexual difficulties, obsessions and compulsions, throughout the 1950s and 1960s. This approach is based on the key principles of learning theory. One such principle is that our behaviour is shaped – or 'conditioned' – by the response it generates in our immediate environment. If we are rewarded for performing some act we are likely to repeat that act; if we are punished for that act, the likelihood of it recurring is reduced. Behaviour therapy focuses on specific triggers in a person's environment that generate problem behaviours, and how such behaviour is rewarded and maintained.

Traditional behaviour therapy can be seen as a reaction to psychoanalytic theories and it steadfastly rejected any explanation of behaviour based on the working of the inner mind. By early 1970, however, research left little doubt that behaviour was as much mediated by our preceptions and beliefs as it is by actual rewards and punishments. The theoretical model of behaviour therapy evolved to include cognitive variables, such as those Ellis and Beck have highlighted. This evolution will be reflected in late 1993 when both the *British Association for Behaviour Therapy* (BABT), and the *European Association for Behaviour Therapy* (EABT) vote to incorporate the term *Cognitive* in their association's title to reflect the currently preferred terms 'Cognitive Behaviour Therapy' or 'Cognitive-Behavioural Therapy' (CBT).

The Cognitive Explanation of Human Suffering

While Ellis and Beck share a common premise in the assertion that human disturbance is created by distorted images of ourselves and others, they differ slightly in their explanation of the source of these negative cognitions. Ellis plays down the role of early experience and has come to the conviction that human beings

> 'have a strong biological tendency to needlessly and severely disturb themselves and, that, to make matters much worse, they also are powerfully pre-disposed to unconsciously and habitually prolong their mental dysfunction and to fight like hell against giving it up.' (Ellis, 1987, p. 365).

Ellis sees people becoming seriously upset because of excessive achievement and approval-seeking demands, because they overreact to the inevitable inconsiderateness of others, and because they have a 'low frustration tolerance'. Major irrational reactions arise out of a lack of acceptance of reality as it is, and a stubborn refusal to stop demanding that self and others be different.

Beck, on the other hand, proposes that negative thinking originates in deeper unconscious beliefs, *assumptions*, laid down in childhood and later. He tends to pay more careful attention to the context in which core beliefs developed, to help individuals make sense of why they continue to hold on to such beliefs, while also challenging them to find more realistic, self-accepting ways of thinking and coping.

Having worked with both Ellis and Beck, I am struck more by differences in their individual style of working than by disagreement between them at a theoretical level concerning the goals of therapy. Albert Ellis is blunt, persuasive, incredibly humorous and unshakeable in his conviction that people can relinquish the irrational in favour of a more rational, flexible way of thinking and living. Beck is more subtle in his approach to the client, relying on empathy tempered with humour to ferret out with clients just what they are thinking about a particular situation. Beck is slow to label someone's thinking as 'irrational', preferring to encourage clients to go out and test beliefs for themselves. Ellis challenges negative thinking in a more direct and forceful way, exposing – even exaggerating – the irrationality and absurdity of his clients' beliefs and confronting them with the choice of continuing to make themselves miserable or 'grow up'.

Both of these approaches appeal particularly to an aspect of

American culture which idealises the individual who can stand his ground, choose his destiny and achieve impressive goals, regardless of interpersonal support. Watching these pioneers working with clients to help them achieve this kind of independence, it struck me that in the context of a culture where many forms of social support have broken down, this approach offered a key to survival as much as an option for recovery.

But healthy personality development balances growth in autonomy with the ability to form and sustain meaningful relationships. In Ireland, our strength has been in the latter domain; we have traditionally emphasised 'belonging' and encouraged loyalties to family and various institutions. CBT may offer us a healthy balance by helping us also build a sense of autonomy and self-reliance. This can be particularly crucial where loyalties are misplaced or where they have become enmeshed in a dysfunctional family system. For individuals in these situations, CBT may help overcome the fear and guilt of standing alone, adopting different values, and asserting or re-drawing boundaries with others.

CBT: How Does It Work?

What distinguishes one therapy model from another is the unique way it answers the question: 'What must happen in ther-apy for someone to become freer in themselves and in their relationships with others?' Effective CBT requires a creative balancing of two components: compassion and accountability. Compassion characterises the empathic response I make to someone who has been hurt by life, in whatever way it has let him down. At some level therapy doesn't remove hurt; it enables an individual to accept and integrate what is broken, without allowing that reality to dominate his self-image. My being present as a therapist in a genuinely respectful way to someone in pain qualitatively changes his experience, and helps him to come to terms with his history in a new way.

Accountability implies that I also challenge clients to become aware and take control of how they continue to hurt themselves and others by replaying the past. To live with oneself and others, while sustaining a measure of self-esteem, requires effort and sometimes a very profound struggle with one's own negative voices. Recovery may also require learning new ways of solving practical problems. Goal-setting, problem-solving, assertiveness training, decision-making, are skills that may be taught in a very structured way within this approach and require committed co-operation if they are to have any impact.

Many of the texts referenced in this chapter describe systematically the range of cognitive and behavioural techniques used to modify distorted thinking and irrational beliefs. Descriptions are also available elsewhere of how this model can be applied to specific types of human problems (Hawton et al, 1989; Brewin, 1989; Burns, 1990). What follows is my personal attempt to convey what I identify as the spirit of CBT, highlighting, in turn, key features of the change process as therapy unfolds. I include those features which are common to good therapeutic practise, what-ever the approach, emphasising that specific cognitive and behavioural techniques should be presented in the context of a trusting relationship, an agreed agenda and an appreciation of factors in the client's life that may either encourage or sabotage progress. This process is summarised in Figure 1 which links the following components:

1) Building and maintaining a therapeutic alliance;

2) Defining a workable agenda;

3) Exploring key elements of particular problems, i.e. 'decentering';

4) Building self-esteem through actively confronting problems and challenging negative thinking;

5) Looking deeper and revising 'core beliefs', the rigid or irrational 'rules of living' that render a person vulnerable to recurrent depression and anxiety;

6) Re-engaging with one's world, testing the validity of newly-acquired perspectives and dealing with inevitable setbacks.

Any given session of CBT might include attention to all or some of these components, or may focus exclusively on one, depending on the stage of therapy and the need of the client:

CBT: THE PROCESS OF CHANGE

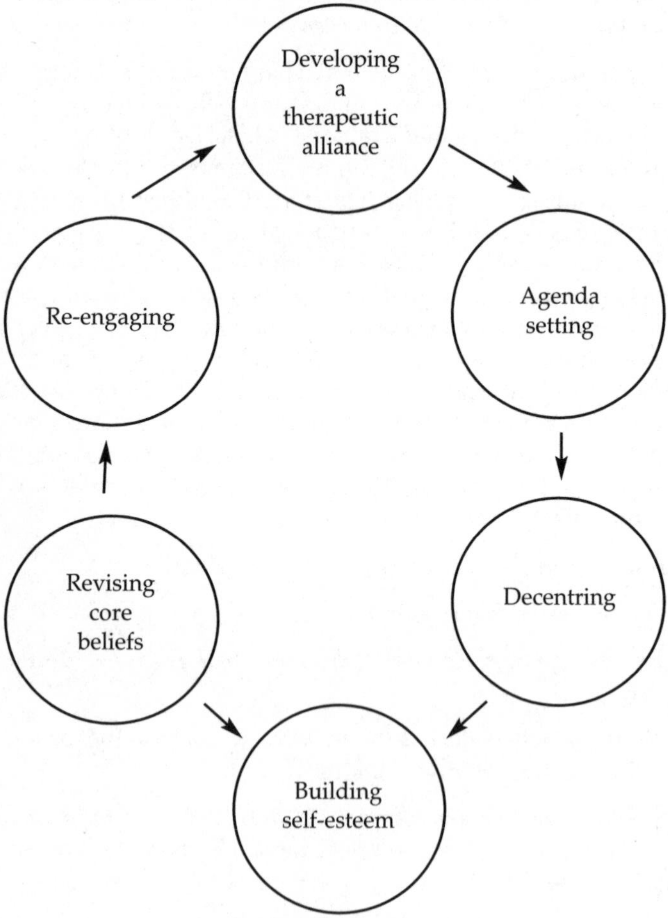

FIGURE 1

1) Developing (and Maintaining) a Therapeutic Alliance

When clients present for therapy they are generally demoralised and unclear as to how exactly they need help. There is a need for the therapist to allow them to tell their story and be listened to in an accepting, respectful way. Gradually, there evolves between the therapist and client a shared understanding of their experience and how they are dealing with their distress. Empathy and intelligent enquiry are crucial if such a mutual understanding is to be achieved. Empathy is not merely a matter of reflecting feelings or conveying reassurances to the client; it is more a constant commitment to grapple with how the client is experiencing his world at any given time. Empathy and cognitive exploration are intimately linked. When empathy is accurately attuned to the experience of the client, the therapist reflects what they are feeling and thinking, and the client becomes more in touch with his experience and more open to exploring his inner world in a deeper way.

The cognitive-behavioural approach regards the therapeutic relationship as a *collaboration* between two parties who work together rather like an investigative team. Beck and his colleagues (Beck, et al, 1979) have repeatedly emphasised that the therapist needs to help clients *discover* how their own perceptions and beliefs are contributing to their distress and guide them towards experiencing alternative ways of construing their world. It is recognised that this partnership is a very human enterprise, fraught with all kinds of possibilities of misunderstanding, insensitivity and frustration on both sides. For this reason, there is a process of feedback built into each CBT therapy session. The therapist asks clients at the beginning or end of a session how they felt during the preceding session, checking to what extent they felt understood, respected, listened to, and whether anything in the session particularly helped or upset them.

It is to be expected that the quality of the alliance between therapist and client will fluctuate frequently over the course of therapy. The relationship may become temporarily strained or ruptured in some way. Generally speaking, something has occurred which has touched a particular sensitivity of the client. 'Ruptures' of this kind are unique windows into key interpersonal sensitivities for the client.

> Mary, aged forty-four, who had been in therapy for some months, became very upset and panicked when time came for me to take a holiday. She came to our last session before the break, said little, and left feeling even more upset and abandoned. At our next session she shared what she had been thinking about my departure, which she had concealed during

the previous visit: 'You (TB) won't hear me out if I tell you what I really feel'; 'You'll see how broken I am and take the high road'; 'If the going gets really tough you'll leave me'. Clearly my temporary absence had touched a vulnerable nerve around the issue of how acceptable it was to be upset and how trustworthy others were in times of need. When she shared her experience of my leaving, there was a genuine opportunity for some healing and consolidation of the relationship to occur. However, during the time she had concealed her negative thoughts and feelings, she believed them utterly and my actual departure and 'failure to hear her out' seemed to confirm her worst suspicions and drive her more deeply into herself. It is extraordinary how people's negative thinking can almost be self-fulfilling, as their behaviour inadvertently provokes the very scenario they most fear.

When 'ruptures' occur in the alliance, it is important to shift the focus away from specific interventions and deal with the relationship in an open, honest manner. While the break may have reflected an over-reaction on the part of the client, it may also be that the therapist has something to learn. Therapists do make mistakes, jump to conclusions, use inappropriate techniques that divert the client away from his agenda, etc. If negative feedback is welcomed, rather than responded to defensively, the air is cleared and therapy becomes more genuine and effective in the process. Furthermore, dealing with negative feelings rather than avoiding or minimising them, prevents anger from becoming diverted into passive-aggressive behaviours such as forgetting to do some assignment between sessions, missing appointments, or simply remaining stuck in the change process.

2) Agenda Setting

Another aspect of developing a sound working relationship with clients is being able to help them translate vague symptoms into concrete, solvable problems which will become the focus of the therapy. Reframing vague symptoms in terms of goals that can be achieved is an immense relief to most clients. This process of negotiation is called 'agenda setting'. It has two components: 1) both therapist and client need to agree on specific problems the latter wants to address, and 2) both need to agree on the methods that will be employed to help solve these problems.

Clients are entitled to know what they can expect in the course of therapy, in terms of what the therapist will do and what they themselves might be expected to do. They deserve to know how you as therapist generally approach these problems, how long it takes, whether or not medication may be involved, the limits of confidentiality, etc. Self-help texts such as *Feeling Good* (Burns, 1980) are very useful resources to explain the model to clients.

> Recently I saw a woman who presented with the complaint of having a 'major identity crisis'. While such a problem might suggest a whole range of possible conscious or unconscious conflicts that needed to be addressed, we spent a good deal of time concretising exactly when and where she experienced the problem and what form it took. Real problems occur in place and time and not just in people's minds, and so I asked her to give me as clear an example as possible from the past couple of days of her 'identity crisis'. She told me about an upsetting event the day before where she had walked into a room of students where she was expected to participate in a seminar. She described how she had feelings of anxiety and panic and was overtaken by an image of herself being small and helpless and stupid. She had thoughts such as 'I won't have anything to say', 'If I open my mouth I will sound stupid and people will think less of me', 'These other people are so cool, I'm so pathetic', etc. Gradually we clarified that she wanted help to feel better about herself in social situations and able to risk sharing her opinions with others. When we both knew where we wanted to go, therapy became focused, relevant and effective. Part of the solution involved clarifying some negative beliefs and images she had carried from her own family experience, but ultimately progress was measured in terms of the behavioural changes that she had wanted to make in her life, which had been agreed by both of us as a workable agenda.
>
> ****
>
> Another client presented with alarming panic attacks and obsessive thoughts about death. Her agenda was that she wanted to 'get rid of these', so she could live a normal life. While I agreed that such symptoms were disturbing and needed to be brought under control, it has been my experience with anxiety disorders that one often needs to accept and under-

stand the symptom before bringing it under control. The latter involved exploring more concretely what happened to her in various situations and elaborating on the content of her negative imagery. While she was most reluctant to accept this as a necessary part of therapy, I discussed my rationale with her and we agreed to include it as part of the agenda. When we did look more closely at the precise images of death that haunted her, it became obvious that these represented in a symbolic way what she was experiencing in her own life. She was married to a man whose career was taking him to different parts of the world and in the process she had begun to lose her identity dramatically, finding herself alone in foreign countries, in the sole charge of their children, unable to work, and increasingly alienated from her husband whose business made excessive demands on his time. In a very real sense, a part of her was 'dying'. This experience again highlighted the importance to both client and therapist of negotiating an agenda that is mutually comfortable. To have simply 'got rid of' her symptoms would have missed the heart of her experience which needed to be acknowledged and acted on in some constructive way.

****

Part of agenda-setting in CBT includes reaching an understanding with clients that they are willing to do self-help assignments between sessions. Such 'homework' might involve keeping a daily diary, recording how they coped with upsetting events, practising specific strategies learned within the session, initiating a new way of handling a difficult relationship. The purpose of homework is to facilitate the carry-over to the client's natural environment of insights and skills achieved within the therapy hour (Bates, 1993).

3) Decentering

Decentering is about learning to observe your own behaviour in any specific situation. Decentering creates a neutral zone where people can watch their own thought processes in action as they interpret a particular event and react accordingly. For example, as I write this chapter I notice my mood is mostly good, as I enjoy the opportunity of sharing how I use the CBT approach in an Irish setting. Occasionally I notice my mood beginning to drag, and inevitably, these feelings coincide with doubts about being too 'wordy' or failing to offer something of practical value to the reader. Such concerns may be valid, but there is an all-too-familiar ring to these negative thoughts. They could easily run riot and drain my energy if I let them. Decentering is that process whereby I become aware of, and accept responsibility for, the way I upset myself. Paradoxically, such an awareness can restore morale and a sense of control as the logic of my mood swings becomes apparent to me.

The Daily Mood Journal:
The Daily Mood Journal is helpful in enabling clients make the links between their thoughts, feelings and behaviour. This form (Table l) is structured to allow analysis of what occurs in response to specific upsetting events that happen between sessions.

TABLE 1

DAILY MOOD JOURNAL			
Upsetting Event	Negative Feelings	Automatic Thoughts	Coping Behaviours (What did you do to deal with this upset?)

In the first column, labelled 'Upsetting Event', the client is asked to highlight a particular time and place where he began to notice a downward shift in his mood during the day. The upsetting event may be an objective happening in his environment, or an inner-world event such as remembering a loss or thinking about the future. By anchoring this exercise in a specific time and place, the client is more likely to stay focused on his actual feelings and thoughts in that situation.

Column 2 of the Daily Mood Journal – Negative Feelings – invites clients to write down the different feelings they had in the particular situation. Emotions offer the best clue as to what is going on within and between people and what precise meaning and interpretation is being given to the current situation (Greenberg and Safran, 1984, 1987). In teaching clients to use this form within the therapy session, I spend a good deal of time on this column. Clients differ greatly in terms of how in touch they are with their own emotional experience and also in terms of the range of feelings they are willing to acknowledge at any particular time. For example, a client may be quite comfortable reporting feelings of anger, but have some difficulty acknowledging underlying feelings of hurt and rejection. Acknowledgement of the latter may in turn evoke a feeling of shame and failure as the client would have no inner permission to feel such emotions or share them with others.

Column 3 invites clients to record their 'Automatic Thoughts'. These thoughts occur spontaneously at a conscious or a pre-conscious level in response to some event. They are described as 'automatic' because they seem to just happen, without any particular deliberation or reflection on the part of the client. They may take the form of specific statements, images, or of an inner dialogue, e.g. 'Oh God, this is terrible!', 'I can't possibly handle this', 'I'm no good at dealing with this kind of situation', 'It's my own fault, I should have been able to avoid this happening', etc.

Clients can have difficulty initially accessing their own automatic thoughts. Because the mind routinely filters out certain cognitive events in its need to pay attention to others, it is not uncommon for clients to fail to notice automatic thoughts while being absorbed by the details of the situation or overcome temporarily by their own emotions. When they begin to take the time to describe what is in their awareness, they also begin to notice their automatic thoughts.

In column 4 clients record their 'coping behaviour' in response to the upsetting event. Lazarus (1966) has described two broad categories of coping responses: on the one hand, there are strategies that cope with one's own emotional reaction to problem situations, such as confiding in a sympathetic friend, taking time out to calm down and gather one's energies, and on the other hand, there are strategies that are specifically aimed at altering a problem situation, such as perhaps seeking information concerning what exactly happened. As clients monitor their typical coping behaviours, they become aware of both positive strategies as well as self-damaging repetitive behaviours that maintain their status quo.

In-Session Decentering:
Decentering is achieved within the session by having clients recreate or anticipate difficult situations. CBT favours specificity and concreteness in working with clients. When a general concern is identified within the session, the therapist will normally seek to recreate a very specific episode where the problem occurred. This brings alive, in an emotionally immediate way, the precise feelings and issues which need to be addressed. Working 'live' within the session to help a client recreate an experience has the advantage of allowing the therapist to notice tell-tale details such as body language, tone of voice, eye contact. By drawing attention to these individual forms of expression, clients can notice aspects of their experience which they have been avoiding.

> Carol, a woman of forty, in the final stages of her first pregnancy, was curiously dismissive of severe headaches she was having ten days before her due date. She had already been admitted to hospital twice in previous weeks for high blood pressure and had been encouraged to keep in touch should her physical condition change in any way. There seemed to be reasonable grounds for concern and caution, but her behaviour did not reflect the need for such worries.
>
> I commented on this discrepancy when I perceived it and asked her how she would feel about checking in with the hospital staff:
>
> Carol: I don't think there is any real reason to bother them.
> TB: How do you imagine you would feel if you did go over for a check-up?
> Carol: I'd feel embarrassed ... and probably silly (shifts around in the chair).
> TB: You certainly look uncomfortable as you describe this. Are there any other feelings you notice as you imagine this scene ?
> Carol: Maybe ... I feel a little afraid.

TB: And what would be your thoughts in that situation, as you imagine yourself visiting the hospital and describing your headaches to them?

Carol: 'Don't be a moanie ... you don't get any brownie points for moaning.'

TB: Are their any other thoughts you might have?

Carol: 'Plenty of people get headaches. I'm just being hysterical' ... Hmm ... (laughs lightly) ... I know where this is coming from ... My mother always made little of her own suffering and was very dismissive of any illness I ever had. PMS was 'hysterical' in her point of view; in fact, she said 'all women are hysterical.'

In the course of exploring a person's thoughts and beliefs in an emotionally immediate way, there is often a spontaneous recall of the historical events that led to their development. Associated memories and accompanying feelings are activated which may be painful, but also cathartic. Understanding that one's beliefs belong to a historical situation where they represented, at a time, a reasonable adaptation to difficult circumstances, relieves guilt and embarrassment for having such beliefs. Also, when clients experience first hand the intimate link between early family experience and current negative thinking patterns, they are much more open and ready for the work of challenging these negative beliefs and revising them.

Many clients experience the same specific negative thoughts every time they are faced with a stressful or ambiguous interpersonal situation. These thoughts arise automatically from deep fears and insecurities they harbour, about being rejected, blamed, or abandoned by others. They routinely mis-read another's behaviour, 'mind-read' and 'jump to conclusions' in the absence of any real evidence. As a result, they are prone to recurrent attacks of anxiety, depression or anger when relating to others. Inevitably, these same negative thinking patterns occur in relating to the therapist. Safran and Segal (1990) have recently enriched the practice of CBT by describing how these interpersonal cognitions can be monitored and elicited within the session. As illustrated by the example of 'Mary' above, they describe how the client's negative feelings towards the therapist can be used to bring into awareness and change fears and prejudices towards others which repeatedly lead them into self-defeating interactions.

4) Building Self-Esteem

As the client observes first-hand his own negative thinking and actions and accepts how they are contributing to his difficulties, he becomes more receptive to trying to act in a different way, and to testing whether or not these automatic thoughts are always true. CBT offers a range of behavioural and cognitive interventions to challenge negative thinking and restore self-esteem (Burns, 1980, 1990). Table 2 presents a sample of these techniques. Cognitive and behavioural interventions overlap in their shared purpose of loosening the hold a particular negative belief has on the client and engaging him in a re-evaluation of his perceptions and assumptions.

TABLE 2

CHALLENGING NEGATIVE THINKING

(Sample of techniques from *The Feeling Good Handbook* by David Burns, 1990)

1. **Examine the Evidence:** Instead of assuming that your negative thought is true, examine the actual evidence for it. For example, if you feel like you never do anything right, you could list several things you have done successfully.

2. **Identify the Distortion:** Write down your negative thoughts so you can see any cognitive distortions you're involved in. This will make it easier to think about the problem in a more positive and realistic way.

3. **The Double-Standard Technique:** Instead of 'putting yourself down' in a harsh, condemning way, talk to yourself in the same compassionate way you would talk to a friend with a similar problem.

4. **The Experimental Technique:** Do an experiment to test the validity of your negative thought. For example, if, during an episode of panic, you become terrified that you're about to die of a heart attack, you could jog or run up and down several flights of stairs. This will prove that your heart is healthy and strong.

5. **The Pleasure Predicting Method:** Predict how satisfying various activities will be on a scale from 0% to 99%. After you complete each activity, record how satisfying it actually turned out to be.

6. **Survey Taking:** Ask people questions to find out if your thoughts and attitudes are realistic. For example, if you believe that public speaking anxiety is abnormal and shameful, ask several friends if they ever felt nervous before they gave a talk.

7. **Externalisation of Voices:** Your therapist assumes the 'voice' of your inner critic and you practise responding honestly, realistically and refuse to buy into attempts to put you down.

Taking Action To Build Self-Esteem (Behavioural Strategies):
Doing nothing is probably the most self-defeating strategy for coping with stress. Behavioural strategies emphasise practical solutions to problems and suggest how the client can act differently and recover self-confidence. They activate clients to verify the truth of self-defeating beliefs so they can put the lie to such beliefs and rebuild self-esteem. For someone who is depressed and inactive, pleasurable activities can be scheduled into a weekly diary, to show them how activity improves their mood and put the lie to the thought 'nothing could make me happy'. Procrastination is tackled through a procedure described as 'graded task assignment' which involves planning very precisely how projects that seem overwhelming can be broken down into 'bite-size' tasks. Completion of each step makes clients feel a lot better and motivates them to achieve the next step. When the job is complete they are in a uniquely strong position to re-evaluate the idea 'I can't do anything right'.

There are also specific behavioural strategies to help clients overcome fears and phobias. Essentially they involve systematic *exposure* of the client to his fears. The process includes listing with the client an inventory of his fears and ranking these from the 'least feared situation' to the 'most feared situation'. Exposure to each situation is rehearsed in the session. As the client confronts each situation he records his progress, noting in particular his 'actual anxiety' at each step and comparing this to his 'expected anxiety' before he engaged in a particular behaviour. If these steps are carefully planned and the client well prepared, he will discover that his anxiety does diminish and these activities can be very rewarding. Such practical experiments alone can suffice to enable the client recover his independence and break a long-standing habit of avoidance behaviour, which only served to keep his fears alive. In common with other behavioural strategies, exposure works long-term by changing the client's perception of the threat as well as their perception of how capable they are to cope with their own anxiety reactions.

Table 3 illustrates a sample of homework from a twenty-one year old woman who had been agoraphobic for over a year following loss of employment and a family trauma. While many issues around her fear of leaving home were addressed, ultimately her avoidance of venturing out alone had to be confronted. During this later stage of therapy she brought in the following record to the session:

TABLE 3

Excerpt from the Diary of an Agoraphobic Client

Date	Outing to	Anxiety Expected 0-100	Time Away	Alone?	Actual Anxiety 0-100
May 10th	Walk to local shop	50	15 mins	yes	30
May 11th	Walk to friend's house	60	25 mins	yes	20
May 12th	Take bus to shopping centre	80	1 hr	yes	50
May 14th	Meet friends in town	90	2 hrs	yes	40

For someone who is demoralised, nothing succeeds like success. It will often be more useful to favour behavioural experiments over cognitive interventions with the very depressed or anxious individual as they may find verbal challenging of their negative thinking confusing rather than helpful.

Cognitive Strategies for Building Self-Esteem:
A key criterion for assessing the success of CBT is establishing that the client has learned to be aware when his own negative thinking comes into play and to challenge such thoughts before they take hold and become destructive. Thus, clients learns to stop themselves presuming what another individual is thinking, and ask 'what evidence do I really have for believing this?' or 'might there be some other way of thinking about this?', or they may stop and review the positive versus negative effects such thinking is having on their attempts to relate to this other person. Since negative thinking associated with depression and anxiety is distorted in very characteristic ways (Beck, 1976; Burns, 1980), a useful skill is being able to identify these distortions, or errors in one's thinking, which prevent one from seeing reality as it is. The best clarification of cognitive distortions is provided by David Burns (1980, 1990).

He defines 'the ten forms of twisted thinking' associated with mood disorders. Table 4 presents examples of cognitive distortions derived from Burns' account in both *Feeling Good* (1980, pp 31-41) and *The Feeling Good Handbook* (1990, pp 8-11)

TABLE 4

TYPICAL COGNITIVE 'DISTORTIONS'

DISTORTION	EXAMPLE
All-or-Nothing Thinking	If I don't do it perfectly, there is no point in doing it at all.
Should	If I respect others, they *should* respect me.
Overgeneralisation	I *never* get anything right.
Discounting The Positive	OK., so I got my work done today, so what? It's only what's expected of me.
Jumping To conclusions (Mind-reading, fortune-telling)	I'm depressed again. Everyone is fed up with with me. I'll never get over it.
Magnification	This situation is awful. There is nothing I can do about it.
Personalization	That dinner didn't go very well. It was my fault. I should have been more entertaining.

The 'triple column technique' is a structured exercise which clients can practice between sessions, as they learn to record negative thoughts, identify distortions and construct rational responses which are realistic and suggest positive coping strategies. Table 5 (overleaf) illustrates this exercise, returned by a twenty-two-year-old nurse who had been getting increasingly anxious and upset coming up to final exams.

One lively way for clients to learn to challenge their negative thinking is by carrying out this inner dialogue as role-play within the therapy session using a technique described as 'externalisation of voices' (Burns, 1990). Initially, the client is invited to try and make the therapist feel put down by confronting him with the litany of his (i.e. the client's) negative thoughts. The therapist responds, from a realistic and constructive position, and shows how these negative thoughts can be disarmed and refuted.

Following this, the client and therapist change roles, so that the therapist has the opportunity to voice the client's negative thinking and the client can practice making his own responses. If the client runs into difficulty, roles are reversed so that the therapist again models how he might respond.

TABLE 5

TRIPLE COLUMN TECHNIQUE		
Negative Thoughts	**Distortion**	**Rational Response**
I shouldn't feel this way	Should	It would be nice if I felt better, but feeling stressed before exams is not surprising. Being ashamed and resentful of my feelings only adds to my problems.
I'm stupid, I always make mistakes	All or nothing Discounting the Positive	I'm human, not stupid; and even I make mistakes! I also have done some things really well on this course.
I have too much to do - I can't manage -I'll mess up this exam and never finish this course.	Catastrophising	I'm just frightening myself by thinking this way. I'd do a lot better to write out what I can achieve today and get on with it.

These techniques are elaborated in much greater detail elsewhere: Beck, Rush, Shaw, and Emery, (1979); Ellis, (1979); McMullin and Giles, (1981); Hawton, Salkovskis, Kirk, and Clark, (1989). Two sources I have found particularly helpful with clients are: *Feeling Good* (Burns, 1980) and Melanie Fennell's chapter on *Depression*, included in Hawton et al (1989).

The former is a wonderfully enthusiastic book describing a wide range of self-help exercises. It is an invaluable source of creative ideas for both therapists and clients. Fennell's Depression chapter includes an excellent appendix for clients, describing in detail how they can learn to plan their time, set realistic goals, and learn to identify and challenge their own particular negative thoughts.

5) Revising Core Beliefs

The deeper work of CBT concerns the very heart of a client's self-image and his beliefs about how he is expected to relate to others. Self-image arises largely from the responses of important others in early life. The attitude of parents, teachers, peers, gradually shapes my self-appraisal. Their behaviour conveys important messages about how acceptable I am, how I am expected to relate to them, and how trustworthy relationships are. Consistency, warmth and reliability teach me that closeness with others is a safe and rewarding experience. In contrast, early relationships characterised by inconsistency, painful separations, repeated disrespect or abuse, will negatively distort my self-perception and reduce my trust in others. I may learn that to survive I must rely only upon my own resources; or that intimacy with others can only be achieved if I am willing to deny my own needs in favour of looking after theirs; or that intimacy can only be achieved if I present myself as dependent and powerless in relation to others.

Core beliefs are the conclusions we draw as a result of early experience. They can take the form of key strategies or 'rules of living' to get us through life, e.g. 'I need and trust the support of others as it makes it much easier for me to live with myself.' Core beliefs are the synthesis of what a person regards as fundamental to survival, and are not easily relinquished. They form a crucial aspect of one's sense of identity. They tend to work as long as individuals can live them out, and provided there is some flexibility which allows individuals to adapt to changing circumstances. However, they can render the individual vulnerable to recurrent stress when they are stated and operated in a rigid, inflexible manner, e.g. 'I must *always* have the approval of others because without it *I can't possibly* feel good about myself.'

Depression is often perpetuated by a specific demand that some high standard of personal performance or approval by others *must* be achieved in order to feel happy. In *Cognitive Therapy for Depression,* Beck (1979) describes how these unconsciously-held assumptions become activated by some critical event, such as a rejection or loss, and in turn generate the negative automatic thoughts and self-defeating behaviours which are so characteristic of depression. In Tom's story, above, it was the crisis of a sudden suspected heart attack that activated his core belief regarding his basic unreliability and brought it painfully to consciousness.

For therapy to have any lasting and prophylactic impact, these beliefs need to be identified and modified. This process can take time. Core beliefs are more than simply arbitrary, biased perceptions that yield to reasonable dialogue or conflicting evidence. They are associated with critical life experiences, sometimes traumatic memories, and thus are heavily invested with emotion. An individual may persist in beliefs of this kind due to strong loyalty feelings towards the family context where they were learnt, and often these loyalties need to be reconsidered before a client can feel they have permission to reject or modify them.

For clients to allow these beliefs and associated memories to become uncovered, they must have achieved the feeling of safety within the therapeutic relationship. At this stage of therapy, the focus becomes what is most vulnerable and personal for the client. Access to such beliefs may be achieved through spontan-eous recall of early memories during the course of therapy, or guided imagery which evokes the context where they were learned, or through ruptures in the therapeutic relationship which open deep insecurities in the client (Safran and Segal, 1990).

Core beliefs or 'silent assumptions' can also be deduced logically using the 'Vertical Arrow' technique (Burns, 1980). This technique involves focusing on a particular automatic thought or concern the client repeatedly reports. Rather than challenging it, the therapist asks the client what exactly would be upsetting if the imagined consequences of this particular concern where in fact to take place:

> Susan, a women of thirty-one, was altogether too nice. This had created problems in her marriage, as her husband had begun to find her less and less attractive, and had ended up in an affair with another woman he found more 'exciting and challenging'. In the course of her therapy, she made a statement, which sounded all too familiar for her, and which the therapist pursued in the following manner:
>
> Susan: I felt upset but I didn't want to say anything and cause a hassle.
>
> (TB: Let's say that happened, why would that be upsetting to you?)
>
> Susan: Hassle destroys the atmosphere.
>
> (TB: Let's say that happened, what would be upsetting to you about this?)

Susan: You could say things you regret – things you would not normally say.

(TB: Let's say that happened, what would be upsetting to you about this?)

Susan: You could end up hurting someone you care about.

(TB: Let's say that happened, what would be upsetting to you about this?)

Susan: This would make me a bitch.

(TB: Let's say that happened, what would be upsetting to you about this?)

Susan: I could end up like my mother.

(TB: Let's say that happened, what would be upsetting to you about this?)

Susan: I saw my mother nag my father too many times as a kid and I *swore* I'd *never* treat men like she did. Conflict destroys a relationship.

This technique systematically uncovers some core belief which is stated in terms of something I *must* do, or others *must* do for me to feel OK about myself. In this case, Susan had reacted to her mother's behaviour by acting out an equally self-defeating 'rule' within her marriage, where she believed she must avoid conflict. As a result, she seriously lost touch with her husband at an emotional level, and their relationship became less real and challenging for both of them.

It is not always of pivotal importance to know the genesis of such an obviously maladaptive belief, but in some cases making the link to the original context facilitates an emotional catharsis for the client and helps the process of changing the belief. Secrecy, shame, and dissociation of the pertinent memories have frequently kept alive an unquestioned faith in these fundamental beliefs. Reliving these traumatic memories may be necessary to allow the original experience to be named, felt, and integrated as part of one's self and one's history. Therapies described elsewhere in this book approach this task of uncovering painful memories in different ways, and many of these can be usefully incorporated within the Cognitive-Behavioural approach. In CBT what is important is that the core beliefs, formed as a result of these experiences, are clearly identified, to allow them to be re-evaluated from the perspective of a free, thinking adult who is now supported within the therapy relationship. The role of the therapist at such a critical point is essentially one of 're-parenting', i.e. providing a secure base where reflection and debate can occur and where one's most cherished rules can be revised.

Reviewing with the client the advantages and disadvantages of a specific core belief can often help to facilitate awareness that such a belief may be self-defeating:

> Michael was a highly successful executive who developed an incurable illness in his mid-thirties. By the time he was forty he was completely paralysed, partially blind, and totally dependent upon constant nursing care from others. While he found some creative ways of continuing to express himself and remain in touch with others, he became prone to very severe episodes of depression. He often described how he felt quite suicidal and regarded his life as totally useless. It became clear that he continued to hold expectations of himself that were quite unreasonable and unyielding in the context of his disability. Having clarified that one of his core beliefs was 'I must be number one, and be seen to be, in order to feel good about myself.' I asked him to review the advantages and disadvantages of this belief. Table 6 illustrates the format we followed in our session, using the Cost-Benefit Analysis technique (Burns, 1990). Initially, his belief in this rule of living was almost 100%, and it was easy for him to describe its 'advant-ages'. However, we looked at it more closely and discovered there were also many serious 'disadvantages' to retaining this belief.

Serious illness confronts each of us with a critical challenge to develop an attitude that encourages acceptance and self-esteem and enables us remain open to whatever possibilities life still holds (Bates, Burns and Moorey, 1989). The challenge for Michael was to revise his belief to allow him to come to terms with his disability and to live out his life as creatively as possible. Therapy has no ready-made solutions for personal crises of this magnitude, but CBT can help to identify and challenge key attitudes that maintain denial and resentment, and prevent adaptation. His 'Revised Belief', arrived at after a number of serious, challenging sessions, is included at the end of table 6 opposite.

While the wisdom of this revised attitude was compelling to Micheal, he resisted it strongly at an emotional level. He continued to see himself in his dreams as physically active, executing

TABLE 6

Cost-Benefit Analysis	
Core Belief:	I must be number one, and be seen to be, in order to feel good about myself
Advantages of believing this	Disadvantages of believing this
I worked extraordinarily hard and achieved success early in my life.	*I devoted all my energies to building a career and none to my family.*
I loved the admiration and respect I gained from others.	*I needed constant reassurance from others that they saw me as a success.*
	I regarded others who were not at the top of their careers as lesser human beings.
	I can see no good whatsoever in my life now that I'm disabled.
Revised belief: For years success meant being number one, but I can no longer live out this demand. My life has completely changed, and 'success' now means accepting myself as I am, with this disability, this 'failure', and working to mend the hurt I caused to my family *and* myself through years of neglect.	

the many tasks of his former profession with complete competence. We worked hard to understand what made it so difficult to accept the stark reality of his disability. What emerged were a library of memories of his mother indulging him with an exaggerated sense of his greatness. He was expected to be 'the best' and nowhere in his childhood was he prepared for personal failure. In essence, he was 'set up' to deny his disability and conceal his pain from others. He had clung to his mother's image of his omnipotence rather than adapt to reality of his vulnerability. Michael was able to express intense anger and hurt at being set up in this way, and this release of emotion helped loosen the cognitive grip of his core belief. It also enabled him claim his right to sometimes fail and he developed an attitude of acceptance about many early memories of failure he had never spoken about. Our work together continues.

I sometimes explain to clients that when self-defeating core beliefs are acted on by them in their adult life they, in effect, recreate and relive something of their past. In essence, they 'go home', and inevitably replay the drama of their childhood with the same emotional consequences, e.g. loneliness, shame, fear, frustration, rage, etc. The therapist's invitation to revise these beliefs is essentially an invitation to leave home. The past is not denied but its power over one's present and future is radically diminished. As autonomy is achieved, clients become free to choose to make significant changes in how they relate to themselves and others.

6) Re-engagement

Personal breakthroughs in recovery and therapy are not always easy to integrate into everyday life. Returning once more to Tom's story: his family were thrilled to see him smiling again, but were at a loss as to how to allow him reclaim his role as 'dad' within the family. Everyone had learned to avoid asking for his help while he was spending his six years being very withdrawn.

It is important to prepare clients for the 'culture shock' they may experience on leaving therapy. Others don't know quite how to take them and there is an abiding suspicion, even resentment, that they are now okay and that the havoc they have caused over the preceding months or years has to be overlooked.

After ten sessions with Tom, I worked with both him and his wife for four sessions, helping them both re-envisage and negotiate his role within the family. It was important for his wife to make room for him to re-enter the family and encourage family members to express their feelings about what life had been like for them in his 'absence'. He has kept in touch from time to time, dropping in for support in the midst of one particular crisis. For the past two years, since he graduated from therapy, he has not been depressed.

Mary, who has trouble asking for what she needed in our session, planned many opportunities outside therapy where she simply 'asked for what she needed'. Susan, who preferred 'no hassle', needed to rehearse several role-plays with important others, and express her annoyance over parental interference in her marriage. Carol went directly to the maternity hospital after the session described above, and 'moaned'! Within hours the hospital team intervened surgically and delivered a beautiful baby boy. The delivery was not without complications and she realised she had to learn to read, respect, and voice her own bodily distress signals a lot sooner.

Another aspect of re-engaging with one's world is the inevitability of experiencing set-backs in the course of this process. Such set-backs are demoralising, particularly when viewed in catastrophic terms as being 'back to square one'. Anticipating the set-backs and rehearsing one's response is part of CBT. Identifying and practising cognitive-behavioural coping strategies which are likely to help can be both a helpful and light-hearted experience, as both client and therapist are working from a position of strength. Practising homework assignments, even in the later stages of therapy, can be a way of structuring clients' re-entry to the world and focusing their attention on crucial skills that need to be consolidated through repeated practice.

How Well Does CBT Work?: Research Evidence

Research on CBT has produced very promising results in a variety of settings. In an analysis of 28 studies involving over 1,300 patients, published in the *Journal of Consulting and Clinical Psychology* (Dobson, 1989) it was found to be equal to, or more effective for depression than drugs, behaviour therapy, and other psychotherapies. Table 7 presents a summary of six of these studies, selected by Hollon (1990) as being the most rigorously controlled of the series. Subjects were either offered anti-depressant therapy (ADT), cognitive-behavioural therapy (CBT), or a combination of both (ADT / CBT). The average number of sessions in the 6 studies was 15, which would be the desirable, but not rigid, goal of CBT. Subjects from each of these studies can be grouped together because treatment was standardised within each of the conditions, comprising Beckian CBT based on his treatment manual (1979), and Imiprimine as the anti-depressant medication in each of the studies.

The six articles reviewed in this way, include Rush, Beck, Kovacs, and Hollon (1977); Blackburn, Bishop, Glenn, Whalley, and Christie (1981); Murphy, Simons, Wetzel, and Lustman (1984); Beck, Hollon, Young, Bedrosian and Budenz (1985); the NIMH Collaborative Study (Elkin, et al, 1989); and Hollon (1990).

Table 7 shows 184 subjects receiving anti-depressant drug therapy (ADT), 170 receiving CBT, and 92 subjects receiving a combination of both treatments, i.e. ADT/CBT. There was a predictable drop-out rate in each of these groups, with roughly a quarter to a third of participants failing to complete treatment. Slightly more subjects dropped out of the drug treatment condition, suggesting that CBT has more holding power for its recipients. Pretreatment measures of depression were made using the Beck Depression Inventory (BDI), a brief 21-item self-rating scale measuring depression. This inventory (Beck, Ward and Mendelson, 1961) is used frequently in clinical settings to monitor progress over the course of therapy, with significant reduction in BDI being regarded as evidence of recovery.

Table 7 shows how each of the groups had roughly equivalent mean scores on the BDI before treatment began. Their scores would place them in the severe range of depression. Following treatment, scores were also fairly equivalent, and in the normal range, with the combination approach ADT/CBT proving to be slightly better than either treatment alone.

TABLE 7

Cognitive Therapy Outcome Research
(Based on 6 Studies)

	Anti Depressant Therapy (ADT)	Cognitive Behavioural Therapy (CBT)	Combination (ADT/CBT)
Number of subjects in 6 studies	184	170	92
% Drop-out	36%	26%	27%
Pre-treatment BD1	26.6	27.3	27.1
Post-treatment BD1	10	9	7.5

Individuals were randomly assigned to each of the above groups in all of the studies included, regardless of whether their diagnosis had been considered 'endogenous', or 'reactive'. The above results would indicate that presumably anti-depressant therapy was effective for individuals who might be included in either group, and that equally CBT was effective for individuals who might traditionally have been expected to benefit only from anti-depressants. With individuals who are severely depressed, a combination of both drugs and therapy can be necessary and effective.

Perhaps of even greater interest are the results, shown in Table 8, grouping three follow-up studies which investigated the rates of relapse, comparing those who had received CBT and terminated treatment with those who had received drug therapy, or a combination, and terminated treatment. Results, in these studies, support the claim that CBT has a lasting *preventive* benefit. The average rate of relapse, defined as experiencing a major episode of depression within a year to two years after termination of treatment, was twice as great among those who received only anti-depressant therapy, in comparison with both other groups.

TABLE 8

Cognitive Therapy: Relapse Rates
(Based on 3 separate follow-up studies)

	ADT	CBT	ADT/CBT
Kovacs et al (1981) 1 year (Relapse Rate)	65%	39%	N/A
Blackburn et al (1986) 2 year (Relapse Rate)	78%	23%	21%
Hollon et al (1990) 1 year (Relapse Rate)	67%	20%	30%

For Whom Is CBT Suitable?

While the above findings are encouraging in terms of the likely benefit of this approach for sufferers of depression in particular, recent attention has been directed more toward understanding what client characteristics are likely to predict a favourable outcome with this approach, and what precisely it is within the therapy that works so well. Clinicians engaged in the assessment of this approach with depression have emphasised its suitability for nonpsychotic, depressed individuals who do not have severe personality disorders. CBT is found to be most effective with clients who are at least willing to try out new coping strategies and do homework assignments between sessions (Burns and Nolen-Hoeksema, 1991) and where there is evidence of a strong empathic relationship between therapist and client (Persons and Burns, 1985). Fennell and Teasdale (1987) studied a small group of individuals who responded with particular rapidity to this approach and compared them with a similar group who responded less impressively. What seemed to distinguish these two groups was the perception of the 'rapid responders' that the Cognitive Model was relevant, made sense of their particular difficulties, and gave them practical ways of taking control of an emotionally chaotic situation.

A very useful resource in terms of the application of CBT with people who have severe problems, is the volume published by Hawton, Salkovskis, Kirk, and Clark (1990). Besides Melanie Fennell's chapter on depression, already alluded to, there are excellent chapters dealing with Cognitive-Behavioural assessment, treatment of anxiety disorders, somatic problems, eating disorders, sexual dysfunction, and chronic psychiatric problems, e.g. schizophrenia, which is a developing area within CBT.

In treating clients with personality disorders, i.e. clients who have a long-standing, severely damaged image of themselves or others, cognitive-behavioural therapists have encountered difficulties that required elaborations of the techniques described by Beck (Young and Lindemann, 1992). The work of Jeff Young (1990) describes emotionally-focused and imagery techniques for addressing the high degree of avoidance, rigidity and interpersonal dysfunction characteristic of this client group.

Recently, CBT has been applied systematically in a variety of medical settings to good effect. It seems to offer a very adaptable and flexible approach that can be used with clients faced with very different problems, e.g. Chronic Fatigue Syndrome (Butler, Chelder, Ron, and Wessely, 1991), Chronic Pain Syndrome (Phillips, 1987), Rheumatoid Arthritis (O'Leary, Shoor, Lorig, and Holman, 1988). In each incidence, techniques such as presenting a psycho-biological model of pain, having patients identify and challenge misconceptions regarding their condition, and encouraging them to take action rather than remain passive were shown to significantly alter their experience of the condition and in many cases alter their specific symptoms.

References

Bates, M.A., Burns, D.D., and Moorey, S. (1989), 'Medical Illness and the Acceptance of Suffering' in *The International Journal of Psychiatry in Medicine*, 19; 3: 269280.

Bates, M.A. (1993), 'The Predictors of Adherence to Homework in Cognitive-Behavioural Therapy', Ph.D. Dissertation, University College Dublin.

Beck, A.T., Ward, C.E., Mendelson, M. et. al, (1961), An Inventory for Measuring Depression, in *Arch Gen Psychiatry*, 4:561-571.

Beck, A.T. (1976), *Cognitive Therapy and the Emotional Disorders* (New York: International Universities Press).

Beck, A.T, Rush, A.J., Shaw, B.F., Emery.G. (1979), *Cognitive Therapy of Depression: A Treatment Manual* (New York: Guilford).

Beck, A.T., Hollon, S.D., Young, J.E., Bedrosian, R.C., BUudenz, D. (1985), 'Treatment of depression with cognitive therapy and amitriptyline' in *Arch. Gen. Psychiatry*.

Blackburn, I.M. Bishop, S., Glen, A.I.M., Whalley, L.J., Christie, J.E (1981), 'The efficacy of cognitive therapy in depression: a treatment trial using cognitive therapy and pharmacotherapy, each alone and in combination' in *Br J Psychiatry*, 139: 181-189.

Blackburn, I.M., Eunson, K.M., Bishops, S.A. (1986), A two-year naturalistic follow-up of depressed patients treated with cognitive therapy, pharmacotherpy and a combination of both, in *J. Affective Disord*, 10:67-75.

Brewin, C.R. (1989), 'Cognitive Change Processes in Psychotherapy' in *Psychological Review*, 96:3: 379-394.

Burns, D.D. (1980), *Feeling Good: The New Mood Therapy* (New York: New American Library).

Burns, D.D. (1990), *The Feeling Good Handbook* (New York: William Morrow and Company).

Burns, D.D. and Nolen-Hoeksema, S. (1991), 'Coping Styles, Homework Compliance and the Effectiveness of Cognitive-Behavioural Therapy' in *Journal Consulting and Clinical Psychology*, 59:2: p. 305-311.

Butler, S., Chalder, M. R., Wesselly, S. (1991), 'Cognitive Behaviour Therapy in Chronic Fatigue Syndrome' in *Journal of Neurology, Neurosurgery, and Psychiatry*, Vol. 54: 153-

Dobson, K. (1989), 'A meta-analysis of the efficacy of cognitive therapy for depression' in *Journal of Consulting and Clinical Psychology*, 57, 414-19

Dryden, W. (1984), 'Rational-Emotive Therapy' in *Individual Therapy in Britain* (ed) W. Dryden, pp. 235-263.

Elkin, I., Shea, M.T., Watkins, J.T. et al, (1989), 'NIMH treatment of depression collaborative research programme, I: general effectiveness of treatments' in *Arch Gen Psychiatry*, 46:971-982.

Ellis, A. (1962), *Reason and Emotion in Psychotherapy*, (Scarcasus, NJ: Lyle Stuart).

Ellis, A. (1979), 'The Practise of Rational-Emotive Therapy' in *Theoretical and Empirical Foundations of Rational-Emotive Therapy*, A. Ellis and J. M. Whitely.

Ellis, A. (1987), 'The Impossibility of Achieving Consistently Good Mental Health' in *American Psychologist*, Vol. 42, 4, p.p. 366-375.

Fennell, M. J. V. (1989), 'Depression' in Hawton et al (eds), *Cognitive Behaviour Therapy for Psychiatric Problems* (Oxford: OUP), 169-234.

Fennell T, M. J. V, and Teasdale, J.D. (1987), 'Cognitive Therapy for Depression: Individual differences and the process of change' in *Cognitive Therapy and Research*, 11, pp. 253-71.

Greenberg, L.S. and Safran, J. D. (1984), 'Integrating Affect and Cognition: A Perspective on the Process of Therapeutic Change' in *Cognitive Therapy and Research*, 8:559-78

Greenberg, L.S. and Safran, J.D. (1987), 'Emotion in Psychotherapy' in *American Psychologist*, 44: 19-29.

Hawton, K., Salkovskis, P.M., Kirk, J, and Clark D.M. (1989), *Cognitive Behaviour Therapy for Psychiatric Problems, A Practical Guide* (OUP).

Hollon, S.D., and Najavits, L. (1988), 'Review of Empirical Studies on Cognitive Therapy' in *Review of Psychiatry* (ed) A.J. Frances and

R.E. Hales, Vol. 7, 643-67. (Washington DC: American Psychiatric Press).

Hollon, S.D. (1990), 'Cognitive Therapy and Pharmacotherapy for Depression' in *Psychiatric Annals*, 20:5: 249-257.

Kovacs, M., Rush, A.J., Beck, A.T., Hollon, S.D. (1981), 'Depressed outpatients treated with cognitive therapy or pharmacotherapy' in *Arch Gen Psychiatry*, 38: 33-39.

Lazarus, R.S. (1966), *Psychological Stress and the Coping Process* (New York: McGraw-Hill).

McMullin, R.E., and Giles, T.R. (1981), *Cognitive-Behaviour Therapy, A Restructuring Approach* (New York: Grine and Stratton).

Murphy, G.E., Simons, A.D., Wetzel, R.D., Lustman, P.J. (1984), 'Cognitive therapy and pharmacotherapy, singly and together in the treatment of depression' in *Arch Gen Psychiatry*, 41: 33-41.

Persons, J.B. and Burns, D.D. (1985), 'Mechanisms of Action of Cognitive Therapy: The Relative Contributions of Technical and Interpersonal Interventions' in *Cognitive Therapy and Research*, 9: 5, p. 539-551.

Rush, A.J., Beck. A.T., Kocacks, M., Hollon, S.D. (1977), 'Comparative efficacy of cognitive therapy and pharmacotherapy in the treatment of depressed outpatients' in *Cognitive Therapy and Research*, 1: 17-37.

Safran, J.D. and Segal, Z.V. (1990), *Interpersonal Processes in Cognitive Therapy* (New York: Basic books).

Simons, A.D., Murphy, G.E., Levine, J.E., Wetzel, R.D. (1986), 'Cognitive therapy and pharmacotherapy for depression: sustained improvement over one year' in *Arch Gen Psychiatry*, 143: 18-23.

Young, J.E. (1990), *Cognitive Therapy for personality Disorders: A Schema-Focused Approach* (Sarasota, FL: Professional Resource Exchange).

Young, J.E. and Lindemann, M.D. (1992), 'An Integrative Schema-Focused Model for Personality Disorders' in *Journal of Cognitive Psychotherapy*, Vol. 6, No. 1, pp 11-23.

CHAPTER 8

Gestalt Therapy and the Self-Organisation Process

Vincent Humphreys

Historical Context and Introduction

It was in the 1950s that Gestalt therapy first emerged as a distinctive approach to psychotherapy. Fritz Perls is generally recognized as the founder of Gestalt therapy even though his wife Laura played a major role in its development. Gestalt has its roots in Germany in the 1920s and 30s where Fritz trained and practiced as a psychiatrist and psychoanalyst. Among the influences that shaped the thinking and practice of Gestalt were (a) Wilhelm Reich, with his view that the body as well as the mind is important in the development of resistances, (b) existential ideals, with its emphasis on man's capacity to make choices and I-thou communication as elaborated by Martin Buber, (c) the work of Gestalt psychologists, who suggest that in perception, man actively creates meaningful configurations or gestalts, (d) Drama, through the director Max Reinhardt with whom Fritz Perls did some theatre work. Perls's love of dramatisation is reflected in his creative therapy techniques. (Parlett and Page, 1990)

Perls put forward a comprehensive theory on the nature of human functioning (Perls, Hefferline and Goodman, 1951). One of his basic assumptions was that a person cannot be considered as separate from his environment. This environment includes physical and social objects. It is in the process of interaction between himself and his environment that man meets his basic needs. Perls describes several ways in which the person interacts with the environment. The most basic of these is through the formation of clear figure/ground relationships. These are called 'gestalts'. If say, a person is hungry, then in a clear gestalt his perception of the environment will highlight food. Other aspects will be in the background and the person will engage the environment to meet this need. As the need is met, this gestalt will recede and others will come into the foreground depending on current needs. As a clear gestalt is formed the contact with the environment is uninterrupted.

Perls proposed the idea that 'problems' arise when our contact with ourselves as well as the environment is interrupted or blocked. In this situation Gestaltan are unclear. He suggested four main ways this happens: through projecting, introjecting, retroflecting and the process of confluence. Introjection is where people take from the environment without evaluation. Much of what they take in is 'swallowed' whole without consideration and integration. Children often introject labels from their parents e.g. lazy, stupid. Retroflection is a process where we do to ourselves what we would really like to do to the environment, such as injuring ourselves rather than hitting out at someone. Projection is when we attribute feelings, thoughts, motives to others which are really our own and confluence is where the boundary between self and the other or the environment is blurred and the person doesn't, either, fully engage the environment or fully withdraw from it. (Polster and Polster, 1973)

As a person engages in these process of retroflecting, projecting, introjecting and confluence basically what they are doing is disowning themselves. Perls used this idea of disowned 'parts' to develop an experimental approach to therapy. He devised innovative techniques to facilitate people to be aware of their 'here and now' experience of disowned 'parts', to 'act out' or 'play' these parts in order to more fully integrate them as part of self. Perls is best known for the creative techniques he developed.

While Perls put forward a theory of human functioning it became embedded (or neglected) in Perl's emphasis on the technical aspects of therapy. Perl's disliked theorizing as he felt it took away from direct experience. However within their theory Perls and his colleagues did anticipate systemic theoretical development with such ideas as 'the whole determines the parts' (Perls Hefferline Goodman, 1951) and the environmental 'field' (Perls, 1973). At the same time it was difficult for the early Gestaltists to further develop and incorporate these ideas into practice because the basis for such thinking had not yet emerged.

Since the development of Gestalt therapy, theory and practice, systemic and self-organisational theories have come to the fore

(Dell, 1985), (Dalenoort, 1989). Kaplan and Kaplan have combined Gestalt theory with self-organisation theories (Kaplan and Kaplan, 1985). What has emerged from this is not a theory of therapy but rather a theory on the nature of human functioning (Kaplan and Kaplan, 1991). From this appreciation of human functioning a therapeutic method has emerged. This chapter gives an overview of this theory of human functioning and then details how it can be applied in therapeutic work with individuals. Some of Perl's ideas and techniques are also described and contrasted with those of Kaplan and Kaplan.

Human functioning is active and unchanged

If we look at human functioning at a micro level, over a very small time span, we discover that our functioning is not static but ongoing, i.e. continuously active and continuously changing. Here the phrases 'continuously active' and 'continuously changing' are used to emphasise that from moment to moment, all our behaviour, feelings, thoughts, images, movements and breathing are being created anew. If, right now, I take a moment to become aware of my ongoing functioning, I notice that I close my eyes, put my hand to my chin, breathe deeply, think about sitting back in the chair, open my eyes, listen to the sounds outside and look at the garden. Thus my functioning is a continuous process of shifting and changing from second to second. Furthermore this shifting process is holistic in the sense that as one 'aspect' of functioning changes, other processes simultaneously change e.g. as images change, breathing, feelings etc. simultaneously change.

We express ourselves as stable

This view of human functioning as continually active and continually changing appears to contradict our day-to-day conception of ourselves. Generally, we experience ourselves as stable and continuous – the same person through time. We describe ourselves in various static terms such as outgoing, intelligent and ignore the fact that we actually function quite differently at different times depending on our 'mood' or 'state of mind'. Theories of personality postulate man as having static personality traits to account for our sense of stability and continuity.

If we accept that our functioning is, in fact, continuously active and continuously changing, then, the question arises as to how is it that we experience ourselves as stable and unchanging i.e. the same through time? We are, in fact, continuously creating this sense of stability on a moment to moment, second by second basis. We usually assume our experiences are given, established, natural. We tend to think of ourselves in macro terms that reflect this stability e.g. as a father, accountant, or sportsman. We do not focus our attention on the choices we are continuously making.

The following example highlights the idea that, we are actively and continuously creating in the present what we experience as stable and continuous.

> Supposing a man is creating or believing himself to be shy. His description would be something like 'I am shy and not very good in social situations'. However, observing him closely we might see him do the following: As he organises himself along familiar lines, he moves slowly in situations with new people, hunches his shoulders, thus giving an appearance of being small. He doesn't initiate conversation. If someone speaks to him he may give short answers and not expand or finish by inviting another response. He stays close to someone he knows, hoping he may initiate conversations. Internally, perhaps he feels uncomfortable, unable to think fluently and his breathing may be short. He probably sees himself as uninteresting. He imagines that others are comfortable, extrovert and at ease with themselves. He is not imagining himself any other way. He further creates this shyness by pushing away any feeling of interest in other people.

All of the above is active, ongoing, and maintaining itself in the present and the individual has a sense of his 'shy stable self'. How he sees the environment, and how he senses the environment perceives him, is consistent with and is supporting how he is currently maintaining and stabilizing himself as 'shy'.

> While in this 'shy' self-organisation the man does not recognise that at other times and in a different social situation, with a few close friends, he organizes himself differently. Here he feels comfortable and at ease. He is interested in the others and actively asks them about themselves. At the same time he talks easily about himself, perceiving what he has to say as important and perceiving others as interested in him. He allows his

sense of humour to come through. His breathing is deeper and his shoulders are relaxed and open.

Even though we experience ourselves as the same all the time, most people know that at times they feel different or that a variety of people and places 'bring out' different aspects of themselves. Thus a person might know he is quiet and easy going most of the time but in a crisis at work he can be energetic and tough. Easy and quiet, energetic and tough, are different ways of organizing ourselves. Most of us know we can organise ourselves differently, although how we shift and change from one self-organisation to another is often out of our awareness. When a person is strongly within on self-organisation e.g. depressed he may know in a conceptual way that at times he is happy but that sense of happiness feels distant and unreachable.

Maintaining self-organisational stability

The process of creating a sense of stability while at the same time being continuously active and changing, is termed self-organisation. The process contains two elements, one of *focal attention* or awareness (that aspect to which we are paying attention to at any given moment) against a *background* of other self-organisational processes which are not currently in the forefront of our attention. Together, these two elements are what is termed a configuration process. As I currently write this chapter my focus of attention is on the content of what I want to write. At the same time, more is happening in the background of which I am vaguely aware, e.g. pressures of time, feelings of unsureness as to clarity and bodily tensions as I sit hunched. The way that I maintain my focus of attention on the content is to push away, or avoid, other vague 'intrusions'. This pushing away is an active process of self-regulation and I am doing it on a current, ongoing, moment to moment basis.

It is between focal attention and that which is in the background that we regulate ourselves, usually towards giving ourselves a sense of stability. We can regulate ourselves towards rigidity or towards more openness and change. Both of these processes are described below:

> Supposing the 'shy' man is at a social function and is in conversation with a woman. Within his self-organizational process of feeling uncomfortable and shy he becomes aware of feeling interested and attracted to her. However he anticipates she would not be interested in him and pushes away the feeling of attraction, thus heightening his sense of self as 'worthless' and maintaining his self-organisation as shy.

Before pushing away the feelings of interest and attraction and by maintaining his perception of the other as not interested, he is regulating himself rigidly as shy.

> Supposing on the other hand the 'shy' man choose to regulate himself differently at the point where he becomes aware of feelings of interest and physical attraction. Although aware of his inclination to withdraw he chooses instead to slow down and pay more attention to these feelings. He discovers he feels more open towards the woman, becoming interested in what she has to say. He takes the risk of talking about himself and even though he is unsure of the consequences feels some excitement. At the same time he tells himself he can cope okay if she proves uninterested in him.

Confluence and contact in self-regulating

This concept of self-regulation is the pointer towards how people keep themselves the 'same' or allow themselves to become aware of their ongoing choices, and allow themselves to risk and discover different self-organisational possibilities. People can discover how to recognise and observe their own moment to moment self-regulatory processes (and for an outside person, eg. a therapist to observe them) and use them as a fulcrum for awareness, choice and more expanded functioning. In Gestalt, this is termed *contactual functioning.* On the other hand, someone can choose not to recognise, to ignore or push away these possibilities and use them as a basis for restricted, familiar, safe or 'rigid' functioning. This is termed *confluent functioning.*

The nature of confluent functioning is along familiar, safe lines, with little or no sense of choice. The consequences of such functioning are usually familiar and bear little risk or excitement. Confluent functioning is fast, thus skipping over the feeling of choice and creating reality out there as given and unchangeable.

When people see reality as given and unchangeable they simultaneously create themselves as 'fixed' in relation to this 'given reality'. People assume they are just being who they are and are responding as they 'have to' or are 'made' to. It should be said that this functioning is in a sense efficient. There is usually no need to explore ourselves or the environment anew. To do this takes time and energy and usually it is enough to rely on past and familiar experiences. Difficulties can be created, however, when we face the unfamiliar. Instead of tentatively exploring the environment afresh and seeing the potential we sometimes tend to stick more rigidly to familiar processes of self-organisation.

Contactual functioning has the quality of touching unfamiliar processes. It involves discovering awareness of choices, and an element of risk and excitement. It includes the process of exploring oneself and the environment, opening up to the possibility of exploring the unfamiliar, and of perceiving the world and self differently. The pace is slower, thus allowing this exploration to occur.

A fuller description of the contact process is given by Kaplan, Kaplan and Serok:

> Contact ... refers to processes of active engagement of the environment that involve a phase of examination and exploration and temporarily, a relative fluidity of experiential boundaries. Contact can be seen as a mode of self-organisation that permits recognition of how one is organising and how one is working at reorganisation. A series of progressive phases are discernable i) 'holding back' on organisational crystallisation, ii) 'allowing' oneself to 'see' and 'hear' more of what exists in self and in others and iii) 'allowing' oneself to simultaneously explore alternatives. (Kaplan, Kaplan and Serok, 1985)

Self and mutual support

I have presented the theory of self-organization from the point of view of individual functioning and I have described contactual and confluent functioning from this perspective. Within this framework I have also described how an individual perceives himself and the environment from within his own self-referential perspective. So, for instance, the 'shy' man may see others in his environment as comfortable and outgoing, thus supporting his own perception of himself as shy.

When two people interact and both are self-referentially perceiving the other in a way that supports their ongoing familiar self-organizations, they are mutually creating possibilities or supports in terms of familiar self-organisational configurations that tend towards the safe, restricted and limited. In this a systemic process arises where two or more people together, in a mutual way, support each others confluent functioning.

> A boss talks to a worker asking him to do something. The worker feels under pressure. He has a lot of other work but feels unable to say this to his boss. He hesitates and appears reluctant and sees his boss as unreasonable and dictatorial. The boss at the same time feels under pressure himself and, seeing the worker as uncooperative, feels 'as if' compelled to push hard for the work to be done.

Both the boss and the employee are mutually supporting a system of restricted self-organisational functioning.

> Supposing on the other hand the boss, when talking to the worker, sees him hesitate. He wonders how the request is being received and decides to put aside his feelings of pressure. He says to the worker 'you are hesitating and I am wondering if this request is okay?' The worker sensing a different and more accepting tone from his boss, still feels unsure about saying he is overworked but decides to take the risk.

Here the mutual support processes are''read' and used differently, that is towards more open, risk-taking contactual functioning. Thus as two people regulate themselves in relationship to each the other they can read and use the ongoing activity of the other in a way that supports restricted (confluent functioning) or expanded self-organisational processes (contactual functioning).

Therapy

From confluence to contact:
In the Gestalt orientation therapy is not something that one person has or one person does to another. It is something that two (or more) people do together. The therapist and the client are all the time engaged in a mutual process that shifts and changes depend-

ing on what each of them does. As described above, any relationship is a mutual support process for either confluence or contactual functioning. In the therapeutic relationship, it is the special responsibility of the therapist to move towards a more and more contactual relationship. This means that the therapist, as well as being open to the client's experience and supporting the client to express this, has to be open to his own experience in the relationship, to take risks to say what is happening experientially for him and to speak of his experience of their relationship together. Through this interactive process the client is supported in discovering how he can organise differently in respect to another, in this case the therapist.

In the therapeutic relationship the focus is on moving towards more contactual functioning, ie. more openness, risk taking and awareness of choice in the here and now process. There are three aspects of engaging the client to support change i) attention to the self-organisation of the client, ii) awareness of the self-organising process of the therapist, iii) concern with the mutual relationship between therapist and client. Each of these is described in more detail within the sections that follow.

As we self-organise to maintain a stable sense of self we are creating our experiential existence – how we experience and perceive ourselves. Most of the time, this process continues without our paying any attention to it. This is confluent functioning. It is as if the self-organising process is 'on automatic' and goes by itself. This self-organising engages the environment and makes the unknown known. All our functioning is a working relationship between what is a familiar, known way of functioning and engaging the unknown. This is the contact process.

The aim of therapy is to gradually move from confluence (the known) to contact (the unknown). There are several aspects involved. These are i) Current ongoing experience, ii) Supporting the client to become aware of 'touching on' or 'pushing away' unfamiliar experiences. This includes the awareness of and use of shifts towards change. iii) Holding on to the familiar. These are not discrete processes, each is embedded in the other.

1. Touching current ongoing experience

The therapist starts each therapy session by focussing on current experience. The client comes into the session possibly expecting to talk about the problem. At the same time other experiences are also present, such as anxieties about coming to therapy, how he will be seen, what to expect etc. The therapist, rather than focusing initially on the 'problem', (which could possibly lead away from personal contact with the client) focuses on current experience perhaps by asking the client how he is feeling coming to therapy. He may then ask the client what he wants to get from the therapy session. The question 'what do you want' is open-ended and often leads to the client talking in terms of movement in therapy e.g. 'I would like to be less hot tempered'.

Here are two examples of touching on current experience at the start of a session.

T. Thank you for coming to see me. I'm aware I feel a little nervous as we meet for the first time. I am also looking forward to getting to know you more, and hoping we can work well together. I am wondering how you are feeling as we start the session together.

C. I'm not sure as I don't really know what to expect. Part of me really wants to be here and part of me is apprehensive.

T. Yes, I can appreciate these mixed feelings. Could you say more about wanting to be here and more about being apprehensive.

Another example

T. As you sit down I notice you sitting low in the chair and also that you are holding your breath. (Client shifts to a different position and seems to breathe a little easier).

C. Well, I realise I hadn't really sat down. I was a bit distracted as I came in.

T. You have shifted in the chair and you seem to be breathing easier.

C. Yes I feel more comfortable.

T. You said you were distracted as you came in. Do you still feel distracted?

C. No, I am beginning to settle down now and I am ready to go on.

As the client talks, as well as paying attention to what the client is saying, the therapist follows the changing and shifting self-organisational process of the client. He is interested in changes or shifts which are expressed in all aspects of functioning, for example, i) *auditory* – tone, pitch, content, speed of speech, emphasis and fluidity, ii) *thought processes* – clarity, confusion, number of thoughts, speed of thinking, images, iii) *feelings* – strength of feeling, range of feeling, connection of feeling to words e.g. strong words without appropriate feeling like being angry in a quiet voice, iv) *movement* – body movement, holding body still, movement towards / away from therapist, shift in eye movement, eye contact, shaking. It is of course not possible to focus on all of these aspects at any one time. The therapists look for two aspects in particular, one is the most striking *self-organisational* process of the client eg. talking rationale while looking at the floor, and the other is any *shifts and changes* eg. looking up and emphasising a word or phrase. Shifts and changes are functioning that may reflect emerging awareness of the unfamiliar.

The therapist will tell the client what stands out most striking to him as they talk together and how he experiences what he sees and hears. In doing this the therapist is supporting the client to appreciate their current functioning and to appreciate shifts and changes that may not be recognised.

C. I don't deserve to get paid for my work.
T. Your voice drops and you look down as you say that. I am wondering how you are feeling?
C. I am not sure, I don't feel anything.
T. That must be difficult to 'not feel anything'.
C. (*looking up at T.*) Well maybe I do feel something.
T. I noticed that you shifted there and were looking directly at me – and I'd like to know two things. How is it for you to look directly at me, and then, what you are feeling?
C. When I looked up at you I could see your interest in what I was saying and that felt good to me and now I am realising I really do feel down about my work and am wondering if I do deserve to be paid for it. (*This latter part is spoken with more strength of feeling*).

In this example as the therapist draws attention to current experience the contact process strengthened in terms of the clients own feelings and also in terms of his contact with the therapist.

To become aware of the current functioning it is necessary to move the focus away (step back) from the content if ideas or problems, to *how* the person is doing what they are doing. The therapist might ask the client 'how you are feeling at the moment as you are talking about ... ?', or 'what are you aware of at the moment?', or 'what is it like for you to talk about this?' These questions are really a means of letting the client know that the therapist is recognising his current experience and asking the client to direct his attention to it.

As well as stepping back, another way of bringing current experience into focus is to slow down the process in order to be aware of experience as it is happening. Slowing down provides a context for more awareness of how self is organizing and simultaneously allows self reorganise. The therapist can support the process of slowing, by slowing down himself and by suggesting to the client to slow down. The term 'slowing down' refers to the possibility of doing what you are doing e.g. talking and at the same time being aware of what it is like to be doing this. I slow down by being aware of how I am regulating my breathing and slowing it down a little. I may ask the client to go slower so I can follow him. This also creates the possibility that he too can follow his own process a little easier.

2. Awareness of and using shift towards change
One way the client keeps himself the same is by not noticing any shifts as they occur. Shifts are small pieces of behaviour which indicate that 'something else' is happening. As the client does not recognise these he is, in effect, avoiding the unfamiliar. The therapist can support the recognition of the unfamiliar by bringing these shifts to the attention of the client.

Client is talking about feeling in a 'one down' position and is sitting low down in the chair. As she talks she sits up a little and continues talking.

T. I see you sat up a little just then as you talked about your boss.
C. I was not aware of that, but now that you mention it, I did.
T. What are you aware of as you sit up?
C. I realise how angry I feel.
T. Do you want to say more about what that is like for you to realise that you are angry.
C. I don't usually let myself be angry or feel angry (*looks at therapist*).
T. I notice you looked at me at that moment – what is happening?

C. I guess you want to know how you feel with my anger.
T. I like it. You seem to have more energy.
C. Yes I can feel more of my own power as I let myself feel angry.

Bringing these active changes to the client's awareness enables him to discover how to recognise and appreciate how he functions and how he changes to allow other self-organisational possibilities to emerge.

Therapy is not only a matter of heightening or increasing the contact process. It also enables the client to be aware of shifts of activity that moves towards greater or lesser contact. This leads to the client having a greater choice and control in their ongoing functioning and in their lives. As noted in the introduction sometimes people know that they organise themselves differently at different times but don't have a specific sense of how they do this. Being aware of the shifts of activity leads to the discovery of how they are shifting and reorganising and being able to choose to do so.

3. Holding on to the familiar
As well as bringing the awareness of shifting process to the client's attention, sometimes the therapist may focus on how the client is holding back from change i.e. how he is holding on to the familiar. The holding often emerges strongly when some change is also emerging and the client pulls back from the change (possibly as he doesn't feel enough safety to explore the change). Examples which might indicate holding are: holding breath, stillness, swallowing back feeling and stopping crying.

Client is talking and the therapist sees something happening with the client. He sees some colour in her face and some swallowing. The client seems to hesitate and then go on talking. The therapist tells the client what he has observed.

C. Yes I can sense some feeling come up, like I am going to cry. I push it down.
T. Are you aware of how you push it down.
C. I hold my breath and I tell myself I shouldn't cry.
T. Can you say more about this.
C. There is a strong sense in me that I shouldn't cry, that it is being silly, that I have nothing to cry about.
T. How are you feeling now as you make these statements?
C. I realize I am not seeing my feelings as important.

By focussing on the holding, clients have an opportunity to get to know their current functioning and to experience its strength. It may also open the way to move on to something new.

Here and now

It was Perls who introduced the emphasis of 'here and now' experience into therapeutic work. While Kaplan and Kaplan also use 'here and now' experience their emphasis is different to that of Perls. In this section I describe Perls' use of the 'here and now' and contrast it with the direction Kaplan and Kaplan take using the concept of self-organisation.

In the introduction I described Perl's concept of projection, (putting onto others disowned aspects of self, retroflection, (putting onto self feelings or actions that a person wants to place outside) and introaction ('swallowing whole without criticism or integration). In all of these processes there are 'parts' of self that are disowned, such as the wish to be angry. In therapy Perls encouraged clients to act out these disowned parts by becoming each of the parts in turn and conversing with the other. Often these disowned parts took the form of polar opposites, for instance a person might be in touch with his ability to be soft. Any number of polarities are possible and each person develops his own. In therapy the purpose of the conversation between the parts was to allow 'each part to live to its fullest while at the same time making contact with its polar counterpart.' (Polster and Polster. 1974)

Perls used this idea of people disowning parts of themselves by incorporating it into one of his great innovations i.e. his theory and use of dreams in therapy. He saw all the characters and objects in a dream as 'parts' of the dreamer and in working with dreams Perls would suggest to the person to play out the various characters in the dream. The following exerpt from a dream therapy session illustrates this and also shows how Perls uses 'here and now' experience. The client is Meg and in her dream there is a dog and a rattlesnake.

P. Ah, now have an encounter between the dog and the rattlesnake.

M. You want me to play them?

P. Both. Sure. This is your dream. Every part is a part of your self.

M. I'm the dog. (*hesitantly*) Huh. Hello, rattlesnake. It sort of feels good with you wrapped around me.

P. Looking at the audience. Say this to somebody in the audience.

M. (*Laugh gently*) Hello, snake. It feels good to have you wrapped around me.

P. Close your eyes. Enter your body. What do you experience physically?

M. I'm trembling. Tensing.

P. Let this develop. Allow yourself to tremble and getting your feelings ... (*her whole body begins to move a little*). Yah. Let it happen. Can you dance it? Get up and dance it. Let your eyes open, just so that you stay in touch with your body, with what youwant to express physically ... Yah ... (*she walks, trembling and jerkily, almost staggering*) Now dance, rattlesnake ... (*she moves slowly and sinuously graceful*) ... How does it feel to be a rattlesnake now?

M. It's... sort of ... slowly ... quite ... quite aware, of anything getting too close.

P. Hm?

M. Quite aware of not letting anything getting too close, ready to strike.

P. Say this to us. 'If you come too close, I –'

M. If you come too close I will strike back!

P. I don't hear you. I don't believe you, yet.

M. If you come too close I will strike back!

P. Say this with your whole body.

M. If you come too close I will strike back!

P. How are your legs? I experience you as being somewhat wobbly.

M. Yeah.

P. That you don't really take a stand.

M. Yes I feel I'm ... kind of, in between being very strong and - if I let go, they're going to turn to rubber.

P. Okay, let them turn to rubber. (*her knees bend and wobble*) Again ... now try out how strong they are. Try out – hit the floor. Do anything. (*she stamps several times with one foot*) Yah, now the other. (*stamps other foot*) Now let them turn to rubber again (*she lets knees bend again*) More difficult now, isn't it?

M. Yeah.

P. Now say again the sentence, 'if you come too close ...' (*she makes the effort*) ... (*laughter*) ...
M. Come here.
P. How do you feel now?
M. Warm.
P. You feel somewhat more real?
M. Yeah. (Perls, 1969. It alics his)

This process of 'being' different 'parts' of self is essentially a technique of making present disowned parts. Also the concept of 'parts' of self give the impression of characteristics which are enduring over time. Kaplan and Kaplan's emphasis is on the *how* of ongoing functioning – how a person is continually organising self in ways that maintain avoiding or disowning and how to discover new ways to reorganise towards change. By appreciating how people are always creating their experiential existence, in the 'here and now' Kaplan and Kaplan, are able to work directly with the here and now, rather than using techniques of *bringing* elements in the present, which is essentially bypassing the ongoing process.

As well as working with disowned parts another way that Perls used the 'here and now' was to'bring the past into the present'. He would suggest that clients re-enact the past in the therapy session. For instance instead of the client talking *about* a relationship with a significant person he would suggest they would imagine the person to be in the room and talk *directly* to him or her and also take the part of the other person and respond. This technique is known as the 'empty chair' whereby the client imagines the person in an empty chair in front of them.

Kaplan and Kaplan's emphasis on current ongoing functioning opens the way to help the client discover how he engages in creating his experience in the here and now and how he can discover and explore changing how he organizes. In this approach, when a client talks about past experiences, the therapist focuses on *how* the activity of remembering these past experiences is affecting the person right now. For instance, if someone is talking about the experience of moving house as a child and the therapist notices some unrecognised feeling, he might ask what it is like to be talking and remembering these experiences. What he is focussing on here, is the person's experience of what it is like for them to be doing what they are doing. Another way of saying this is that the therapist is shifting the focus from the foreground of content, to the background Gestalt of current experience. Foreground and background together form the totality of the self-organising process. Bringing the attention of the client to both processes helps him to be aware of the totality of his current here and now experience. In the therapy the focus is often on the background experience of the present, bringing it into the foreground with such questions as: 'what is it like to be here'? 'how are you feeling as we start this session?' 'what are you experiencing as you talk about this?' 'I see some feeling in your face what is happening for you at the moment?' All these questions are in the present tense and serve to facilitate the client to focus on the 'here and now' experience.

When the client talks about past relationships, rather than enact them, the therapist will gradually bring the focus to how the client is currently organizing in the relationship to the therapist. Exploring directly with the therapist allows the process to be brought alive into an ongoing relationship. It brings the current background experience of how the relationship is being created into the foreground. In fact the very process of bringing the background experience into focus changes the relationship and changes how the client is organising himself in therapy.

Client is talking about how she finds it difficult to talk to her parents and how she becomes tense when she does so:

T. You appear to tense up as you are talking right now.
C. Yes, I am aware that my hands are tense, and my breathing is short.
T. You say you get tense talking to your parents. I am wondering how you are feeling as you talk to me now.
C. I feel tense talking to you now (*Client is quiet*).
T. (*After client is quiet for a while*) What is happening now?
C. I realise I relax more when I am quiet but even as I think about saying something to you I begin to tense up. (*Client puts her head back on the chair and seems to relax*)
T. I am wondering if you are relaxing a little as you put your head back.
C. Yes I do, but as soon as you speak or even start to speak, I tense up again.

T. So, here with me the most comfortable place for you is to be quiet. As soon as you think about talking you feel tense and you also feel tense as I speak.
C. Yes, that's right. (*Client is quiet again*)
T. How are you as you are aware of this?
C. I feel sad. I am also aware that that's exactly how it is with my parents. The only comfortable place for me is to be quiet.
T. I'm aware that as we are talking you seem easier and that you seem more relaxed now with me.
C. Just getting in touch with what's happening has helped. I am also finding it easier as you talk. Not so afraid.

In the above example the therapist asks the client what is happening for him in relationship to the therapist. It is important to note that the starting point can also be the other way round i.e. with the therapist highlighting what is happening for him in relationship to the client. This reflects the therapists current or here and now, experience of the relationship and helps open background experience in both people. If the therapist is feeling sad, bored, excited, angry etc. it may be that there is also something of that going on for the client as well. As the therapist takes the risk to bring out his experience it gives the therapist and client the opportunity of exploring it together.

Client is talking about not making friends and is giving examples of various social situations.

The therapist notices that as he is listening to the client he is holding his breath and feeling a little tense. He also becomes aware that his attention is wandering and he is feeling bored. He speaks to the client.
T. I notice that as you talk, I am holding my breath and feeling very tense. I would like to say something to you and at the same time I feel unsure about interrupting you. (*Client looks more directly at the therapist*)
T. As you look more directly I feel easier, like I sense your interest. As you were talking I noticed my attention wandering and that I was feeling bored. How are you with what I am say ing?
C. Now that you say it, I often have the feeling I am boring people.

As the therapist says what is happening for him it creates a relationship that supports contact, openness, and risk taking, rather than a mutually confluent system, (in this instance of two people being bored). Therapist openness also enables the therapist to have his own experience, separate to the client, while at the same time being touched and affected by the client.

The therapist is not a machine, but a real person with feelings, anxieties, uncertainties, etc. Trying to achieve real person to person contact is the essence of therapy. The more the therapist self-organises in a restricted way say as 'professional therapist' the more the client will be supported to stay with his own self-organisation of 'client'. The more the therapist says what is happening for him or her the more the client will feel supported to be aware and to say how he experiences what is happening. Also, the client will be making assumptions about the therapist anyway, so it is just as well that the therapist says in an active way what he is thinking, feeling and doing, thus giving the client information against which to compare his own assumptions.

Working with process themes

In therapy, the client can discover how he organizes himself in a relationship, how to organise differently and to be aware of the choices he makes in this process.

The therapist will work with whatever emerges during the sessions. He won't have any preset plan of what to cover or do. Each session stands in its own right and the starting point for each session is how the client is organising himself in the here and now. As the sessions progresses, a 'process theme' may emerge which can then become the focus for how the person is functioning and experiencing. A process theme is an aspect of unfamiliar functioning which is emerging and is usually set against some familiar functioning. In the second last example the process theme was 'being quiet' as against 'talking and listening'. Here is another example.

Client is scrunched up, withdrawn, in chair.

T. I am noticing you scrunched up in the chair (Client looks up at therapist)

T. As I was noticing you in the chair I felt some heartfelt feelings towards you and I felt warm towards you, but as I saw you scrunched up I wondered how you would take it from me. As you look up now I feel different, like there is a possibility of you taking the warmth. (*Client is thoughtful*)

T. How are you with me saying, I felt warm towards you.

C. I feel a little easier, but I realise I don't let the warmth in from others. I feel I can do everything on my own. It is hurt I feel from others not warmth.

T. With me you said you felt a little easier as I said I felt warmth towards you. How did you let it in from me.

C. I don't know. I'm not sure I wish I could see the warmth from others, but how do you know it's here?

At this point the client is acknowledging the process theme – in this instance taking warmth (unfamiliar) as against taking hurt (familiar). As the client acknowledges the theme, the therapist can make suggestions that give the client time, space and permission to further explore the unfamiliar functioning – how they are doing it and what it is like to do it. Continuing the example:

T. Perhaps the way to see it is to look. Try looking at me to see if you can see the warmth, and if so, what happens.

This, then, is the start of the client actively trying out something new, in the present, to experience what happens.

C. (*looks*) I can see the warmth on your face as you look.

T. Can you be more specific as to how you see it.

C. Your eyes, I see it in your eyes and slight smile. You look relaxed.

T. As you see the warmth are you aware of anything else that is happening for you.

C. Yes I can feel it inside. I feel touched.

T. Yes I can see that and I also feel touched as you look at me. How did you allow the warmth in?

C. I'm not sure. I think I relaxed a little.

T. What is it like for you to take it in and feel touched.

C. I feel uncomfortable and a little angry with you. I want to push you away.

T. So as you feel the warmth from me there is also a push away … Try looking again and see what happens. (*Client looks longer then looks away thinking hard*)

T. What's happening?

C. As I look at you and feel the warmth two images quickly come strongly to mind. One is of me in my family fighting over food and another is of how I push away my parents as they express warmth towards me. Both those images come very strongly. (*Client then sobs*)

T. The images, in a way, are right now blocking out the warmth from me.

C. (*Sobbing*) Yes, and that's how it is with my parents, I push their warmth away. (*Client goes on then to talk about how although she has a close relationship with her parents. She blocks any warmth from them*)

T. I sense quite a lot of warmth here now between us as we talk. Do you feel it?

C. Yes. As I feel the warmth I get some comfort from it.

By maintaining the focus on what is happening between them, the therapist is supporting the client to appreciate how she is allowing herself to change in the here and now. Although this process needs more work on how the client experiences warmth from others and her resistance to it, a change has occurred in that she has experienced, and knows how she has experienced, taking warmth and comfort from someone else.

Integrating change

Therapy is a process of moving from the familiar (confluence) to the unfamiliar (contact). The familiar, even though it may be painful, is known and stable and easier to cope with than the unfamiliar, which may be uncertain and frightening. For a person to make such a change involves risking and for this he needs support. There is a positive correlation between risk taking and experiencing support ie. the more supportive contact that is given and received the greater the potential for risk taking in therapy.

The challenge for the therapist is to facilitate the client to support himself to take risks in moving from the familiar to exploring, experiencing and integrating the unfamiliar. The therapists attempts to gauge the level of support the client is feeling and to gauge the edge of risk-taking. The risk-taking should not be so small that the client is being supported to stay the same and yet not so great that the client has no familiar base from which to experience the change. One reason that therapy seems to go slowly is that the focus is on what may appear to be very small segments of experience. In effect slowness helps integrate change and helps the person know these changes to be choices he can make. At the end of the therapy session some time is spent looking back on the session in order to highlight what has happened and to support the process of integration and change.

Conclusion

I have described how the combination of Gestalt and Self-organisation theory can be applied in therapeutic work with individuals. The emphasis on mutual support processes between two people also means that the therapy can be applied in work with families and with groups. Here the focus is on how the processes between people are mutually supporting familiar, rigid self-organisational or supporting, the recognition, exploration and integration of unfamiliar self-organisations.

References

Dell, P.F., (1985), Understanding Bateson and Maturana, Toward a biological foundation for the Social Sciences, *Journal of Marital and Family Therapy* 11 (1), 1-20.

Dalenoort, G.J. Ed., *The Paradigm of Self-Organisation* (Gordon and Breach Science Publishers, 1989).

Kapland M. and Kaplan N.R., The Self-Organisation of Human Psychological Functioning, *Behavioural Science,* Vol. 36 1991 p 161-178.

Kaplan, M., Kaplan N.R. and Serok, S., Gestalt therapy's theory of experiential organisation and mutual support processes in psychotherapy and supervision. *Psychotherapy* Vol. 22 1985 No. 4

Page, F. and Parlett M., *Gestalt Therapy from Individual Therapy, a Handbook,* Wendy Drynan (ed) (Open University, 1990).

Perls, F. S., *The Gestalt Approach and Eyewitness to Therapy,* (Palo Alto: Science and Behaviour Books, 1973) p 15-17.

Perls, F.S., (1969) *Gestalt Therapy Verbatim* (Real People Press) p 178-180.

Perls, F.S., Hefferline, R. and Goodman, P. (1951) *Gestalt Therapy, Excitement and growth in the Human Personality* (New York: Delta).

Polster, E., and Polster, M., (1973) *Gestalt Therapy Integrated: Contours of theory and practice* (New York: Brunner mazel) p. 68

Further Reading

Fagan, J. and Shepherd, I., (eds), *Gestalt Therapy: Theory, Techniques, Applications* (Harper and Row, 1970).

Kaplan M.L. and Kaplan N.R., (1982), 'Organisation of experience among family members in the immediate present: A Gestalt/Systems integration' in *Journal of Marital and Family Therapy,* 8, p 5-14.

Kaplan M.L. and Kaplan N.R., (1987), 'Processes of Experiental Organization in Individual and Family systems' in *Psychotherapy,* Vol 24/Fall 561-569.

Oaklander, V., Windows to our Children (Moab, Utah: Real People Press, 1978).

Passons, W.R., *Gestalt Approaches in Counselling* (Holt, Rinehart, Winston).

Perls, F. Hefferline R. and Goodman, P., *Gestalt Therapy: Excitement and Growth in the Human Personality* (New York: Delta, 1951).

Perls, F., *The Gestalt Approach and Eyewitness to Therapy* (New York: Science and Behaviour, 1973).

Polster, E. and Polster M., *Gestalt Therapy Integrated: Contours of Theory and Practice* (New York: Brunner Mazel, 1973).

Stevans, B., *Don't Push the River* (Real People Press, 1970).

Stevens, J.O., *Awareness, Exploring, Experimenting, Experiencing* (Real People Press, 1971).

Stevens, J. E. (ed), *Gestalt Is* (Real People Press, 1975).

CHAPTER 9

The Person-Centred Approach

Rachel Graham

This above all: to thine own self be true,
And it must follow as the night the day
Thou canst not then be false to any man.

Shakespeare (Hamlet. Act 1, Scene 3.)

Personal note

My involvement in the Person-Centred Approach began when Carl Rogers visited Ireland in 1985 for a ten-day workshop on the subject of Cross-Cultural Communication. The workshop had approximately two hundred participants from all over Europe and from the USA. My first experience of being in a group of that size was extremely disorientating and the first two days seemed chaotic, because decisions about the format of the workshop were made by the whole group, an example of real democracy at work! I found this irritating, frustrating, a waste of time, occasionally interesting, infuriating, fascinating and at times I found myself looking at this curious mix of feelings in myself and wondering if I was learning something important.

Many people left in disgust over the lack of structure and organised input from the facilitators in those first two days. I still have a considerable amount of sympathy with their action. However, after two days the group succeeded in dividing itself up into small groups of about ten people each, with one facilitator per group. This was my first experience of being a member of an encounter group and it felt to me like entering another world.

I had been struggling hard to try to regain a sense of control in my life after separating from my husband. Here, suddenly, was a place where I felt listened to without being judged, where I could be a 'separated wife' without feeling labelled as 'bad' and allow myself to experience what being separated really felt like. Here, too, I listened to others struggling with their fears, their sense of isolation and loneliness, their desires and hopes. I began to feel intimate with these people who had shared so much of themselves, and to gain a sense of what a relationship could be when the fear of being judged or ignored as a person was no longer present. I felt excited. At the end of the ten days, two exhausted facilitators took refuge in my house and when I discovered that they ran a course in the Person-Centred Approach in London, I enrolled immediately.

Over the next two years I found myself accepted and listened to in a profound way. A surprising result of this was the feeling of expansion and liberation that accompanied this acceptance. I began to believe in myself, to have a sense of self-acceptance. My fellow participants, who at the beginning of the course had seemed to me a rather unattractive bunch, became well-known to me, many remain good friends. We have been together with our fears, our loneliness, our insecurities, our sadnesses, our anger, our laughter, our joys and our strengths, and I can accept and respect them exactly as they are.

Thus I became a Person-Centred therapist because the nonjudgemental, accepting and listening attitudes that are characteristic of the Person-Centred Approach are important for me. And because I had experienced their healing power I wanted others to be given that opportunity to discover new strengths in themselves and to explore what they wanted out of life.

In this chapter I have referred to the therapist as 'she' and most of the clients as 'he', both because I am a female therapist and because it seems to make for greater clarity to have some degree of consistency. It is not intended to be in any way sexist. I have also generally used the term 'therapy' or 'psychotherapy' rather than 'counselling', but I do not regard the two as distinct and separate processes. 'Psychotherapy' is often thought of as a longer and deeper process than 'counselling'. To me the process is, to a large extent determined by the client, it may be short, as short as one session very occasionally, or it may last as long as two to three years.

The development of the Person-Centred Approach

The most notable characteristic of the Person-Centred Approach is the emphasis it places on the experiential world of the person and his or her inherent capacity to change and develop.

The Person-Centred Approach originated with the American psychologist, Dr Carl Rogers in the 1940s. Carl Rogers died in 1987 leaving behind him a long, productive career whose influence has extended well beyond therapy into education, social work, parenting and intimate relationships, industry, management and cross-cultural communication. He first began to develop his own style of therapy in the 1940s when, as a result of his personal experiences in counselling, he began to believe that the dominant psychiatric and psychodynamic models of therapy involved too many preconceptions of the patient and of what was good for him. He concluded that these labelling and often directive (in his view) forms of therapy were not generally constructive for the patient. He learnt to distrust expert diagnosis or 'labelling' of a patient and to trust instead that the patient would be able, with help, to define his or her own problem and to change in a positive direction.

For example, if a client comes in saying she is depressed, instead of merely labelling the person a 'depressive' Rogers would warmly welcome the client, try to enter and explore the client's world with her, enabling her to develop an understanding of herself and to begin to make choices and changes for herself. Thus 'nondirective' counselling came into being. Rogers adopted the word 'client' instead of 'patient' to highlight the element of choice and freedom on the part of the 'client' and that it was a non-medical, non-manipulative form of counselling.

'Non-directive' counselling emphasised the capacity and resources of the 'client' for self-understanding, self-improvement and self-directed change. To begin with, Rogers focused on the importance of deep, attentive listening on the part of the therapist in promoting change. He also felt that the therapist should 'reflect the feelings' of the client back to him, as if she was holding a mirror up to the client to enable him to see and understand more clearly what he was experiencing. Thus the therapist attempts to put her own judgements to one side and to accurately convey her understanding of the client's personal world.

As far back as 1942, Rogers introduced tape recording into the therapeutic process in order to test and develop his theory further. He was the first therapist to open up the therapy hour to the scrutiny of others. A strong believer in a rigorous scientific approach to therapy, he exhibited a willingness to investigate the conditions that he claimed were necessary to promote therapeutic change.

Despite his efforts to promote a more scientific approach to therapy, he was frequently parodied by critics implying that the therapist sat passively nodding or saying 'Mmm-mmm' or that 'reflection' consisted merely of the technique of reflecting back the feelings of the client or, worse still, of merely parroting his or her last phrase. This is still a fairly commonly heard criticism, but it is based on a gross misunderstanding of the theory. These criticisms impelled Rogers to further clarify and refine his approach. He pointed out that empathic listening required the ability to enter into another's world and understand it as if you were that person, and that 'reflection' represents the therapist's attempt to accurately convey that understanding of the client's world. In later years he regretted ever having used the term 'reflection' (1986 p.127, *Rogers Reader)* preferring either 'testing understandings' or 'checking perceptions' as more accurate terms for the therapist's task of capturing the client's meaning.

As his research developed and knowledge expanded, the focus shifted toward the internal, phenomenological world of the client and the term client-centred therapy was adopted. Rogers argued that the human being, like any biological organism, has a natural tendency to develop in the fullest possible way within the constraints of the environment. Just as a plant will seek out the light, so, in an analogous way, will a human being seek the opportunity to grow and develop in a positive direction. So the ultimate goal of therapy or 'the goal of social evolution' was, according to Rogers a 'fully functioning person'.

In order to become 'fully functioning' a person must experience the right facilitative conditions. These conditions are that the therapist should be a real person, not hiding behind her professional status, be accepting of the client, and be sensitive and understanding of the client's experience. The more that these qualities are realised, the more successful the outcome is likely to be for the client.

This theory was elaborated and extended into the realm of human relationships and personality theory. In 1961 Rogers published his now classic text *On Becoming a Person.* It was originally intended primarily for professionals but it turned out to have huge general appeal. His popularity probably peaked in the late 1960s and the 1970s as his writing and influence expanded into new areas. His books covered the following topics: Education: *Freedom to Learn* (1969), relationships: *Becoming Partners: Marriage and Its Alternatives* (1973), intensive personal growth groups: *Carl Rogers on Encounter Groups,* and politics: *Carl Rogers on Personal Power* (1977). With the recognition that his work had many applications beyond the therapeutic encounter, Rogers adopted the title 'Person-Centred Approach' in preference to client-centred therapy, although many practitioners throughout the world continue to define themselves as 'client-centred.' To Rogers, the Person-Centred Approach was a philosophy of life and 'a way of being' in every day life, not merely an attitude to practice in the therapy room.

Carl Rogers' influence was immense. He was a leader in the Humanistic psychology movement, which became known as the 'third force' (the other two being Behaviourism and Psychoanalysis); and in 1963 he helped to found the Association for Humanistic Psychology. He was also president of the American Psychological Association. His impact was probably more profound in the United States of America than it has been in this country or the rest of Europe. Nevertheless there are Person-Centred networks all over the world.

Rogers carried on actively participating in groups and writing until his death in 1987. Personally a shy, quiet man, he never sought publicity and actively declined a 'guru' role, despite pressure from many followers. This attitude can be seen as an integral part of his philosophy according to which mutual respect and equality in relationships are paramount. His optimism and hope for the future seemed unshakeable, many would add unrealistic. Certainly his initial and overt influence is waning and has been for some time. In the pressurised world of today, the quick fix directed by an 'expert' may be a more popular option than the truly democractic approach of Rogers. However new variations on Rogers' ideas seem to be increasingly appreciated in the helping professions, e.g. 'gentle'[1] teaching with the mentally handicapped. And it seems as though there is a recognition of the fact that the more extreme forms of behavioural intervention, with little or no attempt to consult the recipient, just do not work. Whether this form of democratic person-centred relating will spread into the wider political arena, as Rogers had hoped, remains doubtful.

Philosophy

Rogers' philosophy grew gradually out of his experience with clients in therapy and in groups, from watching them struggle to achieve a sense of meaning in their lives. He came to have a conviction that if people are given a space, where they can experience freedom from the judgements and expectations of others, they can come to terms with their humanity in a constructive way. He believed that human nature was basically trustworthy and *constructive* rather than destructive. He had a far more optimistic view than most psychologists or Christians in the Western world. From Freudian pessimism to original sin, he challenged the traditional view of the human being as a creature that needs to be kept under strict control.

He argued that any psychotherapy has some value orientation and a view of human nature, whether this is implied or explicit. The preference in Person-Centred therapy is that these values are made explicit. So the human being is seen as inherently:

> positive, forward-moving, constructive, realistic and trustworthy. (*Rogers Reader*, p.403)

This is not just simple naïvety on Rogers' part. He genuinely believed, after many years of experience of clients in therapy, that he could see nothing he would call destructive in a person's basic nature. In the therapeutic relationship the therapist provides, as far as it is possible to provide, a safe, non-threatening, accepting atmosphere. Here people may express all kinds of violent feelings, bitter hatreds, anger, rage, sorrow, bizzarre or anti-social desires.

As these 'bad' feelings come out, at first there is a sense of relief: 'Someone has heard these awful things about me and is still listening and doesn't seem to be angry or upset with me,' followed by an acceptance, 'Yes, these feelings do exist in me and they're really pretty normal,' then a shift toward a more positive focus and a sense of moving on, 'I want to live for today, not spend the time thinking about my problems.' Thus, when we are allowed to express ourselves most fully, to acknowledge our 'bad' feelings as well as our 'good' feelings, we begin to gain a sense of balance in our lives and our fear of losing control lessens its grip.

If we have grown up in a family where it was not permitted to express some or any of these 'bad' feelings, we learn to fear, repress or deny them in order to feel loved or liked. Rogers argues that, when we allow ourselves to become aware of and express these feelings, fear diminishes and we become increasingly free to express and develop ourselves more fully.

There is evidence that the views a therapist holds may well influence the outcome of her clients in therapy (see Weakland, Fisch, Watzlawick & Bodin 1974). If a therapist learns to accept and trust her own nature, in the way Rogers appears to have trusted his, it seems likely that this might facilitate her clients in learning to trust themselves. A therapist who is convinced that she knows best what is good for the client is not likely to encourage the development of self-responsibility. Conversely a therapist who believes that the client knows best what he needs, is likely to nurture that self-trust, e.g. Cl: 'I don't know what to do. My life is a total mess. I can't go out without feeling terrified. Can you help me?' Replies to this initial plea for help could vary immensly. The appeal is basically for the expert to 'make it better', and is similar to that of a patient to his doctor. However if the therapist then makes an expert pronouncement such as 'Yes, I can help you. We have a programme I can guide you through which will decrease your fear,' the responsibility for change is immediately taken by the therapist.

The person-centred therapist would not take this approach. Rather she would listen carefully to try to understand the personal experience of the client. Her response might be more along the lines of, 'You are feeling that your life is chaotic and you can barely even cope with going out. It's hard to know what to do but you would really like some help.' This response may not, on paper, seem as immediately helpful as the first one, but it is geared toward checking out the therapist's understanding of what the client has said and keeping the sense of responsiblity for what is going on with the client. This is important in maintaining a more equal balance of power in the relationship. The confirmation and support given by the therapist gives the client space to begin to work out his own solutions.

Toward the end of his life, Rogers paid increasing attention to the intuitive side of himself and to mystical experience. Aspects of Zen thinking, with its emphasis on personal experience and learning, were particularly appealing to him and he was fond of quoting Lao-Tse. One particular sentence sums up Rogers' philosophy very succinctly:

> If I keep from imposing on people, they become themselves.

What is therapy like?

First Session and Clients' Expectations

A client deciding on therapy or counselling for the first time will usually be very unsure of what to expect. She or he may have learnt about a therapist from a variety of different sources, such as the recommendation of a friend, the family doctor or from another therapist. Some clients will be more prepared than others, but it is a difficult step to take, one which many people still feel rather ashamed of, and nearly everyone feels anxious and vulnerable when they first knock on a therapist's door. Previous experience of professional helpers can sometimes have left the client feeling uncomfortable, intimidated and powerless. White coats, big desks, closed doors, distant buzzers, unwelcoming waiting areas and abrupt manners can all contribute to and heighten anxiety. I do my best to allay these anxieties immediately. The first contact is often by telephone and a friendly voice can help calm a client's more extreme fears.

When a client arrives for his first appointment the balance of power is all on my side, I know the process whereas he is often not only nervous about his difficulties but has little idea of what is going to happen, so it is important to do as much as possible to make him feel at ease. Meeting him at the door, warmly introducing myself and shaking hands are all ways I can show respect for the client as a person. I like to arrange the seating so that I am on the same level as my client (i.e. one chair should be much the same height as the other) and there is no large desk or any barrier between the two of us. The seats should be near enough so that touch is possible but not too near that it feels threatening to the client. (Some clients may require more distance at first in order to feel safe.) The room should be comfortable and welcoming.

Sometimes a client will begin to talk immediately, in which case I would aim to listen empathically, not interrupting or imposing a structure, taking my lead from the client. If, on the other hand, the client is quiet and looking a bit lost, I might start with something like, 'Well, we have about an hour together. What brings you here?' The response that follows will often make clear some of the client's expectations. If he says, 'I've tried everything. I've been from doctor to doctor and they haven't helped me. The last doctor I went to wasn't much good either but he suggested I come to you. So here I am, what can you do?' It is immediately clear that he expects the therapist to 'do' something for him and that he looks to her to supply a solution.

This is quite a common and reasonable expectation, if it is based on the medical model of physical care. So my response should try to show the client that this situation is different. In this case, he seems to have tried a number of different avenues and not found any helpful. It is therefore particularly important for the therapist not to mislead the client and to be 'congruent' or honest about her beliefs. A response along the lines of, 'You've been to a lot of places looking for help and haven't got much satisfaction. And you are wondering, without much hope perhaps, if I can help', shifts the focus onto looking at his feelings rather than trying to supply a quick solution.

Therapy Contract

Sorting out the therapy contract needs to be done at the first session. Any contract will have a number of external constraints, such as finance, the rules of the office or institution that the therapist might work for, the availability of the client and the therapist. I do not generally work to a rigid time frame, prefering to talk with each individual client to work out a mutually agreed upon contract. Some clients choose a time limited agreement, and there is a lot to recommend this since it can facilitate change. It might also allay a client's anxiety about being 'taken for a ride' by a therapist greedy for money. If a time frame is agreed on, it remains something that can be changed and the 'f1nal' session is an assessment of progress, after which a new contract can be negotiated or the client can decide to stop. Open-ended contracts might also benefit from an occasional 'review' session to assess progress. I try to make it clear that it is ultimately the client's responsibility to decide on the nature of the contract and on whether to continue therapy or not.

I generally begin with weekly sessions of about fifty minutes to an hour. This seems to be the norm. If a client comes a long way, I can arrange for a longer session at less frequent intervals. Toward the end of therapy, clients quite often like to meet less frequently, fortnightly for example. As with the length of contracts, the frequency and the length of time of each session can vary, occas-ionally a two-three hour session can be helpful.

The New Client

The person who enters therapy for the first time is often someone whose sense of self-confidence and worth as a person has been damaged, sometimes very deeply. This poor 'self-concept' is acquired, usually over a long period of time, through feedback from people you need or love in your life. All kinds of people set themselves up as experts when it comes to human behaviour: parents, teachers, priests, colleagues, friends, brothers and sisters, will often readily advise you on what you should be doing. It is easy to begin to feel that other people know better than you what you should do with your life. It is pretty common to find thoughts such as 'I should go to college', 'I should stay in this job, it's secure', 'I should get married', 'I should stay with my husband/wife', 'I should not be angry with my parents'. A sense of futility and despair at ever being able to fulfil all these expectations can set in.

Karen Horney[2] once referred to these feelings as 'the tyranny of the should'. Your need for love, approval and affection means that you try hard to please the important people in your life, and in this process your sense of self-worth can be lost. In Rogers' terminology, you have lost a sense of your 'organismic self' – that is a basic reliance upon your *own experience.* This 'organismic' self is naturally trustworthy and, left to itself, it will strive toward constructive growth and life enhancement. Rogers believed that all human beings are born with this 'self-actualising' tendency to fulfil their true potential, but the demands of people and the environment interfere with this to a greater or lesser extent.

Thus, a client who is in a state of 'incongruence' is no longer in close touch with his own deep, organismic experience but has been trying to live up to what he *should* be. This discrepancy between what he is aware of and what he might be experiencing at a deeper, denied level, causes anxiety. He is trying to live up to an 'ideal' self based on the expectations of others which he has incorporated into his self-concept, while denying his 'real' or 'organismic' self. For example, a man who had seen himself as a dutiful son felt he owed his parents a lot, and that he must therefore always feel loving toward them. As he opened up to his feelings, he discovered that he felt very angry with them and he began to see himself as a person who can admit to angry feelings. Admitting to his anger enabled him to understand that he also loved his parents deeply.

'Softer' feelings can also be pushed down out of awareness. A client who had been accused by his brothers and friends of being a 'sissy' found it hard to allow his warmth and affection to surface for fear of being ridiculed. For a long time he had firmly believed that his strength lay in being alone. Yet he was haunted by a feeling of loneliness, of being separated from people by a 'glass wall', of being an outsider and of not fitting in. He wanted to please people but didn't know how to and was afraid of being rejected. As therapy progressed he gradually felt safer to explore these feelings and to allow them to surface, discovering that he was no longer ridiculed or rejected, he gained in confidence. He finally began to find a sense of strength and power in trusting his 'soft' side that he had previously repressed. He now trusted in his own judgement, his 'real'or 'organismic' self rather than a self that he 'should' be, composed of the expectations or desires of others.

Rogers refers to these 'ideals' adopted by the client as 'conditions of worth', that is conditions that are imposed upon you by well-meaning others. So that you internalise the idea that if, for example, you are 'quiet,' 'affectionate,' 'good', 'studious,' 'tough,' or 'macho', you will be respected, loved and cared for. A client who has been trying to live up to these 'ideals' imbibed from family, people in authority and assorted 'experts', will often come to a therapist looking for yet more advice. The person-centred therapist will try not to fall into the trap of offering it, because it would go against the basic premise that a client has within himself the resources to find a way forward. I want to offer the kind of relationship in which the client feels safe to explore his feelings and find them accepted. I do this by trying my best to provide the three conditions described below.

Therapist Attitudes

The core of Roger's theory centres around what he calls three 'necessary and sufficient conditions' for successful therapy to occur. It is the responsibility of the therapist to provide these conditions, which are:

1. 'Empathy' – the ability to enter into the client's personal world and to convey her understanding accurately to the client so that he feels truly understood.
2. 'Unconditional Positive Regard' – an acceptance of the person as a human being who is worthy of being valued no matter how they have behaved or how they are behaving.
3. 'Congruence' – genuineness, no hiding behind a professional role, being fully present as a whole person.

If all three of these conditions are present in the therapist, along with a minimal amount of receptivity on the part of the client, then according to Rogers, growth and change will occur in the client While these three necessary qualities of the therapist sound simple and easy to grasp, appearances are deceptive, and it represents an ideal toward which I struggle. I try to be accepting, to see the full humanity of each person in front of me, to empathise sensitively and not to be afraid of my own feelings and impulses. Each time I am with a client, the degree to which I succeed in doing this will play a major part in determining how successful the therapy is.

At the beginning of a therapeutic relationship, the position taken by the client can vary widely; while one may be very ready to make changes, another may find it very difficult to accept that he has to take personal responsibility for the changes that he desires, the hope for a magic formula dies hard.

Conor had thought about coming for at least six months, but hadn't felt ready. At the first session he was so intent and clear about the changes he wanted to make that my task as a therapist was minimal and the client seemed to be changing so fast that it was hard for me to keep up with him. My task at this stage was mainly that of accepting, clarifying and verifying what was happening, as the client had already taken full responsibility for the changes. It seems to me that in this situation I would have had to have been an extremely clumsy therapist to stop the process of change.

Empathy

Empathy is a process whereby the therapist chooses to accompany the client into his perceptual world, to experience alongside him his way of seeing things, his understandings and personal meanings. Feeling at home in this world of the client involves leaving aside your own judgements, perceptions and experience and being sensitive to the moment by moment changes, to the fear, the anger and the confusion of the client as it emerges. If I succeed in this I can sometimes sense meanings of which the client is barely aware. I can then communicate back to the client my sense of his world, but whereas he is uncertain and fearful, I can be a more confident companion on his journey.

I need to continue checking with the client that my responses are accurate and to be sensitive to any misperceptions on my part. It is important that I do not 'get lost' in the client's world. Despite the fact that I can experience much of what the client is feeling, it is essential that I can return to my own frame of reference. To protect myself from being overwhelmed I must feel secure in myself. This is necessary for the client's sense of confidence in the ther-apist because if the client is feeling fearful, isolated or insecure, he must have the security of knowing that the therapist remains calm and rational.

An empathic attitude is not easily captured in a couple of responses because it is part of the whole process and can build on past understandings between therapist and client. Empathy training has often been rather limited and reduced in some therapy training courses to little more than a technique by focusing trainees on an isolated anecdote in a book and requiring a written response to this anecdote which 'reflects the feeling.' This represents a superficial understanding of the empathic process in therapy. The nature of the client's response will reveal the level of empathy that has been achieved, If the client feels understood it has an impact on the process, often moving it to a deeper level.

A high level of empathy is hard to achieve..Research has shown that many therapists fail to reach even a moderate degree of empathy with their clients. Yet it has also been shown to be a powerful indicator of a positive outcome to therapy. When the therapist can sustain only a very low level of empathy, however, it can sometimes result in a setback for the client. Although, in contrast to this finding, other studies indicate that the *intent* to be empathic on the part of the therapist can be enough to facilitate a positive change in a client. This suggests that the client's perception of the trustworthiness of the therapist is an important part of the process of therapy.

An example might help to illustrate different levels of empathic responses. (From low to higher levels of response.)

Cl: I don't want to stay on at college, but my parents think I must get a degree and then a job. I want to be free and feckless. I know I need to have a career, but I just don't feel ready, I don't know what I want to do.

1. You should get a degree.
2. Your parents are pressurising you to finish your degree.
3. There seems to be a feeling stemming from your parents that you really ought to finish this degree, yet it doesn't give you the time or the space to find out what you really want out of life.

This third response led to an exploration of his need to develop himself and to know himself better, to work out what his values were, as distinct from his parents' values.

An accurate empathic response by the therapist does seem to encourage a deeper exploration on the part of the client. I have also found it beneficial to couch my reply in a tentative and open-ended way. This way of responding is not only a means of checking that I am on the right track, but also of focusing the client on what might be more to the edge of his awareness. Often it is these feelings, lying just beneath the surface, that when brought to light result in huge changes in the way a client views particular issues.

Body language can often give a strong clue as to what is going on at a deep level. A client can be smiling and laughing but avoiding your eyes. He may be talking about deep pain while smiling. He may sound perfectly calm but hold out a tight fist. If a therapist is immersed in the empathic process, this includes a body awareness and an overall sense of the issues, not merely attention to the words. Is this empathic quality natural? Are we born with it or do we learn it? All children grow up with an abilty to judge their parents' or caregivers' moods and reactions and by the time they are adults this sensitivity to others is generally an integral part of us.

Using this sensitivity empathically is a choice we can make. Research on empathy indicates that it is largely a learned ability. Training can increase accurate empathy and it is more commonly seen in experienced counsellors.

Empathy can be a volatile quality and personal issues belonging to the therapist can easily interfere with the process. It is, for this reason, particularly important for me to be very self-aware and attentive to issues that might block my ability to empathise. Blocks can include any major issue that is troubling me outside of the session, or my own needs or fears arising in the session. Even the 'need to be helpful' can sometimes be a block to staying with the client in the present moment. Preconceived ideas about what 'should happen' or what the client will feel in his or her particular position can prove to be a harmful distraction. Because it is practically impossible for the therapist to keep fully aware of all these potential blocks, it is important to get some form of outside supervision. As I have become more self-aware and confident, I am beginning to trust myself more. This leaves me freer to be empathic without fear.

Unconditional Positive Regard

Unconditional positive regard can be defined as an attitude of acceptance of the full humanity of the client and a trust in the innate potential of each client. I try to consistently maintain this attitude regardless of a client's behaviour.

It is this 'regardless of the client's behaviour' that often causes problems for people new to this approach. It can be extremely difficult to maintain a positive attitude to a person who I find intimidating, who is expressing contempt and hatred for everyone he or she works with, or who is always utterly depressed and self-deprecating. A lot of effort in the Person-Centred learning programmes go into exploring and challenging the underlying prejudices and fears of trainee therapists. This should continue for the practicing therapist in ongoing supervision or groupwork. This exploration is part of the process of learning to become self-accepting, to tolerate and openly admit to difficult private feelings.

Unless we accept what we are we cannot change. This applies to both the therapist and the client. In my training, for example, I was quite fearful of men being angry with me, and felt threatened, angry and rejecting in return. This is still a difficult issue for me but one of which I am more aware and significantly less frightened. By acknowledging these fears, I have become more accepting of them in myself and therefore more able to acknowledge difficulties when they occur, and to accept a client who is angry. This accepting attitude does not mean that I like or approve of a client's worst behaviour, but that despite his behaviour I continue to value him and to see him as someone with potential to change and develop. As a therapist I do not have the role of approving or disapproving of a client's feelings, I merely accept that these feelings exist and that I want to go on listening and understanding them.

If I am willing to accompany the client into his world, eventually his revelations could mean that the very person I believed I could never accept is right there in front of me. A therapist colleague, for example, had always insisted that she would never be able to work with a man who sexually abused children. However, when a client who had been with her for about six months one day admitted to abusing his children, she found that her knowledge of this man's world and her feeling for him as a human being overcame her previous barrier to working with abusers and she did not reject him. While she in no sense condoned his behaviour, she could stay with him and they could explore together the deeper meaning and source of his behaviour. It is clear also that her attitude of acceptance, in this case, was present at the beginning of therapy. This enabled the client, after six months of building up a relationship, to feel safe enough to risk talking about his abusing behaviour.

The offering of unconditonal positive regard is particularly important for people with a low opinion of themselves. A poor 'self-concept' can set up a cycle of self-defeating behaviour: 'I've nothing interesting to say, no-one wants to listen to me, people don't like me, I feel isolated, no-one wants to be with me, I've nothing interesting to say.' This cycle is immediately broken if you find a therapist who is interested in you and in what you are saying. In these circumstances, clients often express great surprise that someone will listen to them and also at what they uncover in the process of expressing themselves. Even in the first session a client can realise that 'I never knew I felt sad.'

Each client has a particular way of expressing him or herself and vulnerability will show itself in different forms. Accepting a client involves appreciating their own idiosyncratic patterns of speech and metaphors. A client who is a nun, for example, might use many religious metaphors. Working class Dubliners may have a distinctive and rich use of language. A football or hurling fanatic may use metaphors relating to these sports. A teenager may use very different language than a middle-aged business person. Adaptation to and an understanding of these varying means of expression help a client feel accepted on their own terms. A particulary colourful metaphor can act as a catalyst in cementing a relationship. For example a client used the metaphor of 'killing the leprechaun' inside him and picking up on this vivid image led to a deep exploration of the unacceptable side of himself.

Most relationships in the real world are conditional; we continue to love someone often on condition that 'they don't change too much' or we like someone as long as 'she doesn't let me down'. In therapy the focus is solely on the needs of the client, which makes unconditionality slightly easier to achieve. It may not be possible to be totally unconditional; perhaps it is more realistic to say that in the therapy situation I try to be unconditonal and succeed in achieving only a relatively unconditional stance. Many therapists have opted to retain the title 'client-centred', reflecting perhaps their feeling that outside the therapeutic relationship it is impossible to maintain this 'unconditionality'. Rogers, however, intended the term 'person-centred' to extend beyond the therapy session and into our everyday lives. This is a very demanding task but it seems to me very worthwhile to attempt it.

Congruence

Congruence can be defined as a match in the therapist between her deep feelings, her awareness of these feelings and her ability to articulate them. For example, when I am faced with a client who is talking rapidly without pause, I might suddenly realise that I have lost concentration and haven't heard what he has been saying. If, instead of bluffing or covering this up, I examine my feelings carefully and realise that I had become bored, admitting my boredom and looking carefully at what happened can encourage the client to respond more genuinely, perhaps finding out that he was bored with himself too! Congruence has been referred to as 'genuineness', 'realness' or 'authenticity' in the therapist. A congruent person is someone who is not afraid to be herself, who doesn't hide behind false fronts or roles (like that of 'therapist'!), someone who is fully present, with you as a complete human being with all her strengths and failings. It is worth quoting Rogers at this point:

> ... in the relationship the therapist is transparent to the client, openly being the feelings and attitudes that at the moment are flowing within her. It clearly involves the element of self-awareness, meaning that not only are feelings and experiences available to the therapist but that she is able to live and be those feelings in the relationship. It means that this is a direct, personal encounter with the client, a meeting with him on a person-to-person basis. It means the therapist is *being* herself, not denying self. (Rogers and Sanford, 1984, italics in original)

The effect of this self-awareness and honesty is to make the relationship 'safer' for clients, because they begin to trust that the reactions they are getting from the therapist are real, genuine feelings rather than a formula response.

Rogers argued, on the basis of research findings, that congruence is the most critical element of the theory. Congruence is probably the most difficult aspect of the person-centred approach to learn and to communicate appropriately. It can be easily misunderstood. It does not mean that the therapist blurts out anything that enters her head or imposes her problems onto the client, but it does mean that she can select out of her feelings which ones are persistent and have a direct impact on the relationship. It is likely, of course, that any persistent, hidden feeling will be having an impact on the therapeutic process. If, for example, a therapist's boredom remains hidden, it can have a very negative effect on the client, such as exacerbating a feeling of worthlessness.

In many respects 'congruence' distinguishes person-centred therapy from other forms of therapy, although some forms of Gestalt therapy which emphasise a person-to-person encounter, use the therapist's awareness in a manner akin to the notion of congruence. Learning to trust in my own responses as a person connecting with another person is extremely important. Many other therapies tend to have a more 'professional' approach to their clients. By this I mean that they take a clear-cut role of 'therapist' and do not regard being authentic, real or genuine as part of their job.

The Person-Centred Approach puts a high priority on this 'genuineness' or lack of a professional 'front', because it is often through this authenticity that a client learns to trust himself and others again. Sometimes he has already lost faith in himself through a more distant, objective treatment. Hopefully with a Person-Centred therapist he would feel, 'Here's a real person, who isn't busy analysing and diagnosing me.'

The common veneer of polite manners can mask real feelings. It can be very difficult to stop ourselves being 'insincerely' friendly because we may have a strong sense of the 'rightness' of these behaviours. If, however, I allow myself to become aware of and accept deep-seated feelings, even unpleasant ones, such as anger, boredom, irritation and confusion – can paradoxically free both myself and the client to move on.

Example of therapist congruence

Cl: I always was fed up, almost looking for a problem, but it's beginning to turn.(*Pause. He smiles.*) It's going, it caused so much pain ... My wife's pain ... My pain. I'd love to turn the clock back and change it. (*He is still smiling*)

T: I'm confused because, on the one hand, you are smiling yet, on the other, you are talking about a lot of pain.

Cl: I'm smiling because I know I want to get rid of the pain. (*pause*) ... I'd be embarassed to cry here, I've been through a lot ... hard to ... I'm hurting a lot. (*Sobs*)

In this example, unless the therapist had admitted her confusion, it would have been difficult for the client to stay with his pain or to acknowledge his embarassment. It also highlights the fact that when a therapist has the courage to say what she is really feeling, it can help the client to clarify his own feelings and perhaps to go a little deeper. In this case it also clarified, for the therapist, what had been going on for the client.

An admission of weakness or of a mistake, with an apology, can help a client to be less fearful and more accepting of his own perceived weaknesses. Trust often takes time to develop and cannot develop easily in a relationship where the therapist is not authentic, i.e. denies aspects of her feelings.

I find it extremely hard to stay consistently congruent, but genuineness is a particularly important part of person-centred therapy, in that it contributes greatly to the equalising of the relationship. If I am willing to reveal my feelings and 'mistakes' in the relationship with my client, it can increase the client's courage to become more open himself. Through his experience of my honesty he can learn to become less afraid of revealing his own hidden feelings.

The client's response, to a 'risky' congruent statement from the therapist usually results in a re-engagement in the empathic process at a deeper level. For example, when a long-standing client suddenly began playing a 'one-up-manship' game with me I felt very confused. When I admitted this confusion the client quickly admitted she was trying 'to get one up' on me because she felt I was superior and she needed to feel in control. It became clear that she started trying to manipulate me because she had been feeling totally out of control. This provided an opportunity to open up some deep-seated feelings about power and control in her life.

At its purest, a therapist's congruence provides an undistorted reflection of the effects of a client's behaviour on another human being. But at other times it will involve admissions of the therapist's own issues intruding on the process. To quote Rogers:

> When the therapist is feeling neither empathic nor caring, she must discover what the flow of experiencing is and must be willing to express that flow, whether it seems embarrassing, too revealing, or whatever. (Rogers and Sanford, 1984)

I recently experienced an example of this interference when I had to give a counselling session soon after I had my handbag stolen, with a lot of personally valued objects along with it. As we started, I found myself feeling rather distracted and upset still. I acknowledged what was going on and it helped me to let go of those feelings and to focus on my client. It is clear that this is not an easy option. Often I will have no idea of what effect my congruent response will have on the client and it is still a very risky process for me.

If I have managed to convey an acceptance of the client, then an honest response from me should not be experienced as threatening. When a client is sure of being valued, it creates a trust between client and therapist that is earned rather than one based on the power of the expert. It is based on the known, on the experience of being together. It has no mystery, nothing remains hidden. It is just two imperfect human beings responding to one another.

At times when I trust myself most, I experience a close link between congruence and empathy. Deep involvement in the empathic process, for example of a client experiencing for the first time the terror and pain of early sexual abuse, has brought out a response of tears on my part, as a result of both an understanding of and a spontaneous reaction to feeling the pain of the client. That is to say that when I am truly immersed in the process, congruence and empathy can become intermingled, experienced as a direct and immediate response to the client. Responses at this level feel intuitive or instinctively right. At this point, Rogers' three 'necessary and sufficient conditions' have merged and united. Empathy, (understanding the client); congruence, (the therapist's reaction), and acceptance of the client as he is, have become one and the same thing. To some it might sound as though the therapist is in danger of losing her sense of self in this, but it is, in my experience, a moment in which the client feels truly and deeply understood and affirmed in his own right. The feeling of being together actually confirms an emerging sense of identity in the client. So that although it might seem as though this sense of unity would encourage dependence, it paradoxically gives the client strength, making him more capable of independence and of trust in himself.

I often ask clients at the end of therapy what they found most helpful. Feedback for me has included the expected and the unexpected. Examples of things clients have said include:
1. 'Accepting me whatever I was like. Knowing that any feeling I had was O.K. even the fear of crying for three days, that was still O.K., the fact that you said you would stay with that.'
2. 'It was helpful that right from the beginning you made it clear that it was my responsibility. That even if I wanted to commit suicide, that it was my choice and that I could always choose that. It gave me a freedom to choose life.'
3. 'Time and money were not an issue. And you made it clear that this was your responsibility and not something I had to worry about.'
4. 'Believing in me.'
5. 'When you told me you needed to go to someone for supervision so that you could improve your work, then I felt it was O.K. to come to you for help. If you need help and could admit it then I felt that maybe I could admit it too.'

6. 'When you said that it was difficult for you to reach me at times ... and that this time you had seen something of the real me, I felt touched.'

The last two points are simple examples of the therapist's congruence being experienced by the client as powerful instruments in their own process of change, giving them more courage to reveal themselves to me. A process is set in motion in which the client becomes increasingly congruent, more in touch with his own emotions and he is increasingly capable of being open to his immediate experience and to other people.

Towards the end of therapy many clients have experienced a renewed sense of self-discovery and self-direction, increasing self-confidence and a sense of excitement about life. One client described to me a sudden intense, sensual pleasure in eating a bar of chocolate, like 'experiencing it for the first time'. This sense of newness and wonder often accompanies the opening up of a person to his feelings and experience. Paradoxically, as you learn to please yourself more, you also find that your relationships with other people are deeper and more satisfying. 'Becoming a Person' (the title of Rogers' classic book) involves learning to accept and like yourself, and to open yourself up fully to your experience, with no need for defences to protect you – this is a *process* which continues, it moves forward, changes and develops. A person who is living fully now is in a process of 'self-actualisation'.'Self-Actualisation', according to Rogers, is not a goal to be achieved, rather you can become a 'self-actualising' person.

Recommended reading

Kirschenbaum, H. & Henderson, V. L.,(eds), *The Carl Rogers Reader* (Constable, 1990).
Gives a representative selection of Rogers' writing across a range of topics – therapy, research, science, education, philosophy of persons, political implications.

Kirschenbaum, H. & Henderson, V. L., (eds), *Carl Rogers: Dialogues* (Constable, 1990).
A series of conversations and dialogues with important psychologists and philosophers, including B.F.Skinner, Martin Buber, Paul Tillich, Michael Polanyi, Gregory Bateson and Rollo May.

Mearns, D. & Thorne, B., *Person-Centred Counselling in Action* (Sage Publications, 1988).
A lively, engaging, extremely clear, thorough and thought provoking description of the Person-Centred Approach by two British practitioners. Useful for therapists, counsellors and prospective clients.

Rogers, C., *On Becoming a Person* (Constable, 1961).
Rogers' classic which includes the philosophy of the approach, its place in the Behvioural Sciences, a theory of creativity, applications in social work, in education and to family life and interpersonal relationships.

Rogers, C., *Client-Centred Therapy* (Constable, 1965).
A full account of the theory, process and research in Client-Centred therapy, includes applications such as play therapy, education, administration. Emphasis on an open, developing theory.

Rogers, C., *Carl Rogers on Personal Power: Inner Strength and Its Revolutionary Impact* (Constable, 1978).

An exploration of the wider applications of the Person-Centred Approach, and its potential political impact.

Rogers, C., *A Way of Being* (Boston: Houghton Mifflin, 1980).
A series of personal essays, including 'Growing Old: or Older and Growing.'

Rogers, C., *Freedom to Learn in the 80s* (Columbus, OH: Charles Merrill, 1983).
Updated version of 'Freedom to Learn', applications of the Person-Centred Approach to education.

Footnotes

1. see R.S.P.Jones, R.E.McCaughey, and E.M. Connell, 'The philosophy and practice of gentle teaching: Implications for mental handicap services', *Irish Journal of Psychology*, 1991, vol 12, no 1, pp.1-16.

2. Karen Horney, *Neurosis and Human Growth* (Norton, 1991) Reissue of 1970, Chapter 3, *The Tyranny of the Should*, p. 64-85.

CHAPTER 10

An Integrative Approach to Psychotherapy

Body-Psychotherapy, Process-Oriented and Psychoanalytic Psychotherapy

Patrick Nolan

My approach to psychotherapy views the person as a body - mind unit. By this I mean that psychological and body processes are parallel and have a reciprocal effect on each other. I also believe that the person has within, a potential towards development and growth. Psychotherapy can provide a setting in which people may engage constructively in the struggle towards maturity with the hope of discovering more creative ways of living. My approach attempts to work with the whole person, responding to the needs and uniqueness of each individual, without being over directive or limited by a particular technique or theoretical approach. While technique is important the outcome of therapy is also dependent on the therapist-client relationship, on the therapeutic environment and on the motivation and maturity of the clients.

In developing my approach to psychotherapy, particular teachers and therapists have inspired me by their depth, conviction and way of being. Their ability to meet me at a deep level, to re-cognize the hidden depths within me, has been as important as their particular theoretical orientation. The influence of these people, together with my training in both humanistic and psychoanalytic psychotherapies has shaped my thinking about psychotherapy. I have also been inspired through working therapeutically with people over the last twenty-five years.

In this chapter, I will look at the history of psychotherapy, in particular how the approach of body psychotherapy, relationship-centred therapy and process centred therapy developed. I will continue by outlining my understanding of what humans being are; how they develop and how this relates to the notion of change. Finally, I will examine how I integrate these concepts in practice, working with the whole person, body and mind. I will illustrate the different sections with cases from my own practice, these cases have been altered to preserve anonymity.

A wide range of therapies has emerged since Freud first developed psychoanalysis. Theoretical principles form the basis of each school of therapy; they also provide an identity and a sense of security to practitioners. However if the boundaries between schools are too rigid they may limit the possibilities of practice. In the last thirty years there has been a growing tendency among psychotherapists to ignore the ideological barriers dividing schools of psychotherapy and to define what is common among them and what is useful in each of them. This trend is, I believe, influenced by the fact that no one approach is suitable for all clients, problems and situations. Another factor borne out by research [1] demonstrates that no one therapeutic approach is clearly superior or more effective than another.

A solid theoretical understanding is necessary to work more effectively. However it is important to be mindful of Winnicott's caution[2] that theories make good servants but bad masters. The individual process of each client and the uniqueness of each therapeutic encounter therefore provides the primary direction of the therapy.

I have found that working with both the body and the mind is both possible and fruitful. This integration leads to a richer understanding of people that includes both the emotional and energetic life of the body and their mysterious, imaginative and symbolic nature.

A Historical Perspective – Freud, Ferenczi, Reich Fairbairn and Perls

In examining how the ideas of body-oriented psychotherapy and a relationship-centred approach gradually entered the domain of psychotherapy, I will begin by acknowledging the origins of psychotherapy in Freud.

Freud made ingenious discoveries about the human psyche; in 1892 in collaboration with Breuer he discovered that hysterical symptoms are based on highly significant, but forgotten scenes from the past. He believed that the symptoms arose when the person was unable to discharge feelings about the traumatic experience. In *Studies on Hysteria,* 1895, Freud stated that it was the emergence of emotion along with memory which had the therapeutic effect.

Freud soon discovered 'free association' which involved the patients relating all the thoughts that pass through their minds. He recommended his 'fundamental rule' – that analysts must maintain their normal sympathetic passive objectivity and should not respond to the patient's wishes and cravings. He suggested that therapists should be a mirror to their patients, reflecting, through 'interpretation' the patient's flow of ideas. Interpretations were intended to make unconscious phenomena conscious, that is, to help patients to understand their present reactions and thoughts in relation to their forgotten personal history.[3]

Following the introduction of free association, Freud became increasingly aware of a force within the patient opposing treatment. He called this force 'resistance' and believed it fended off the memory of forgotten experiences. The forgotten memory was due to a process that he called 'repression'; the aim of the repression was to transform emotionally strong ideas into weak ones in order to protect the person from painful experience. 'The theory of repression,' Freud wrote, 'is the foundation stone on which the whole structure of psychoanalysis rests.'[4]

The techniques of free association revealed a second phenomenon which Freud called 'transference'. Its main characteristic is the experience of feelings towards a person that do not belong, but originate with someone else. Essentially people in the present are reacted to as if they were somebody from the past. It is a repetition, an unconscious replay of an old relationship. A simple example of transference is of a woman whose experience of her domineering father may interfere with her perception of her husband; she may react to her husband as if he were dominating her like her father.

Freud believed that neurosis resulted from traumatic events in childhood and from inner conflicts. The memory of these experiences became unconscious, however this repression led to neurotic symptoms such as depression.[5] The task of the psychoanalyst is therefore to help patients to remember these traumatic unconscious events. They may be repeated in the transference relationship or through slips of the tongue. Through the analyst's interpretation patients are enabled to work through these inner conflicts. For Freud working with dreams[6] which he regarded as the royal road to the unconscious was an important route in uncovering the unconscious of the patient.

Theoretically, Freud defined the aim of psychoanalysis from the 1920s as 'overcoming the patient's resistance, removal of infantile amnesia and making the unconscious conscious.'[7] Although Freud's work developed in a way that emphasised the psychological sphere, he expressed a continued interest in the biological aspect of human problems. He stated in 1923 that the ego is 'first and foremost a body ego.'[8] An important implication of his statement about human development is that the lack of certain human body sensations will limit ego development. Even as late as 1933 Freud remarked in a letter to an American psychiatrist, Joseph Wortis, that 'Analysis is not everything, there are other factors … so long as the organic factors remain inaccessible, psychoanalysis leaves much to be desired.'[9]

Freud was a courageous innovator, whose genius created the basis for psychoanalysis. Two of the most influential and adventurous analysis in the 1920s were Sandor Ferenczi and Wilhelm Reich. They extended Freud's work focusing not just on the content of the patient's material but on the form of the patient's communication.

Ferenczi, a close and loyal colleague of Freud, proposed a more flexible approach to working with patients. He discovered in his practice that following Freud's fundamental rule that the analyst should be impersonal was ineffective with many clients. He found that they were unable to get beyond 'dead points' in the therapy. Around 1918 he developed his 'active techniques' to deal with these difficulties. While working with a patient diagnosed as hysterical he noticed an erotic quality in the way she crossed her legs when reporting love fantasies relating to doctors. Ferenczi[10] suggested that she lie without crossing her legs. When she did so she experienced intense physical and emotional reactions that led to the emergence of repressed memories and recalling important traumatic causes of her illness.

Ferenczi believed in varying the therapeutic style depending on the patient. He questioned whether a patient's lack of progress was always due to resistance or whether it was partly due to the inflexibility of the therapist. He recognized that muscular relaxation led to the release of feelings and to the flow of free association. 'I have since learnt that it is sometimes useful to advise relaxation exercises and that with this kind of relaxation one can overcome the physical inhibitions and resistance to free association.' He argued that maintaining an aloof or sympathetic passivity after inducing the patient to recollect or re-experience an original trauma, might in some cases merely feel like a repetition of the original trauma.

Ferenczi attempted to clarify the interpersonal relationship in analysis and was the first to emphasise the therapist's role in this relationship, for example, in countertransference. Countertransference includes the analyst's emotional reactions to the patient. If the analyst is conscious of these reactions he may use them to deepen his understanding of the patient's process.

Balint[11] echoed Ferenczi's views by highlighting the importance and uniqueness of each therapeutic relationship. He acknowledged that the therapist must fulfil his function of mirror *vis a vis* the patient as Freud recommended, but emphasised that it must be a living mirror that reflects in its own way the patient's truth to him.

Reich[12] was the first analyst to develop a systematic approach to understanding how people use body mechanisms as a defence against feeling and memory. From 1920 to 1930 he was the director of the Vienna Seminar for psychoanalytic technique. It was during this period that he developed his method of 'character analysis' in which he found a way of working with resistance in the patient. He believed that the character resistance expresses itself not only in words but in such behaviour of patients as their manner of speaking, or their facial expressions. He insisted therefore that simply paying attention to the content of 'what' the patient says will not lead to deep change. Change will only happen by interpreting the attitude of people, and by highlighting 'how' they actually behave.

Reich[13] later developed a method called 'vegeto-therapy'. This method worked directly with the physical basis of character resistance that expressed itself in the form of muscular tension. He believed that the neurosis was psychologically anchored in these tensions which acted as defences. According to Reich this muscular defence, which he called 'armouring' referred to the total muscular tensions in the body. It protected individuals against threats to their primary needs. He stated that 'the lasting frustration of primary natural needs led to a chronic contraction of the organism.' He insisted that it was important to pay attention to and work with the muscular tension or armouring of the patient. This view opened the possibility of combining a verbal and a physical way of working. Reich wrote: 'When a character inhibition would fail to respond to psychic influencing, I would work on a corresponding somatic attitude. Correspondingly when a disturbing muscular attitude proved difficult to access, I would work on it characterological expression and thus loosen it up.'

Reich's basic thesis was that there was a physical and a psychological unity in the individual. He called this unity a 'functional identity' of muscular armour and character armour referring to the character attitude of the person.

Following Reich's death in 1957, different schools of Reichian therapy developed. John Pierrakos and Alexander Lowen developed bioenergetic analysis in America. In Europe many schools sprang from the work of Ola Raknes. Ferenczi and Reich have had a strong influence on many schools of therapy. In particular Reich has had a major influence on the humanistic schools for example the Gestalt school of psychotherapy and Ferenczi has influenced the object relations school of psychotherapy.

Fairbairn,[14] a Scottish psychoanalyst, made important contributions to the development of psychoanalysis. He held that the primary wish of every child was to have satisfying relationships and that the deepest trauma for children is that they are not loved or that their love is not received. This disappointment has the effect of splitting the original sense of unity of self which children experience. Children turn to the inner world of internalized images in the face of traumatic disappointment in relationships.

The therapeutic relationship according to Fairbairn includes not just the relationship involved in the transference but the total relationship existing between the patient and therapist as persons. He believes that making a real contact in the present has the effect of repairing the splits in the ego and the inner object world, which occurred through disappointments in primary relationships. The therapeutic relationship gives the client an opportunity, denied to him in childhood, to undergo a process of emotional development with a reliable and beneficent parental figure. Fairbairn stresses that all other factors such as insight, recall of infantile memories and catharsis depended on the therapeutic relationship.

Perls[15] who developed Gestalt psychotherapy was influenced by the work of Freud and Reich. Perls focussed on the clients experience in the present. He paid attention to the person's thinking, feeling, expression, bodily sensations and imagination. Perls believed that in becoming aware of themselves people could integrate parts of their personality which had been disowned. He has had an important influence on the emphasis which therapists have placed on the process within therapy.

The brief outline above concerns the main innovators of an approach to therapy that incorporates a more holistic view of the person. It sets the background for an analysis of the way in which diverse therapeutic approaches may be integrated in the context of my view of what a person *is*.

Some Basic Assumptions

What a person 'is' and the nature of health and disturbance

My work is based on the assumption that each human being is unique and needs recognition of his or her uniqueness. Essentially the person is a mystery and no model of therapy can adequately capture this mystery. I also assume that the human being is a psychosomatic unity with both an instinctual and a spiritual nature. Every experience happens simultaneously on a psychological and physical level. People have within themselves a strong potential for development, growth and maturity and their search for emotional contact with others is inherent from birth.

Recent research[16] confirms that the young baby has an innate capacity for interpersonal relating. There are considerable self healing capacities within the body and psyche. My belief is that much of the progress in therapy, depends on the emergence of these resources. This progress is related to the client's willingness to engage in the deepened struggle within themselves; this may involve facing deep pain which they may have avoided or repressed. I believe that in facing and accepting their inner difficulties and suffering within a therapeutic relationship it is possible for people to reintegrate these experiences and become more whole. This is similar to Proust's view when he writes: 'We are healed of a suffering only by experiencing it to the full.'[17] My views in this regard have been influenced by the work of Carl Rogers,[18] A. Maslow,[19] D. Winnicott[20] and C. Jung.[21]

Based on these assumptions, I can now explore the development of the person and look at some aspects of health and disturbance.

Natural Progress towards Health

The primary impulse of every child is to satisfy its needs, whether this be for food, comfort or love. The drive towards living, emotional development, integration of the personality, and towards independence are immensely strong. If the parents provide good enough conditions for children in which they feel loved and feel that their love is accepted they make progress. If people in the environment accept and respond to their needs, they will progress towards health and maturity. Winnicott[22] understands this progress as being the evolution of the individual in psyche and soma. The environment that affects the individual involves home, community and wider cultural inlfuences, including lang-uage, laws and customs.

The environment interrupts the individual's progress when it does not provide sufficiently for the individual's growth needs. When this happens the child usually protests, for example through screaming or crying, when it experiences a stressful situation. If the parents are sensitive to the children's state they will usually find a way of enabling them to move beyond the traumatic experience. Wise parents will sense when it is appropriate to limit the child and when it is beneificial for children to find their own solutions when faced with frustration.

There are many situations where the parent's response is not sufficient. Bowlby[23] described what can happen to infants who are separated from their mothers for instance, through hospitalisation. The immediate reaction is to protest, if the separation continues the child goes through a period of despair and finally becomes detached, often adjusting to the separation in a lifeless false way.

Let us give a fictional example of a young boy who experiences painful abandonment through hospitalisation. The normal reaction of the child would be to feel sad or angry and to express these feelings at being separated from his parents. If the traumatic situation continues, his tendency will be to hold back his feeling by restricting his muscles and breathing. The inhibition is structured into the organism in the form of a muscular contraction and prevents the expression of the feeling. If the stressful situation continues over a long period the muscles and other tissue in the body may become slack and lifeless – the child usually withdraws from the world and resigns. In this process the body freezes to numb the distressful experience. On a psychological level the child experiences the absent or frustrating person or situation as a 'rejecting object' and attempts to control or limit the painful experiences by internalising them. The child withdraws and seeks comfort from this internalised image of the experience or person. When emotional contact in the outside world is frustrated, he turns to his internalised object. In time, the child, comes to repress the memory of the experience. The body-mind reaction may not only result in an inner blueprint for future mis-perceptions of people, for example in transference, but also plays a part in creating a 'false self'. Let us consider a different kind of example drawn from my own practice which demonstrates how a person may cope with abuse:

> Rose had been physically and sexually abused by her father as a child. She had repressed any memory of the experience and as an adult thought of herself as dirty, evil and monstrous. On a body level she experienced terror and self disgust, and she looked as if she were under siege. She had a frightening expression on her face and held her body as if ready to take flight. It was as if she had internalized the terrifying experience and based her identity, her way of relating, on this image of herself. As a child she survived by repressing the memory, while at the same time freezing her body and internalising the experience. It would have been too frightening for her to keep these horrific memories in her conscious mind. This led to her feeling constantly terrified of people. She attempted to deal with her fear by eating compulsively and avoiding contact with people. Her fear of contact was such that she was unable to cope with a regular job. In the early stage of therapy I felt it was important to help her to feel safe in relating to me. As therapy continued it

was possible for her to allow the horrifying events in her past to become more conscious and to begin to face these nightmares. Rose may never feel safe enough with people to experience normal social relationships. However she has managed to gain enough security through therapy to deal with her anxiety more effectively. She has managed to take a regular job and consequently has improved her self image.

Formation of the False Self

When children are alienated from their inner world they will adjust by developing what Reich called 'the mask', a false self that is related to the character defences described elsewhere. This is similar to what Jung[24] called the 'persona' which he saw as a compromise between the individual and society. The false self is a response to frustration of the children's needs, and serves as a protection of their 'real self'. Children develop this compromised self to get acceptance and love from their parents, who do not accept the more spontaneous real self. This false self is compliant and builds up a set of false relationships as a compromise solution between their needs and the demands of the environment. This is a response in both the body and the psyche. Katherine Brown[25] writes that the 'denial and repression of the instincts and the self have built an ego that is minimally rooted in the body. The existing ego is a body ego; it is a mental construct or a false-self system.' The degree of falsity of the self relates partly to the degree to which the environment is not responsive to the real needs of the child. When people lose contact with their inner world of feelings, thoughts, needs or imagination they are likely to have trouble in finding their own individual direction in life and in relating to other people in a mature way. I will now give another case example:

John had internalised an unsatisfying situation and developed a false self. His mother ran the home in a very regimental, tyrannical manner and put unending pressure on him to be perfect. For example, she would wake John up in an aggressive manner in the middle of the night to make him correct his homework. She would beat both him and his siblings severely if they opposed her rule. She terrorised him. By the age of five he had adapted to her will by becoming a 'good boy' – he developed a mask which was pleasing, helpful and dutiful, however his behaviour was mechanical and based on a fear of which he was unaware. He was out of touch with his own inner life and driven by his mother's tyrannical way of being which he had internalised. He later transferred this mechanical manner to other relationships in his life.

When I first met John, he suffered from severe panic attacks and bouts of depression and feared any conflict. He was unable to be close to his wife and two children, suffered from disturbed sleep and had poor concentration. He presented himself in a very frantic 'mechanical' manner. His body was rigid, like a taut string. His wish was simply to rid himself of his anxiety and get on with life. He also put both himself and me under enormous pressure to achieve results immediately in therapy. He soon realised that his depression, driven quality and lack of real contact either with his own inner world or with others was because he had internalised the merciless pressure his mother had put on him. In submitting to his mother's will he had avoided her roth; he had also cut off his own needs and wishes, developed a false self in the form of a happy, efficient facade.

Developments of Psychosomatic Reactions

In a supportive environment children are normally able to experience and express their feelings and vegetative reactions. These vegative reactions relate to the vegative nervous system, which governs the involuntary reactions in the body. These include for example, blushing, trembling or blood pressure due to fear. These responses enable the mind to assimilate the experience in a healthy way. However when parents fail to give adequate attention to the children, disturbances may follow. The defensive reactions described above help the children to protect themselves from intolerable experiences, whether these be feelings inside which are too frightening, or situations in the outer world that are too painful to bear. However, repressing the memory and feeling not only limits the potential of the person, but in extreme circumstances may also lead to symptoms such as depression, severe anxiety, obsessional rituals or phobias. Emotion is not purely a mental or physical event; it is intrinsically psychosomatic. By this I mean that experiences or feelings that are too stressful for the mind to integrate may manifest themselves through physiological malfunctioning and body tensions. In extreme cases they may result in psychosomatic symptoms. A simple example would be of an infant who holds his breath in a situation of severe anxiety, for example if his father attacked him. In extreme cases this mechanism may develop into a symptom of bronchial asthma in situations that arouse anxiety. However, not all cases of asthma have their origin in stress. Psychosmatic symptoms and disorders have a complicated etiology of which the unexpressed unconscious conflicts and emotions are only a part.

> To illustrate: Hanna came from a family in which the parents were constantly bickering. These arguments at times became violent. She was very close to her mother and supported her in these battles. Consequently her father often beat her and made derogatory remarks about her body. The constant treat and lack of autonomy resulted in her developing severe anxiety and obsessional rituals in which she constantly cleaned herself. She had come to believe she was dirty inside. In her teens she developed anorexia - she stopped eating: symbolically, it had become unsafe for her to swallow any more abuse. Hanna experienced fear in her relationship with me. In the transference she experienced me as being antagonistic and cruel. Gradually as she realised that her fear and anger were related to the abuse she had experienced from her father, she felt less anxious. This in turn lessened the anxiety that she experienced in other situations in her life. She became more secure with people and was able to develop more long term meaningful relationships.

Other Factors

Of course the relationship with parents is not the only reason for the individuals' ills and itt would be onesided to lay all the blame on them. Temperamental, organic, genetic and social factors also effect the child's development. It is obvious to most parents that each child is unique. It has its own way of being from the beginning. Recent research shows that infants differ in their capacity to show the parents what feels right or wrong, to modify negative experiences or to compensate for lacks in the environment. [26]

Good enough care from parents does tend to prevent serious neurosis. However, stress and conflict are part of life and the individual child will experience the inevitable disturbances associated with living. The conflict arises out of the clash between the demands of family and society on the one hand and the inner needs and desires of the individual on the other. Winnicott[27] believed that true neurosis is not necessarily an illness, and first we should think of it as a tribute to the fact that life is difficult.

In addition to getting one's needs met, development also involves the inevitable frustration of having to enter into society's pre-existing order, this includes language, laws, customs.[28] The manner of the transition from the protected world of the mother into this reality has a strong impact on a child's development towards health. Proper boundaries and limits within the family will help the individual to develop a balanced sense of reality. As the mother is usually the person who provides the primary emotional care for the children, the father can fulfil an important function here.

I will continue by examining the idea of therapeutic change, in a way which incorporates the historical background and my understanding of the psychological health and disturbances as described above. This will lead subsequently to a presentation of an integrated approach to psychotherapy.

Change within Psychotherapy

The nature of change in psychotherapy depends on the particular client and therapist. The maturity, motivation and current psychological and emotional state of the client determine what change is possible. Important factors include the client's reasons for coming to ther-apy, their motivation and their understanding of the nature of personal change. The last two factors may alter during therapy.

Change is paradoxical,[29] it happens when people accept who they are, rather than attempting to become what they are not. The more people recognize, accept and allow whatever they experience within the therapeutic relationship, the more this awareness may lead over time to the healing of old wounds. This may be difficult and painful, the journey may be compared to Dante's[30] metaphor when he wrote the entrance to purgatory is at the deepest point of hell. The therapeutic process may bring us to these depths. However from this point it is hoped that the person may find a more constructive way of living.

As a therapist I may lose contact with the process within the relationship if I am too concerned about the therapeutic goal or structure of the therapy. It is my responsibility to attend to the cues of the client both bodily and psychologically as they emerge within each session.

The process of change within the therapeutic relationship is as important as the goal as illustrated in the following case:

> Henry came to therapy to get rid of panic attacks that prevented him from leaving his home. He realised during therapy that these attacks had their origin in his inability to separate from his overprotective mother. He then saw the necessity of understanding more about this relationship in order to free himself from his panic attacks. As he understood more about the link between his panic and his overclose relationship with his mother his symptoms gradually eased and he was able to slowly feel secure enough to leave his home.

I cannot change the client. What I can do is to provide a framework within which change may happen and I can be present to the client during this process. Research (Nolan 2002) shows that clients should be motivated to look at their own problems and to take some responsibility for dealing with them, if the therapy is to continue effectively.

Repressing both painful and joyful experiences has been necessary for people to survive difficulties in childhood. They develop a neurotic compromise and present a mask. For therapy to be effective, the client must be willing to explore the deeper experiences behind the mask. It is the relationship which provides the holding environment in which these experiences can be managed:

> John (Page 265) became aware of his false way of behaving. This realisation left him feeling less defended, and at times confused about who he was. It was also hard for him to accept how he had idealised his relationship with his mother. This image of his mother was an inner security to which he had clung, it had helped him to tolerate his mother's dominant manner. However, his inability to perceive this relationship realistically perpetuated his anxiety. It was in facing the reality of the horror of his early experience that he began to free himself from his symptoms. His experience of the therapeutic relationship helped him to modify these inner traumatic experi-

ences of his family and gain a new meaning and freedom towards these experiences in his past. In the course of therapy his panic attacks and bouts of depression vanished. He seemed to have a clearer sense of his own identity and was more confident and relaxed in his way of relating to other people. Towards the end of therapy he started training in a profession which he found more satisfying.

I can now attempt to incorporate my understanding of the person and how change happens in going on to examine my approach to working with people.

An integrated approach to the practice of psychotherapy

The model of therapy which I use draws on several theoretical and technical approaches: psychoanalytic, humanistic, body-oriented and Gestalt theories. I find that standardisation of a rigid technique is inappropriate as it does not allow me to make the necessary response to the individuality of each person. It is therefore necessary that my actual therapeutic approach be flexible enough to respond to the uniqueness of each client.[31]

In describing my approach, it is useful to begin by considering some of the important issues in focusing on the body in psychotherapy. This leads to a description of how I work with the process in therapy including work on a body level, work with awareness, work on the analytic level and on a relationship level. I will then examine the phases in psychotherapy and finally outline some other elements in this integrated approach.

The body in psychotherapy

'Man has no body distinct from his soul.' *William Blake*

In western society many people believe that their minds and bodies are essentially different. This dualitic way of thinking has deep roots in our philosophy as well as in the physics of Newton over the last three hundred years. St Paul[32] stated this view in an extreme way, when he expressed his contempt for the body. Descartes, the most articulate philosophical proponent of this view proclaimed 'I have, on the one hand, a clear and distinct idea of myself as a thinking, non-extended thing, and on the other hand, a distinct idea of my body as an extended, non-thinking thing. It is therefore certain that I am truly distinct from my body, and can exist without it.'[33]

In recent years developments in quantrum physics,[34] give hope for a new world view which is more holistic, less fragmented way of looking at ourselves. This perspective transcends the dichotomy between the mind and the body and understands them as manifestations of the same energetic process. This point of view has not many parallels to Reich's idea of 'functional identity' of the body and mind.

In using a body oriented approach I view psychological and body processes as being parallel and as having a reciprocal effect on one another. The body speaks a language that antedates and is as important as verbal expression. By paying attention to the lang-uage of the body as expressed through movement, pose, posture, attitude and gesture, I can complement work on a verbal level. As a body oriented therapist I analyse not only the psychological problem of the client; I also attend to the physical expression of the problem, in the body structure and movement of the person. Practising therapists can only effectively incorporate a body oriented approach into their work after many years of training, practice and supervision, This will enable therapists to work at a body level in a mature, sensitive and balanced way while maintaining their necessary objectivity. These methods could include for example body reading, body awareness, the mobilisation of energetic processes within the body through movement, direct touch or work on the breath.

There are many people who may benefit from the introduction of a body oriented approach to psychotherapy. By working on a body level, I may help the client to become aware of the physical and psychological resistances that have built up over the years to feeling or recalling repressed memories. This is particularly important when clients use words in a way that avoids contact with others and which diminishes their own experience of themselves. Intellectual recognition without emotional experience does not go deep enough to resolve the basic conflicts within a person:

> When John (page 265) first came to therapy he had no idea of what caused his symptoms of anxiety. He spoke in a very fast mechanical tone without any feeling. When he eventually remembered some of the traumatic events of his childhood, he remained untouched as he spoke about the disturbing details of his mother's cruelty. Through working on a body level he

was able to connect in a more real way with his deeper experience. He was able to re-experience his terror of his mother in the session, and in time his anxiety lessened.

It is necessary to respect and trust the dynamic transforming quality of the person's body-mind process. Neurotic tendencies or symptoms are not simply negative or disturbing traits; they are indicators of how the person has protected his or her emerging self. It takes time for people to recognize these well established defenses. In therapy I only focus slowly on the body in some cases after several months or a year of verbal therapy. This period affords an opportunity to establish a working alliance and to make a realistic assessment of the most appropriate way of working. It is important that I explain the reasons for introducing a body orientation at a particular point in therapy. I have to give due consideration to the history of the person, the stage of therapy, the therapeutic relationship, including the transference and the countertransference. It is important that I do not complicate the goal and motivation for introducing a body focus with my own needs. I should make this decision based on the essential therapeutic needs of the client.

By being guided by what emerges from within the client both in the verbal and body level, I will be more likely to respect the defences of the person and avoid the risk of myself or client being flooded with material from the unconscious. This principle is particularly important when I am incorporating more active approaches, such as a body oriented approach to therapy.

The bodily and mental cues of the client guide me and when ample time is allowed, change will happen organically from within the person. This development will occur when the time is right and when the ego is prepared to assimilate the experience. Progress in therapy will be related to the desire of the client, rather than to my demand, goal or my technique.

Incorporating a body oriented approach can evoke regression, that is experiencing and acting from a younger age; however I believe that it is counterproductive to intentionally induce these experiences through special techniques. It is not my task as a therapist to gratify the needs of clients during these states. Allowing somebody to experience the very personal drama and tension of being in need can be invaluable in finding out the personal meaning of this experience. It is important for me as a therapist to be with the clients, accepting and recognizing their experience while they are in this regressive state without attempting to explain it. There will be plenty of time to try to understand these experiences when the client has emerged into a more 'adult' state.

Psychological work and the dissolution of the body armouring should proceed hand in hand.[35] I always coordinate working with the body by attempting to understand the corresponding psychic events. I sometimes spend many months trying to integ-rate what has emerged through working on the body level as will be seen in the case of Brian.

> Brian, an articulate, intelligent, man in his thirties was in a stable relationship and reasonably successful in his profession. Despite that he felt inferior to both his colleagues and to authority figures. I had worked with him over several years in group psychotherapy. In the group he expressed a wish to be more assertive, (in fact he was well able to assert himself). Although a popular group member he expressed unease about being close to other group members, saying that if he was close to people he becomes unsure of himself and feared losing his sense of himself. In one particular session in the group, I worked with him on a body level in a standing position, attempting to open the breathing in his chest, to help him to get more deeply in touch with his experience. Through this work he felt his sense of power and became aware of wanting to be more separate from his mother. While he was standing, he felt a sense of power, his breathing was flowing freely and he was full of rage and passion. When he moved to a lying position, his body became immobile, his breathing became restricted and his body changed to being still and cold. His face which had been very expressive while standing was now mask - like and empty. He reported that he felt 'nothing', 'dead'. I then worked on a verbal and analytic level to begin to understand what his 'nothing' meant. He had not separated from his mother in a way in which he felt like a person in his own right. Also he had never felt recognised by her. He felt as if he was 'nothing', when his mother dominated and dismissed him. He coped with this by appearing very independent and rational and at the same time lost touch with his deeper emo-

tions. However, inside, he continued to have a sense of inferiority which plagued him and left him feeling empty. During the work he was able to feel his previously repressed need – he longed for his mother's interest and love. This experience evoked a feeling of grief in him, as he realised that he had never experienced the sense of recognition from her. He could receive the support and acknowledgement that the group offered as he showed this more real part of himself. We worked through these insights over the remaining months of the group and later in individual therapy. Through his work Brian managed to understand his relationships more clearly and in time be began to experience a greater sense of worth in relation to people in authority.

Apart from direct responses from the client I can assess the effect of a particular body intervention by observing the impact it has on the therapeutic relationship. I also pay attention to the nature of clients' dreams to give me an indication of the wisdom of a particular way of working. I also gain important information about the clients' processes by being aware of how my own body resonates to the many subtle tensions and emotional states in the client. This is a process which Wilhelm Reich called 'vegetative identification.'[36]

There are many clients with whom I would work only on a verbal level, for example if the therapeutic relationship is erotically loaded:

Helen was sexually abused as a child by her father. His way of relating to her was intrusive, consequently she had difficulty in maintaining a clear sense of herself when with men. It was important to provide an atmosphere in which she felt accepted and listened to. Working exclusively on a verbal level seemed most appropriate. This way of working helped her to get a better sense of herself with me and, in time, with the other men in her life.

Some people have a tendency to avoid contact in the present by taking flight into feeling and regression.

For example, Petula suffered from shyness in relation to men. She avoided contact with me in the present by constantly regressing into past experiences. It gradually became clear that it

> was more important to explore her fear on a verbal level and to challenge her flight from contact with me in the present. By encouraging her to talk more about her shyness, it was possible to face and understand these experiences. Working on her relationship with me in this way helped her to face her anxiety and dread with other men in her life. As the therapy progressed she was able to tolerate going on dates and eventually formed a long term relationship with a man.

In body psychotherapy we find the same transference phenomena as in strictly verbal therapy. Because I work on a physical as well as verbal level, this brings both the transference and the counter transference more sharply into focus. It demands a greater ability to handle the resulting emotional tensions. The work on transference is illustrated in the following case:

> Harry had been in group psychotherapy with me for many years. He was in a stable, satisfying relationship and was successful in his career. He felt safe in the relationship with me. His father was an alcoholic and had habitually beaten him on the jaw. Harry's physical stance was one of bracing himself to take the punishment. In particular his jaw had a gritted iron like quality which, when worked on in earlier stages of therapy, had resulted in enormous bursts of rage. He dealt with his father's violence by developing a defiant attitude – 'you won't break me, I can take it'. This attitude had softened while in therapy and he now he was more ready to experience his deep terror of being at the brunt of his father's attacks. In one of his sessions, in which I noticed a slight cowering tendency around his face and shoulder. I touched this area gently and immediately terror spread throughout his body as he collapsed weeping. Because of transference he experienced terror of me, believing briefly that I would beat him. He realised that this was the depth of fear which he had once experienced as a child at the hands of his father. His infantile weeping lasted for about twenty minutes, after which he was able to recount the horrific stories of how his father had constantly humiliated him sadistically on returning drunk from the pub. His loosening of his defences gradually allowed him to go closer to his wife and to be more sensitive in his way of relating to her.

There are a number of other valuable approaches to working with the body such as the Feldenkreis method, schools of massage, schools of dance, that enhance body awareness, increase the aliveness in the body, and change old body habits that are dysfunctional. The factor that distinguishes my body psychotherapeutic approach from these schools is that it recognises and works with transference and counter transference; the therapeutic relationship is always included in the therapy.

I will now go on to consider a process-centred model of psychotherapy.

Focusing on the process in psychotherapy
In using a process approach I incorporate a body oriented, psychoanalytic as well as work with the therapeutic relationship and with awareness. A process oriented approach to psychotherapy views and works with the person in a holistic way; including thoughts, feelings, imagination, sensory experience, motor impulses and expression.[37] These elements all function interrelatedly and from a body-mind unity. They form, develop and change within the context of relationships. In the course of therapy or in the process of an individual therapeutic session it is possible to work with the different levels of the body-psyche. Helping a person to move more fluidly between these levels of functioning has an integrating effect.

Let me illustrate how the process of a person may move between these different levels in a fictitious example of a therapeutic session: a woman may have a conflict with a friend (present relationship in life), she may experience a similar conflict with the therapist (therapeutic relationship on a real and/or on a transference level). As she works with her experience of this conflict she may remember a similar pattern of conflict with her mother (memory of past relationship). This memory may lead to the person feeling angry with her mother (emotion) which may lead to an image of a swan with its wings tied, this might symbolise the way she felt restricted by her mother. As she focusses on this image, it may develop into the swan freeing its wings (imagination). At the same time she may sense a tingling in her right arm (sensation), which may lead to an impulse to express her rage physically through her arms (motor expression).

I will give another example to show how focussing on a body sensation may lead to a past memory: in a session a man may experience a tightness in his throat and a quiver in his voice as he talks about his father. As he becomes more aware of this bodily sensation by working with his voice and breathing he may feel sad or frightened, and self conscious in relation to me. As he explores this emotion he may recall feeling overexposed or unprotected in his family as a child. He may have felt ridiculed by his father whenever he tried to process himself resulting in his feeling overexposed and fearful (see figure).

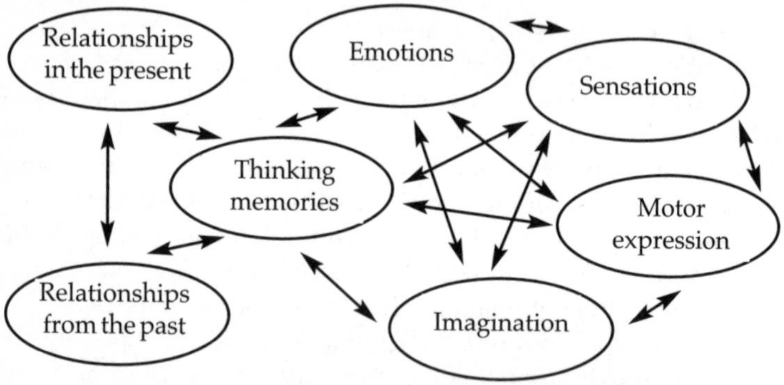

Figure: A process oriented model of therapy

Another example of the process of shifting focus is in my work with Denis:

> Denis felt constant fear in relation to men, and experienced a paralysing anxiety whenever he had to meet groups of people. After some months of analytic and body work, he began to work at a deeper level and became more aware of the sadistic way his brother had beaten him. During a week-long course his dreams showed that he was struggling with his feelings about his inner conflict. His dream images changed from his feeling terrorised and being a passive victim to becoming more active and assertive. In one particular session he had an image of being surrounded by a stone wall, which symbolised the domination of his brother. As we worked on this image it transformed into a powerful lion with which he could identify. This imagery led to body sensations of acute pain in his right

leg where his brother had beaten him badly. His body had been numb, like 'frozen history', the therapeutic work allowed a gradual unfreezing. As he became more aware of the sensations in his legs, Denis experienced and expressed his powerlessness and then his rage towards his brother. This experience helped to come to a greater understanding of his fear of men. In the following months of therapy he continued to work constructively on these issues and in time his fear lessened and he managed to socialise in a more relaxed way.

My approach to therapy uses whatever the process demands at a particular moment and as a therapist I do not know what direction a session will take. My own intuitive and organismic responses are vital in attending to the cues from the client. Appropriate interventions evoke whatever is ripe or ready to emerge from whatever level. They, together with a continual reassessment of the therapeutic relationship with the client, will help to reveal what is emerging in the client and what direction the therapy indicates.

The unfolding of the client's conscious and unconscious experience through dreams, fantasies, body experiences and symptoms will, within the context of the client-therapist relationship, determine the direction of the therapy. I think it is important to be aware of and be able to work with these different levels. Brian's case (page 273) illustrated this. It was important to move from working on a body and emotional level to working on the level of thinking and memory. This shift in focus emerged from what was happening within him; my task was to sense what was emerging and to facilitate this. The whole nature of Brian's session changed when he lay down; the feelings that emerged while working on a body level, led to his old feeling of deadness, this memory to-gether with the defended nature of Brian's body indicated that the session should continue on a verbal level.

Phases of Psychotherapy

Although the distinctions between the stages of therapy described here are artificial, they may help in understanding the therapeutic process. Each personal process is so different that it is difficult to describe a typical session or therapeutic process, the following is therefore a general summary.

In the initial phase of therapy I attempt to establish a working alliance with clients that will enable them to work effectively in the therapy. As a therapist I try to create an atmosphere, which may enable clients to feel safe enough, despite their anxiety, to begin to reveal themselves. The need, motivation and maturity of the client and the personality and style of the therapist will determine the nature of the therapy.

The beginning stage provides a structure in which the client may experience trust and confidence in the therapy. The initial interview may take one or two meetings and will involve hearing about people's life including details of present concerns, personal and family history together with any other information that seems relevant. This interview provides a basis for a mutual decision whether it is right to work together. It also provides an opportunity to clarify practical aspects of the contract such as finance, style and estimated length of therapy. A contract for psychotherapy includes such things as frequency of meetings, payment and the confidentiality of what happens in therapy.

There are a number of rules and ethical principles to protect the trust and 'working alliance' between the client and I. These rules, sometimes unspoken, provide a clear professional boundary and ensure that I, as a therapist do not misuse my position of power and trust. They also provide limits for the client. I do not allow physical violence in therapy, however, I may facilitate physical and emotional expression in a contained way within a session. The contract also forbids any sexual contact between the client and I.

For people who do not understand what therapy involves, it may be necessary to 'educate' the person about the procedure in therapy. Clients may have unrealistic expectations of the therapist and it may for example take time for them to realise the therapy is not so much being told about oneself as having an opportunity to come to a deeper experience and understanding of oneself.

This stage will also involve becoming more aware of patterns, which are causing problems in the person's life, and to begin to identify the source of these problems.

In the middle stage of therapy the client may begin to rely more on the therapist. As a deeper sense of rapport develops, issues about increasing dependency and trust are evoked. The client and the therapist may become more aware of this fear and resistance to experiencing deeper levels within himself.

Unconscious resistance and fears may appear in different ways. Clients may repeat old patterns of behaviour in the transference relationship with the therapist – for example a man may imagine that I am like his mother. He may realise the significance of the resistance, through understanding a dream or through imagery work in which he is encouraged to attend to internal images which may arise. He may also allow resistance, fears or old patterns to become conscious, through working on a body level. Recalling these memories may be emotionally painful and demands a good working alliance with the therapist:

> Henry mentioned elsewhere (page 275) was reluctant to acknowledge that he developed symptoms as a result of his merged relationship with his mother. He experienced it as a betrayal to view his mother in a negative way. His inability to think clearly about her was a symptom of the symbiotic nature of the relationship. As Henry became more willing to talk openly about his relationship with his mother, he came to see how he limited himself by this symbiotic relationship. His openness had the effect of giving him a greater inner distance and perspective from his mother and in time he was able to leave home and enter into a sexual relationship with a woman for the first time.

The final stage of psychotherapy is often taken up with issues of separation and loss which clients have experienced in their lives, and in relation to the termination of therapy. These issues are far more important for personal development than is generally realized. People tend to avoid the painful feelings around separation and loss.[38] This stage of therapy provides an opportunity to deal with these issues. The ending is something which is mutually agreed by the client and myself, I attempt to work toward finishing in a way which respects the individuality of each person. In many cases it involves working towards a mature relationship, in which the client will be ready to separate.

In approaching the end of the therapy, the client's experiences of previous separations may be evoked. These may include for example, experiences of birth, weaning, birth of a sibling, loss of one or both parents and marital separation. It is important to see what has been the client's reaction to these experiences and to ensure that the traumatic situations are worked through and not just reenacted in ending therapy. This is illustrated in the case of Dominic who had been in therapy with me for three years:

> Dominic reacted angrily to what he considered my casual way of finishing therapy, even though we had worked towards finishing over a period of months. As we explored his anger it became clear that he had not come to terms with his brother's death. His brother had committed suicide some years before. The reality of losing the closeness and trust which had developed during therapy evoked his anger which he felt towards his brother for committing suicide. His reaction showed the necessity of doing more work before he would feel ready to finish therapy in a constructive way. As he worked during a further period in therapy, he was able to understand how he had denied his feelings of loss and sadness about his brother's death. He was also able to feel his grief about losing his brother.

Now I will look more closely at the therapeutic setting and the relationship.

Other elements in an integrative approach to psychotherapy:

The therapeutic setting and the relationship in psychotherapy – A client centred stance

Therapy is a holding environment in which change happens within the structure of the relationship over time. The setting provides an atmosphere of empathy and frankness with the intention of being free from moralising and judgement. For many clients the regularity of therapy itself may at times be the most important aspect of therapy. It may like a lifeline, or a platform from which to build sense of trust in relating.

The relationship between the client and I is a central therapeutic factor that provides the basis for all other therapeutic processes. Research[39] demonstrates that the therapeutic relationship is a more significant factor than any particular method of therapy. Any therapeutic intervention or technique is dependent on the quality of this relationship for its impact. It is only when clients understand what happens within this relationship that valuable experiences, or particular therapeutic interventions become meaningful. These experiences involve inner thoughts or feelings, past memories, the relationship to the therapist or to family and friends.

> Recalling the case of Hanna (page 265), it was important that she recognise the origin of her anger and fear towards me. I had to take a neutral stance to allow these feelings to emerge, to act as a mirror and to help her to understand what was happening. It was also important that she feel that I was on her side in her inner struggle with her cruel and sadistic father. Hanna trusted that I was not a threat to her. She was thus able to move beyond her paralysing fear and gain an inner security. This security allowed her to feel less threatened in other aspects of her life.

Therapy is a relationship in which two people are interacting. The client's experience affects the therapist and the personality and mannerisms of the therapist colour the process of the client. It is therefore necessary that I as a therapist be aware, both of how I affect the development of therapy and to sense my own feelings and reactions. I have a responsibility to continue to work on my own problems to help the client to develop. It is my willingness to engage in my own struggle towards maturity, as opposed to perfection or saintliness that will enable me to find a depth within myself. This, together with my reliability, enables me to be present in a way that may awaken the unconscious trust of the client. This trust is essential for the clients to risk remembering, re-exper-iencing and revealing their inner hidden pain both to themselves and to me as the therapist.

Each therapist adopts a style of being with the client that is congruent to him or her and fits their individuality. A method-oriented approach of the therapist may limit the therapy. The wider my view of the client, the more aspects of the client's whole self I can include. It is essential that I base the nature and direction of therapy on the clients's concerns.

Knowledge and theory are necessary, but they cannot replace an ability to tune into and to respond to the manifold experiences within the therapy. The awareness and sensitivity that this brings will prevent me from being too impersonal and objective, using techniques in a detached manner. I endeavour to involve myself emotionally so that I can sense and be affected in a human way by the client's experience, yet preserve sufficient distance to function clearly as a therapist. If I as a therapist become too emotionally involved, it may blur the professional boundary, and interfere with my ability to make sense of the therapeutic process.

I have attempted to show how I combine a psychonanalytic, body oriented, relationship centred and process oriented approach in working with people. I have also tried to emphasise that given the right atmosphere, people may, through engaging in their own struggle, begin to find their own meaning and truth. The process is different for every person and I as a therapist will not know what direction this process will take. As Irving Howe has said:

> What determines the direction a man will take? Sometimes the delicate manoeuvres between his will and desire, sometimes the heat of his vanity, sometimes the blessing of his innocence …

Howe's quote serves to remind us of the uniqueness and mystery of each person.

Notes

1. Stricker, G., and Gooen-Piels, J., 'Integrative and object relations focused approaches to psychotherapy: Theoretical concerns and outcome research', chapter 3 in (eds.) I. S. Nolan and Patrick Nolan, *Object Relations and Integrative Psychotherapy,* (London: Whurr, 2002).

2. Winnicott D.W., *The Maturational Process and the Facilitating Environment* (London: Karnac, 1990).

3. Freud, S., *The Dynamics of Transference* (London: Hogarth) 12:97-108, 1912.

4. Freud, S., *On the history of the Psycho-Analytic Movement,* Standard Edition, XIV, 16, (London: Hogarth, 1924).

5. Freud, S., *On Psychopathology* (Harmondsworth: Penguin, 1979).

6. Freud, S., *The Interpretation of Dreams* (Harmondsworth: Penguin, 1986).

7. Freud, S., *The Ego and the Id, The Standard Edition of the Complete Psychological Works of Sigmund Freud* (London: Hogarth Press, 1923).

8. Ibid.

9. Paner, H.W. Freud: *His Life and Mind*, (New York: Howell Soskin, 1947).

10. Ferenczi, S., *Further Contributions to the Theory and Technique of Psychoanalysis* (London: Hogarth, 1980).

11. Balint, M., *The Basic Fault* (London: Tavistock, 1968).

12. Reich, W., *Character Analysis* (London: Vision, 1950).

13. Reich, W., *The Function of the Orgasm* (New York: Meridian, 1971).

14. Fairbairn, W.R.D., *Psychoanalytic Studies of the Personality* (London: Tavistock Routledge, 1986).

15. Perls, F. Hefferline, R. and Goodman, P., *Gestalt Therapy* (Harmondsworth: Penguin, 1974).

16. Broder, M., 'Developmental theories in the process of change', chapter 6 in (eds.) I. S. Nolan and Patrick Nolan, *op. cit.*.

17. Proust, M., *Rememberence of Things Past* (C. K. Scott Moncrieff, 1913).

18. Rogers, C., *On Becoming A Person* (London: Constable, 1986).

19. Maslow, A., *The Further Reaches of Human Nature* (Harmondsworth: Penguin, 1971).

20. Winnicott, D.W., *The Maturational Process and the Facilitating Environment* (London: Karnac, 1990).

21.Jung, C., *On the Psychology of Unconscious, The Collected Works of C.J. Jung*, Bollington XX, (Vol 7, 2nd ed.m) (Princeton University, 1966).

22. Winnicott, D.W., *Through Paediatrics To Psychoanalysis* (London: Karnac, 1990).

23. Bowlby, J., *Attachment and Loss* (London: Hogarth, 1969).

24. Jung, C. G, 'The Relation between the Ego and the Unconscious' in M. Adler, M. Fordham, W. McGuire, H. Read, R. Hull (trans), *The Collected Works of C. G. Jung*, Bollinger Series XX, Vol 7, 2nd ed. pars 202-406, (Princerton: Princerton University Press, 1966).

25. Ennis Brown, K., The Shadow and the Body, unpublished thesis, Antioc University, 1987.

26. Broder, M., *op. cit.*.

27. Winnicott, D. W., *Through Paediatrics to Psychoanalysis* (London: Karnac, 1990).

28. Lacan, J., *Ecrits* (London: Hogarth, 1977).

29. Fagan, J. and Sheppard, I., (eds) *Gestalt Therapy Now* (Harmondsworth: Penguin, 1972).

30. Mark Musa, A., (ed.), *The Divine Comedy*, (London: Penguin, 1984).

31. Nolan, P., 'Object Relations as a context for an integrative approach to psychotherapy', chapter 2 in (eds.) I. S. Nolan and Patrick Nolan, *op. cit.*.

32. Rom 7:24-5.

33. Descartes, R., *Discourse on method and meditation*, (Canada: Penguin, 1968).

34. Zohar, D., *The Quantum Self* (London: Flamingo, 1991).

35. Brown, M., *The Healing Touch* (Life Rhythm, 1990).

36. Reich, W., *The Function of the Orgasm* (New York: Meridian, 1971).

37. Wrangsjö Björn (ed), *Krpoos-orienterad psykoterapi* (Sweden: Natur och Kultur, 1987).

38. Kubler-Ross, E., *On Death and Dying* (London: Tavistock, 1982).

39. Stricker, G., and Gooen-Piels, J., *op. cit.*.

Further Reading

Boadella, D., *Biosynthesis* (London: Routledge and Keegan Paul, 1987).

Lowen, A., *The Language of the Body* (London: First Colier Books, 1971).

Lowen, A., *Bionergetics* (Harmondsworth: Penguin, 1975.

McDougall, J., *Theatres of the Body* (London: Free Association Books, 1989).

APPENDIX A

Training courses in psychotherapy

The following training courses and training organisations have been accepted by the Irish Council for Psychotherapy for a number of years for the purposes of individual accreditation:

Clanwilliam Institute, Family Therapy course, Dublin.

Mater Hospital Family Therapy course, Dublin.

Tivoli Institute, Humanistic and Integrative Psychotherapy course, Dublin and Galway.

Dublin Counselling Centre

Centre for Biodynamic Psychotherapy , Tracht, Kinvara, Co. Galway.

Cork Counselling Centre, Cork.

Irish Gestalt Centre, Dublin.

Masters in Psychotherapy, University College Cork.

Masters in Humanistic Psychotherapy, University of Limerick.

Psychoanalytic Psychotherapy course, St Vincents Hospital, Dublin.

Group Analytic training course, St Vincents Hospital, Dublin.

Psychoanalytic Psychotherapy course, Trinity College Dublin

Child Psychoanalytic Psychotherapy course, Trinity College Dublin

Institute for Creative Counselling and Psychotherapy, Dun Laoghaire.

Turning Point Psychotherapy course, Dun Laoghaire.

Please note: This is not an inclusive list. The ICP, 73 Quinns Rd, Shankill, County Dublin can be consulted before making any application for psychotherapy training.

The Contributors

1. *Ross M. Skelton* is a founder member of the Irish Forum for Psychoanalytic Psychotherapy, an organisation of practicing analytical psychotherapists in Ireland. He is also a founder member of the Irish Institute of Psychoanalytic Psychotherapy. A lecturer in Philosophy and Psychoanalysis at Trinity College, Dublin, he is the co-founder of the M.Phil in Psychoanalytic Studies.

2. *Michael Fitzgerald* is a consultant child psychiatrist based in Dublin. He is the only psychoanalyst in the Republic of Ireland recognised by the International Psychoanalytic Association. He initiated a number of psychotherapy training courses as well as founding the Irish Forum for Psychoanalytic Psychotherapy, The Irish Council for Psychotherapy and the Irish Forum for Child Analytic Psychotherapy. He is also a founder member of the Irish Institute of Psychoanalytic Psychotherapy.

3. *Rita McCarthy* trained in London as a Jungian analyst. She is a member of the International Association for Analytical Psychology and the Irish Forum for Psychoanalytical Psychotherapy, and a founder member of the Irish Institute of Psychoanalytic Psychotherapy. Along-side private practice, she is also engaged in teaching and writing about analytical psychology.

Patricia Skar is a Jungian analyst trained at the C. G. Jung Institute, Zürich. She is a member of the International Association for Analytical Psychology and the Irish Forum for Psychoanalytic Psychotherapy. In addition to private practice, she also lectures in various psychotherapy training courses in Dublin and is a founder member of the Irish Institute of Psychoanalytic Psychotherapy.

4. *Miceal O'Regan* was a Dominican, a psychologist and psychotherapist. He was Director of Eckhart House, Institute of Psychosynthesis and TranspersonalTheory. He died in 1997.

5. *Dorothy Gunne* trained in psychoanalytic psychotherapy in the U.S.A. and has completed family therapy training with the Clanwilliam Institute and an M.Psych.Sc. in Constructivist psychotherapy at U.C.D.

Bernadette O'Sullivan, having practised as a Clinical Psychologist in the public service, went on to study Personal Construct Psychology and Therapy at the London Centre for PCP. She chose the subject of agoraphobia for her Ph.D thesis (1984) because of her interest in women's issues. The latter continues to be a major focus in her work.

6. *Edmund McHale* is a Clinical Psychologist and Family Therapy trainer and practitioner. He is the executive chairperson of the Clanwilliam Institute. Married, with two children, he lives in Dublin, having trained and worked in the U.S.A. and England.

7. *Anthony Bates* is senior Clinical Psychologist at the Department of Psychiatry, St James's Hospital, Dublin. His therapy training after graduation in 1977 from UCD was in Gestalt Therapy. During the early 1980s he trained at the Center for Cognitive Therapy, Philadelphia, with Aaron Beck. In 1985 he returned for a further five years to the University of Pennsylvania, became licensed as a psychologist, and worked at developing the cognitive-behavioural model with David D. Burns. During this time he conducted his doctoral research on the role of self-help in recovery from depression.

8 *Vincent Humphreys* has a background in psychology and social work. He trained in Family therapy at the Mater Child and Family Centre and in Gestalt Therapy at the Gestalt Centre of Nof Yam, Israel, under the direction of Netta and Marvin Kaplan. He has presented workshops in Ireland and Israel.

9. *Rachel Graham* has a psychology degree from Trinity College, Dublin, and a Person-Centred Approach Diploma in Counselling and Psychotherapy. A former lecturer in psychology at Trinity College Dublin, she is working as a therapist and staff development officer for Beacon Lodge, a residential home for young mothers and their babies in London, as well as maintaining a private practice.

10. *Patrick Nolan* After following a career in social work, Patrick trained at the Institute of Biodynamic Psychology in London and

later at the Institute of Psychosynthesis in Dublin. He has also completed the training at the European Institute of Organismic Psychotherapy and the training course in psychoanalytic psychotherapy at the school of psychotherapy, St.Vincents Hospital, Dublin. He is currently completing an M.Sc. in psychotherapy at University College Dublin. He has worked as a psychotherapist for twenty-five years. He lives in Dublin where he maintains a private practice.

Edward Boyne is a writer and psychotherapist. He is involved with the training of therapists through the Tivoli Institute, Dublin and Galway, as well as working in private practice.

Vincent Browne is a journalist and broadcaster.